RACE AND SOCIETY

For Milun and Nayan
...the future of hope at its brightest

RACE AND SOCIETY

TINA G. PATEL

Los Angeles | London | New Delhi
Singapore | Washington DC | Melbourne

Los Angeles | London | New Delhi
Singapore | Washington DC | Melbourne

SAGE Publications Ltd
1 Oliver's Yard
55 City Road
London EC1Y 1SP

SAGE Publications Inc.
2455 Teller Road
Thousand Oaks, California 91320

SAGE Publications India Pvt Ltd
B 1/I 1 Mohan Cooperative Industrial Area
Mathura Road
New Delhi 110 044

SAGE Publications Asia-Pacific Pte Ltd
3 Church Street
#10-04 Samsung Hub
Singapore 049483

Editor: Natalie Aguilera
Editorial assistant: Delayna Spencer
Production editor: Katherine Haw
Copyeditor: Sarah Bury
Indexer: Elizabeth Ball
Marketing manager: Sally Ransom
Cover design: Shaun Mercier
Typeset by: C&M Digitals (P) Ltd, Chennai, India
Printed in Great Britain by CPI Group (UK) Ltd,
Croydon, CR0 4YY

Library of Congress Control Number: 2016933339

British Library Cataloguing in Publication data

A catalogue record for this book is available from
the British Library

ISBN 978-1-4462-8738-5
ISBN 978-1-4462-8739-2 (pbk)

At SAGE we take sustainability seriously. Most of our products are printed in the UK using FSC papers and boards.
When we print overseas we ensure sustainable papers are used as measured by the PREPS grading system.
We undertake an annual audit to monitor our sustainability.

CONTENTS

ABOUT THE AUTHOR

Dr Tina G. Patel is a Senior Lecturer in Criminology at the University of Salford. Tina's research and teaching interests relate to race/racism, surveillance and crime prevention, and discrimination in the criminal justice system. Tina specializes in undertaking qualitative research with excluded communities, who have often been presented as problematic and deviant. Tina has a number of publications in these areas, and is also the co-author of *Race, Crime and Society*, published in 2011 by Sage.

ACKNOWLEDGEMENTS

During my time in academia, there are a number of inspiring people I have been lucky enough to have met, studied under, worked alongside, and taught – you all know who you are. There would not be enough space here to name you all and to record just how grateful I am to you for your intellectual support, academic guidance and critical engagement. For your love and much needed 'reality checks', my heartfelt thanks go to my family (Patel & Hamilton), especially DPH. A very special thank you to MDPH and NDPH for making me smile and demanding that I stop working and play! More formally, thank you to all those at SAGE for providing me with the opportunity to produce this book. Thank you also to the anonymous reviewers for your feedback and thoughtful comments.

Dr Tina Girishbhai Patel

1

INTRODUCTION

INTRODUCTION

This chapter introduces the subject area of race and society, highlighting in particular its worthiness as a valid area of sociological investigation. The chapter then discusses the use, history and significance of the terminology adopted in this book. A discussion then follows of the aims and purpose of this book as a whole, outlining what you can expect from its subject coverage and how best to use its pedagogic features. In this chapter, key terms, such as 'race', 'racism' and 'post-race' analysis, will also be introduced. The aim of the chapter is to establish the structure, purpose and value of this book specifically within the context of race and society. The case of Rachel Dolezal is discussed to illustrate the complexity of assigning racial labels. The key question raised by the chapter is: Why do we need a rethink of issues relating to race and society?

KEY TERMS

- Post-race

- Race

- Racism

RACE AND SOCIETY

The idea of **race** actually predates the origins of the term, in that humans have a very long tradition in seeking to understand and organize differing population groups according to somatic, psychic and cultural characteristics (Rattansi, 2003: 239). Race has always influenced social relations. As a concept, race has been used to determine status, leading to privilege or disadvantage – depending on the racial group to which an individual was assigned. In this sense, it has been argued that wherever there is race, there is **racism**. This is 'the unequal treatment of a population group purely because of its possession of physical or other characteristics socially defined as denoting a particular race' (Scott and Marshall, 2005: 544). Although racism has been directed against all groups, historically, European expansion during the sixteenth century onwards saw racism being directed against black and minority ethnic populations. This led to Western society assigning privilege to white bodies. Here, whiteness was presented as normative, moral and of superior status. It was a privileged position that emerged from centuries of practices in which whiteness has remained unchecked and unchallenged. This allowed white subjects to define the racial (or ethnic) 'other' in ways that suited their social, economic and political motivations (Patel, 2013). As a consequence, all those falling outside whiteness experienced exploitation, disadvantage and discrimination, for instance limited political rights, removal of reproductive abilities, genocide and slavery.

Today, race (along with other variables) continues to determine social status. This is despite the fact that its status has now been identified as problematic – highlighted by the use of the term in inverted commas ('race') or, in some cases, the refusal to use the term at all. Despite its contested status, the ways in which we are racially labelled go on to shape our social experiences in significant ways. Therefore, although we may not agree to the actual existence of race, we nevertheless should recognize that it has very real meaning for many in society. Race informs how we are treated by other lay members of society and those acting in an official capacity. Perceptions about race influence our access to resources and services. For some, race determines life chances, as in the case of 27-year-old Brazilian Jean Charles de Menezes, who, having been 'mistaken'[1] (Sir Ian Blair, quoted in *The Daily Telegraph*, 31 January 2006) for a suspected terrorist, was shot seven times and killed by London Metropolitan Police officers at Stockwell Underground station on 22 July 2005 (Justice4Jean, 16 December 2013). In Western societies such as those found in Europe, America and Australia, there is currently another episode of heightened 'concern' about particular raced bodies and their numbers in the 'host' country. Here, black and minority ethnic groups in particular have been the focus of panic and hostility in terms of immigration, asylum and citizenship issues. This is evidenced by the continual negative attention given to these groups. Consequently, we have a situation in society today where certain individuals continue to be racially defined as undesirable and as a result go on to experience various citizenship curtailments. This is especially interesting and worthy of sociological study, given that society is now more complex, diverse and susceptible to change. The key question is, if we now have more types of society than we have ever had, why do so many social collectives continue to organize themselves along racialized lines?

It has also been argued that we are now living in **post-race** times. Post-race refers to a deconstructive approach to identity and social relations, in an attempt to move beyond traditional constructions of race and to argue that society has progressed with race equality. However, one of the key arguments of this book is that society still depends on human interaction that is socially constructed. In terms of race, we are still faced with an era that is marked out by racialized events. However, these events are presented as non-racial, specifically by being referred to as 'natural' concerns in employment, trade, security and population numbers. This is evident in racialized events of the recent post-race era, including the 'war on terror', failed multiculturalism and community cohesion, and the widening of European borders and employment movement rights. The socially constructed nature of society means that discussions about race and society are presented within a narrative which connects race with culture with multiculturalism with national identity with community cohesion with wider social relations. Accusations of racially discriminatory practices are defended with reference to inclusiveness and legalistic measures for combating racism, which in reality are met with society's continued securitization of black and minority ethnic populations, resulting in attempts to control, regulate or ultimately remove them from society. It does this by constructing new forms of racism, what Kundnani (2001) calls the 'new popular racism', and Fekete (2001) and Sivanandan (2006) refer to as 'xeno-racism'. These newer forms of racism combine different types of discrimination in varied ways, for instance anti-Muslim racism, Islamaphobia and xenophobia, in order to produce a particular type of cultural discrimination that is context-specific and popularized as acceptable within post-race times. This is because they are viewed as not being (biologically) racist in nature, but more about community conflict and national security (Patel, 2013).

What remains clear is that race and society, specifically the inextricable and complex relationship between them, plays a significant role in human behaviour, social order and future direction. In all aspects of public and private social life, race and society combine to impact on the lives of individuals in very real and meaningful ways. This continues in recent times despite claims to a post-race era. This book will discuss in more depth the various key ways in which race and society are conjoined subject areas worthy of sociological study. In particular, there is a focus on unresolved issues or those areas where a new level of analysis is warranted.

―――――――――――――――― **ACTIVITY** ――――――――――――――――

List all the ways in which 'race' is and is not important in contemporary society. How and why should sociologists address the issue of race when studying society?

TERMINOLOGY

Before we can proceed further with debates centring on the concerns of this book, clarification is needed on some of the key terms of reference that are used in this book. Race talk is a complex, political and contested process (Patel and Tyrer, 2011: 2). This means that any terms used at this specific point in time will always be open to critique and somewhat outdated – this is as it should be. It is fitting, therefore, to give the following disclaimer: I recognize that the terms used, although not ideal, are fitting within this specific space, time and context. The decision to use them has not been a simple process, but the outcome of much thought. The pursuit for more fitting alternatives should never be abandoned.

It was during the American Civil Rights Movement of the 1960s, and later similar activism in Britain, that the term 'Black' became mobilized as a positive political term – represented with the use of a capital letter to indicate the unified inclusion of all those people who suffered racially based inequality, discrimination and violence. Although referring to all those of non-white skin colour, the term was commonly applied to those of African, Caribbean and South Asian origin. However, it is argued that the term can no longer be viewed as a singular politically based racial label with the same set of meanings for all those under its category. The term is therefore now more commonly used in lower case typology: *black*. In addition, the term is rarely used on its own, but often as part of a broader racialized category, for example, black and minority ethnic (Patel and Tyrer, 2011: 2).

The term *black and minority ethnic* is often used to refer to all those who consider themselves to be part of a group within the non-white category. The term is rarely used as a singular racial label, indicating a move away from an essentialized notion of a singular or universal black identity. In this sense, it is often also accompanied by more specific racial labels, for instance *British South Asian*, which is used to refer to those individuals with recent origins in South Asia, who were born, raised and living in Britain, or *African Caribbean* (or sometimes just African or Caribbean, or even British African Caribbean), which is used to refer to those with recent origins in the Caribbean and/or Africa (Patel and Tyrer, 2011: 2). The inclusion of the word 'minority' is used to refer specifically to this group's unequal access to resources and power, rather than having numerical significance – see Wagley and Harris (1958) for a useful outline of the characteristics of minority groups.

The terms *white* and *white European* are used to refer to those who are of non-black and minority ethnic background. In particular, it refers to those individuals with recent origins in Europe. At its most basic, the term is often used in crude biologically based ways, often to refer to all those with white skin pigmentation and recent European heritage. Whiteness (as discussed later in this book), has often been held up as a non-raced category – as applying to those experiencing a normative and privileged status. More recently, the term 'white' in particular has been used as a basis for the ethnic politics of extreme right-wing movements (Moore, 2003: 329).

ACTIVITY

Recall three recent instances where race has been significant. What type of language was used to talk about race? On reflection, did the language that was used accurately describe its subject? Why or why not?

STRUCTURE OF CHAPTERS

Work on how processes of race-related issues, for instance racial discrimination, go on to impact negatively on some groups has taken as its starting point the polarization of race into categories akin to blackness and whiteness. Although important, such an approach is time/context specific. This means that it is limited in its contribution to race issues arising in contemporary society, which are now more diverse and complex than ever before. This book focuses on the processes and impact of racial categorization in contemporary society. In doing so, it moves away from analysis, which, although not entirely irrelevant, is nevertheless now somewhat limited in its understanding of how and why race issues unfold as they do in contemporary society. Thus, a new generational approach to the study of race and society is offered. The following chapters provide an introduction to the main concepts and relevant key theories, including post-developments of these theories. They also highlight the central debates of race issues in contemporary society, working through any under-examined and unresolved issues. Although descriptive in places in order to explain approaches and to locate facts, the book encourages and facilitates critical thinking through its use of case studies and pedagogic features, such as study questions, suggestions for further reading, and so on. The following chapters offer discussions that move away from essentialist and polarized explanations of raced interaction. Instead, there is emphasis on the social construction of race issues. This highlights the intersectional and multifarious nature of race – and its related conceptualizations, in other words, ethnicity, multiculturalism, mixed-ness, religion, nationality, and so on. In doing so, the book as a whole highlights and generates appreciation of how race has morphed into newer forms of categorizations in contemporary society as well as offering an avenue for a more relevant and progressive way of thinking about race and society.

Within this analytical framing, the following chapters make up this book:

Chapter 2 on **categorizing race** begins by discussing the ways in which race has been categorized and argues that its essential and polarized tendencies are problematic. The chapter then describes some of the key historical patterns of racial categorizations and encourages readers to appreciate the need for an updated social constructionist approach in studying the role and significance of race in contemporary society. The theory and concepts covered in the chapter include: Afro-centrism; Black power; black deviance; colonialism; critical criminology; essentialism; ethnocentrism; eurocentrism; scientific racism; and social construc- tionism. The case study in the chapter concerns the online racism that followed Nina Davuluri's crowning as Miss America 2014. The key question raised in the chapter is: What are the key markers of race in contemporary society, and how do they differ from the markers of previous generations?

Chapter 3 on **understanding society** discusses the sociological definition, role and function of society, with a particular focus on the formation of contemporary society and its new and distinct features that are of analytical interest. Readers will develop an understanding of how we think about society and the significance of social rela- tionships, norms and values on our everyday lives. The theory and concepts covered in the chapter will include: apartheid; assimilations; the Chicago School; commu- nity; culture; denizen; social exclusion; social norms; and symbolic interactionism. The case study described in the chapter is the Alphaville gated community in Brazil and its perpetuation of a racial divide. The key question raised in the chapter is: How powerful are 'rules' in society, and why do we usually obey them?

Chapter 4 on the **representations of race** discusses some of the key ways in which race and racial groups come to be represented and consumed, especially in matters relating to space, locality and society. This provides readers with an avenue for recognizing and questioning the significance of power in the construction and consumption of racialized representations, as well as their stigmatic impact on those it deems undesirable. The chapter highlights the use of racialized representa- tions on a regular basis by the mass media, politicians and criminal justice authorities, because they are considered to have a vested interest in generating fear, panic and concern about race and some racial groups. The chapter will draw on the theory and concepts of black deviance; browning; labelling; moral panics; stigma; and white victimhood. In using the Rochdale and the 'Asian sex gang' event as a case study, the methods used to construct a non-racially-based crime as a racialized event is examined. The key question raised is: What is the impact of the media over-focusing on particular race issues?

Chapter 5 examines **identity and the place of race** and discusses the ways in which race is embedded in notions of identity, space and citizenship. Readers will be able to appreciate how social groups are formed and identified along racial lines, and how notions of citizenship are actually informed by ideas about desirability/ undesirability. The theory and concepts covered in the chapter include: cultural capital; globalization; heterophobia; hybrid identity; and mixophobia. The case study in the chapter concerns immigration and the 'Life in the UK' test, also known as the British citizenship test. The key question raised is: How are identi- ties negotiated according to raced spaces?

Chapter 6 discusses **the other 'isms'** and argues that an analysis of race in contem- porary society cannot be in isolation from other social variables. The discussion begins by examining the ordinary and everyday nature of racism and the difficulties this presents for challenging it. The chapter then highlights the complex and varied nature of race, specifically the significant interconnections with aspects of gender, sexuality, age, class and the urban environment. The chapter draws distinctions and evidences the multifarious nature of identities in society and the measurement of these against racial categories. The theory and concepts covered will include: Black feminist critique; critical race theory; intersectionality; postcolonial theory; and underclass. The case study in the chapter concerns the media's reporting of the 2012 gang rape of Jyoti Singh Pandey in Delhi (India), in particular the ways in which other social variables were factored into the portrayal of victim/offenders. The key question raised is: How is a raced hierarchy influenced by other social variables?

Chapter 7 on **masking racism in society** considers the ways in which practices emerging from crude and discriminatory racialized categorizations have serious consequences for some members of society. In particular, there is a focus on how the meanings of such crude racialized categorizations have become popularized and permitted, relatively speaking, within a wider context of national identity/ pride, and the security of this and related interests from perceived dangerous others/ outsiders. The theory and concepts covered in the chapter include: ethnicity; critical whiteness studies; Islamaphobia; and xenophobia. The case study included in the chapter discusses the experiences and perceptions of whites who choose to convert to Islam. The key question raised is: To what extent is the new language of race a reworking of older racist ideas?

Chapter 8 on **race in social institutions and organizations** considers the significance of race in those key social institutions and organizations which are viewed as having significant power and influence in contemporary society over how we construct views about race, label bodies and think about ourselves in relation to others. The theory and concepts covered include: black criminality; institutional racism; positive discrimination; and tokenism. The case study in the chapter is about racism in football. The key question raised in the chapter is: Are there particular spaces where problematic ideas about race and society are especially powerful and, if so, what is the impact of this for progressing thinking about race and society more widely?

Chapter 9 considers **human rights, equality and legislation** in terms of their relationship to human rights and the law on equality and anti-discrimination. Readers will develop knowledge about some of the key legislation in this area. The chapter then discusses the limitations of this legislation for addressing newer and unresolved issues around race and society. The legislation covered includes: the Immigration Acts of 1971 and 1978; the Race Relations (Amendment) Act 2000; and the Racial and Religious Hatred Act 2006; and their equivalents in Europe, USA and Australia, such as the Civil Rights Acts of 1964 and 1991 in the USA and the Commonwealth Racial Discrimination Act 1975 in Australia. The concepts covered include: citizenship; ghettos; hate crime; positive action; and public policy. The case study in the chapter concerns the CCTV surveillance in

Birmingham (UK), and how this surveillance was viewed as a racially regulatory mechanism and was consequentially successfully challenged by residents. The key question raised in this chapter is: How sufficient is existing legislation for protecting the rights of those who suffer disproportionately from race discrimination and inequality?

Chapter 10 looks at **researching race and society**. The chapter begins by describing some of the traditional research practices into race and society, and highlights their limitations for contemporary race and society issues. The chapter then offers direction on how research can be undertaken, namely with an approach that would offer a more qualitative and in-depth understanding of the key issues, built on trust and support for its research subjects. It is argued that the suggested approach would access data from those directly involved in matters, and this brings with it greater validity. The theory and concepts covered in the chapter include: critical research; feminist epistemology; the over-researched; post-positivism; and racial minority perspectives. The case study in the chapter concerns the victimization and abuse of research subjects as well as the unethical methods used in the Tuskegee Syphilis study. The key question that is raised is: Do some racial groups have valid reasons for being suspicious of researchers?

Chapter 11 is the **conclusion**, which brings together the key points of the preceding chapters and succinctly presents the book's main arguments. In particular, it focuses on the validity of the argument that claims that we are living in a post-race society, and the implications of this claim for those who feel that they are subjected to the discriminatory consequences of racial constructions. The case of right-wing extremism on the internet is considered as a way of examining the common and popular repackaging of racism within the context of claims to post-racialism. The chapter will emphasize the need for us to rethink our approach to the study of race and society, and will offer some suggestions to be factored into the analysis of newer and unresolved issues around racialized constructions and social relationships. The key question raised in this chapter is: How can we satisfy the need for a rethink of issues relating to race and society?

HOW TO USE THIS BOOK

The purpose of this book is to offer a conceptual progression of knowledge, understanding and critical thinking of newer and unresolved issues relating to race and society. On this basis, each chapter provides subject discussion (literature, concept and theory), knowledge application (case study), and avenues for developing analytical skills (study questions). For those who are fairly new to the subject, it is recommended that each chapter is read in sequence. For the more subject-developed reader, the chapters can be read non-sequentially or in isolation from one another. In order to fully grasp the subject area, however, it is strongly recommended that the various pedagogic features of each chapter are fully engaged with.

Case study: The 'blacking up' of Rachel Dolezal

There is a long history in the entertainment industry of 'blackface' – a term used to refer to how people of white ethnic background present themselves as black. This was often done by using crude racial stereotypes and by altering one's physical appearance in order to 'appear' black, such as darkening the skin and changing hair type. In most countries, this practice has now been abandoned, although there are some exceptions to this, for instance, as illustrated in the 2009 Australian television broadcast of a Jackson Five parody group (Jackson Jive). However, the practice of 'blacking up' one's appearance is more than just entertainment. It speaks more widely about identity, rights and power, and as such the practice can be seen as denigrating the humanity of African Americans. Today, fictional characters continue to use 'blacking up', but often as part of a story and/ or message about racial prejudice and inequality. For instance, consider Robert Downey Jr's character Kirk Lazarus in *Tropic Thunder*. Lazarus is a white Australian who is so ridiculously committed to his role as an African-American sergeant that he has gone through medical procedures to have his skin darkened (Rose, 2015). Similarly, there are Sacha Baron Cohen's two characters, *Ali G* and *Borat Sagdiyev*, whom Baron Cohen uses to illustrate the everyday racist and xenophobic attitudes of white populations. These characters have actually done much to illustrate the continued practices of racism and its normalized contexts.

However, the practice of 'blacking up' in reality is far less common. Indeed, it is almost unheard of. Why, after all, would one who is in a privileged position want to inhabit another position where they will experience disadvantage and discrimination?[2] There is, though, the case of Rachel Dolezal, who in June 2015 was accused of having lied about her racial identity and other aspects of her biography. It was claimed that Dolezal was actually of white ethnic background (her parents are both white and primarily of *Czech*, *German* and *Swedish* origin) but had spent a significant amount of her life masquerading as black African American. The denial of her heritage as African American came from Dolezal's estranged parents, who stated that their daughter had been trying to 'disguise herself' as African American for a number of years. To accompany this statement they released family photographs, including one of Dolezal as a blue-eyed teenager with straight blonde hair (Mosendz, 2015).

Claiming that she was of black African-American heritage and that she had been a victim of white racism on numerous occasions, Dolezal had worked as an American civil rights activist, and was a key figure in the National Association for the Advancement of Colored People (NAACP) in America – notably as the president of the NAACP chapter in Spokane, Washington. Ironically, it was later found that in 2002, Dolezal (known at the time as Rachel Moore) had unsuccessfully sued Howard University for discrimination relating to 'race, pregnancy, family responsibilities and gender...', alleging that, among other things, she was denied scholarship funds and a teaching assistant position (Begley, 2015). Dolezal claimed that the removal of her artwork from a student exhibition in 2001 'was motivated by a discriminatory purpose to favor African-American students' over her (Begley, 2015).

(Continued)

(Continued)

Aside from the accusations of race-falsification, there are a number of interesting points about racial identity that emerge from the Dolezal case. First is Dolezal's continued self-identification as 'black', a label based, it seems, on cultural self-perception and aspiration. For instance, in one interview, Dolezal was quoted as saying that she has long identified with the black community, and that even as a child, 'I was drawing self-portraits with the brown crayon instead of the peach crayon...' (Dolezal, cited in Kim, 2015). It can be suggested that, although not based on biology or ancestry, Dolezal's racial identity is nevertheless a genuine one, not least because she perceives herself to be black African American. Thus, a Sociological logic goes, whether real or imagined, Dolezal's racial identity is black African American – albeit not a typical one. However, Dolezal's 'blacking up' upsets the practice of 'passing', which is where (usually) members of a black and minority ethnic population group pretend to be 'white' in order to counteract the racism and disadvantage of a given society, for example, in Apartheid society. In this sense, then, black and minority ethnic 'passing' as white is a survival strategy. Dolezal's version of 'passing' was not based on survival, and her imagining of blackness, which, as she claimed, was to create positive social change, was in reality an unnecessary theft of blackness:[3]

> If Rachel Dolezal wanted to be a true radical, one dedicated to transgressing and undermining white supremacy, she would have acted upon Noel Ignatiev's wisdom and publicly denounced Whiteness – without masquerading as a black woman. ... To do this, Dolezal need only have continued her work with the NAACP and publicly renounced Whiteness and (to the degree possible) the unearned advantages that come with white skin privilege. (Devaga, 2015)

At its Sociological core, the Dolezal case tells us that racial labels are socially constructed, and the right to change and adapt one's racial self-identification is not without its challenges.

ACTIVITY

What are the motivations for 'blacking up'? Did Rachel Dolezal make any significant contributions to racial equality by 'blacking up'?

CONCLUDING THOUGHTS

This chapter has briefly discussed how 'race' is a social variable which continues to have an impact on the life experiences of population groups. Often this impact is negative, limiting the chances and freedoms of people who are of black and minority ethnic origin, in particular. Despite the claims of living in a post-race society, race – in a 'newer' form that draws on older racist logics – continues therefore to be a powerful signifier and feature of society. Thus, it is worthy of continued study and critical discussion. In particular, the chapter has encouraged its readers to ask questions about why there is not only still a need for study into race and society matters, but, further, why that study needs to move beyond claims to be living in a post-race society. In addition, the chapter has offered a note on the adopted terminology of the book – with the acknowledgement that these themselves are not problematic terms in need of future revision – as well as an outline of the following chapters and guidance on how the reader can best use the book.

MAIN POINTS

- Ideas about race can privilege some and disadvantage others.
- Whiteness holds a privileged status in society.
- Post-race analysis notes a progression with race equality.
- Race terminology is still problematic and inaccurate.

STUDY QUESTIONS

1. Is there such a thing as race?
2. In what ways does race determine life chances?
3. Are we really living in post-race times?
4. Why is agreement on race terminology difficult?

FURTHER READING

Britton, Nadia J. (1999) 'Racialized identity and the term black', in S. Roseniel and J. Seymour (eds.), *Practising Identities: Power and Resistance*. London: Macmillan. pp. 134–154.
Garner, Steve (2010) *Racisms: An Introduction*. London: Sage.
Kundnani, Arun (2001) 'In a foreign land: The new popular racism', *Race and Class*, 43(2): 41–60.

REFERENCES

Begley, Sarah (2015) 'Rachel Dolezal will break her silence on Tuesday', *TIME.com*, 15 June 2015 (http://time.com/3921964/rachel-dolezal-howard-university/).
Devaga, Chauncy (2015) 'What we can't afford to forget about Rachel Dolezal: A master class in white victimology', *The Salon*, 22 June 2015 (www.salon.com/2015/06/22/what_we_cant_afford_to_forget_about_rachel_dolezal_a_master_class_in_white_victimology/).
Fekete, Liz (2001) 'The emergence of xeno-racism', *Race and Class*, 43(2): 23–40.
Griffin, John H. (1961) *Black Like Me*. Boston, MA: Houghton Mifflin.

Justice4Jean (2013) 'The Jean Charles De Menezes family campaign', *Justice for Jean Online*, 16 December 2013 (www.justice4jean.org/).

Kim, Eun Kyung (2015) 'Rachel Dolezal breaks her silence on TODAY: "I identify as black"', *Today News Online*, 16 June 2015 (www.today.com/news/rachel-dolezal-speaks-today-show-matt-lauer-after-naacp-resignation-t26371).

Moore, Robert (2003) 'Whiteness', in G. Bolaffi, R. Bracalenti, P. Braham and S. Gindro (eds.), *Dictionary of Race, Ethnicity and Culture*. London: Sage. pp. 329–330.

Mosendz, Polly (2015) 'Family accuses NAACP leader Rachel Dolezal of falsely portraying herself as black', *Newsweek*, 12 June 2015 (www.newsweek.com/family-accuses-naacp-leader-rachel-dolezal-falsely-portraying-herself-black-342511).

Patel, Tina G. (2013) 'Ethnic deviant labels within the "war on terror" context: Excusing white deviance', *Ethnicity and Race in a Changing World*, 4(1): 34–50.

Patel, Tina G. and Tyrer, David (2011) *Race, Crime and Resistance*. London: Sage.

Rattansi, Ali (2003) 'Race', in G. Bolaffi, R. Bracalenti, P. Braham and S. Gindro (eds.), *Dictionary of Race, Ethnicity and Culture*. London: Sage. pp. 239–245.

Rose, Steve (2015) 'From Ali G to Rachel Dolezal: The colourful history of blacking up', The *Guardian*, 21 June 2015 (www.theguardian.com/us-news/2015/jun/21/rachel-dolezal-ali-g-blacking-up).

Scott, John and Marshall, Gordon (2005) *Oxford Dictionary of Sociology*. Oxford: Oxford University Press.

Sivanandan, Ambalavaner (2006) 'Race, terror and civil society', *Race and Class*, 47(1): 1–8.

The Daily Telegraph (2006) 'Met Chief admits serious mistake over De Menezes', *The Daily Telegraph*, 31 January 2006.

Wagley, Charles and Harris, Marvin (1958) *Minorities in the New World: Six Case Studies*. New York: Columbia University Press.

NOTES

1. Some of the 'mistaken' elements in the Jean Charles de Menezes case referred to the pheno-typical similarities between himself and the suspect, Hussain Osman. Menezes and Osman were of different ethnic backgrounds, although a composite picture showing half of each man's face was constructed by the police to support their claims about why they mistook Menezes for Osman. It was later found that the image had been altered, making similarities between the two men appear greater than they were.

2. Unless, that is, the practice of 'blacking up' is exactly to experience/research the difference in treatment, such as in John Howard Griffin's (1961) *Black Like Me* project.

3. For instance, Dolezal would have been equally able to pursue racial justice as a white woman, like many white activists before her.

2

CATEGORIZING RACE

INTRODUCTION

This chapter will provide a contextual background to the ways in which race has been so far categorized, namely in essentialized and (black–white) polarized ways. The limitations of this for contemporary analysis is then highlighted. After reading the chapter, the reader will be able to describe historical patterns of racial categorizations, and to appreciate the need for an updated social constructionist approach to studying the dynamics of race in contemporary society. The theory and concepts covered in the chapter include: Afro-centrism; Black power; black deviance; colonialism; critical criminology; essentialism; ethnocentrism; eurocentrism; scientific racism; and social constructionism. The case study in the chapter concerns the online racism following Nina Davuluri's crowning as Miss America 2014. The key question raised in the chapter is: What are the key markers of race in contemporary society, and how do they differ from the markers of previous generations?

KEY TERMS

- Afro-centrism

- Black deviance

- Black power

- Colonialism

- Critical criminology

- Discrimination

- Eco-racism

- Essentialism

- Ethnocentrism

- Eurocentrism

- Prejudice

- Racialization

- Racism

- Scientific racism

- Social constructionism

- Whiteness

WHAT IS RACE?

Race, as we understand it today, differs from the scientific typology concept adopted by the biologists of the last few centuries. Such scientific racism used 'biological determinism' to argue that there were innate, biologically based (and thus natural) and unchangeable differences between humans. European global expansion from the late-fifteenth century onwards saw scientific explanations about 'race' becoming popular (Mason, 2000). By the mid-nineteenth century, there was firm support for what is called 'Enlightenment Thinking' – a discipline of 'race science', which critics have now come to refer to as '**scientific racism**'. Some key contributors to this thinking included Immanuel Kant (1724–1804), David Hume (1711–1776) and Charles Linnaeus (1707–1778). They proposed hierarchical ideas about race, in particular white superiority and black inferiority. However, these were themselves tied to mistaken ideas about human biology, with common views being that blacks were closer to apes than whites, which we now know of course to be untrue (Ely and Denney, 1987). Genetic analysis has found that there is far greater genetic (biological) variation between people previously defined as being of the same race, in comparison to similarity levels between people of different races. Indeed, it has actually been found that the biological differences between humans, regardless of race, are relatively minor. In fact, Tizard and Phoenix (2002: 2) argue that 'when genes have been mapped across the world it has been found that trends in skin colour are not accompanied by trends in other genes ... 85 per cent of genetic diversity comes from the differences between individuals of the same colour in the same country, for example, two randomly chosen white English people'. As Carol Mukhopadhyay (2011: 205) argues, this means that the current use of racial categories is 'arbitrary, unstable and, arguably, biologically meaningless. Individuals cannot reliably be "raced" because the criteria are so subjective and unscientific. And the meanings of "race" have changed over time.'

The contact made between Europeans and non-Europeans during the European expansion from the fifteenth century onwards, first led to the concept of race gaining scientific interest. However, given that contact was made on an unequal basis – underpinned with exploitative motivations, scientific inquiry was inevitably biased. This later played a key role in the development of notions about a supposed natural order. Within this order, white (which was seen as the colour of the Europeans who embarked on 'explorations', which later became conquest, control and ownership missions (Mason, 2000)) was associated with goodness, purity, intelligence, Christianity and godliness. On the other hand, blackness (which was the colour of all non-Europeans subjected to exploratory and conquest encounters) was associated with evil, dirt, stupidity, sin and the devil. From this developed a racially based hierarchical scale where white races were placed at the top and black races located at the bottom. Social scientific consideration of '**whiteness**' is relatively new, largely because whites were not considered to be a racial category; rather, they were the assumed norm, an unmarked territory and essentially the marker of the human race. As Dyer (1997: 3) notes, 'in other words, whites are not of a race, they're just the human race'. Recent work has centred on the deconstruction of whiteness as a norm, and how those belonging to its category experience relative privilege in comparison to their non-white (or lesser white) counterparts. As a category of people, those considered to belong to the white race are initially defined by phenotypical markers. As Jensen (2011: 22) notes:

> White people have white skin, which actually is not really white, of course, but a pale/pinkish/off-white shade that has come to be labelled as white. Associated with that skin pigmentation are a variety of other physical traits regarding, especially, the shape of noses and lips and the texture of hair. White people typically can trace their ancestors to Europe, especially the United Kingdom, northern Europe, and Scandinavia.

However, as Jensen (2011) goes on to point out, in reality, whiteness is not about physical features or ancestry. Rather, whiteness is about power, privilege and status. This is discussed in more depth in later chapters, but for now it is necessary to recognize that such scientific claims were actually used as a way of maintaining white superiority as well as justifying practices such as colonialism. **Colonialism** refers to the processes whereby certain European societies had extended their political, economic and cultural domination of other countries. Colonial 'discoveries', and later neo-colonial rule, were marked by unequal power relations, labour force exploitation (slavery), violence (physical, mental and sexual), and the systematic destruction of traditional communities. Some examples from modern history include the Spanish in the Americas and Africa, the Portuguese in Brazil, the British in India, France and Germany in Africa, and Holland in Indonesia (Melotti, 2003a: 39). In this sense, the popularity of race science must also be examined within the context of wider social developments of the era (Mason, 2000: 7).

One of the key texts in support of scientific racism was that offered by (slave owner) Edward Long in 1774, *History of Jamaica*. In contrast to the Christian theological idea of race as lineage, such as that all humans are of the same species and are descendants of Adam and Eve, with black races having degenerated, Long used the idea of race as type, arguing that black and white races were completely different species of human beings altogether – a theory based on Long's claims of physical and cultural characteristics being prominent in each race. For instance, this included the claim that black races had a 'bestial fleece', as opposed to hair like that of the white race, as well as an inferior level of intelligence to that of apes, again unlike that of the white race, who advanced well beyond primate intelligence (Banton and Harwood, 1975, cited in Rattansi, 2003: 242). Robert Knox's *Races of Man* (1850) went further with these scientific examinations and developed specific racial typologies, such as skin colour, hair texture, and skull shape and size. Indeed, so powerful was the belief that phenotypical features were clearly identifiable and unique to different races that these typologies influenced the racial classifications of the nineteenth and twentieth centuries (Rattansi, 2003: 243). Race today still involves the drawing of boundaries between people, often using phenotypical markers, such as hair texture, skin pigmentation and facial features, to do so (Pilkington, 2003: 11).

Although race-type ideas were popular in their time, they have since been (scientifically) discredited, most notably by their inability to account for evolution (Pilkington, 2003: 12). Although Charles Darwin's theory of evolution soundly challenged the idea of race-types, a belief in inherent racial differences, albeit social rather than biological ones, lived on in the work of social Darwinists, such as Herbert Spencer (1820–1903), Thomas Malthus (1766–1829) and Francis Galton (1822–1911). This helped to support the idea that evolution was a process of struggle and competition between groups for survival (Pilkington, 2003: 13). This helped to maintain the idea of a racial hierarchy – a natural order which rewarded those with the intellect and skills to overcome struggles in order to survive:

> There is in the world a hierarchy of races ... those nations which eat more, claim more, and get higher wages, will direct and rule the others, and the lower work of the world will tend to be done by the lower breeds of men. This much we of the ruling colour will no doubt accept as obvious. (Charles Murray, 1900, cited in Pilkington, 2003: 13)

Most notably, widespread discrediting of any lingering race science ideas occurred following the end of the Second World War, when the horrors of Nazi Germany and its practices in pursuit of advancing the Aryan race[1] were publicly revealed (Mason, 2000: 7). More recently, though, there has been a surge of interest in genetics, socio-economic status and race. For instance, writers of population genetics have interpreted scientific data to argue that there are genetically based differences in IQ levels, which would further explain socioeconomic gaps between racial groups (see, for example, Herrnstein and Murray's *The Bell Curve* (1994)).

Indeed, it is fair to say that social scientific work on disproving race science ideas has not been supported by all social scientists. Considered as an 'academically validated' type of scientific racism, it can be found in the overlapping relationship between the Eugenics Movement and biological criminology, which was most popular in the USA and Europe from 1900 to 1930 (Webster, 2007). The Eugenics Movement in particular based its work on an attempt to improve the quality of human stock, which for them involved reducing the numbers of lower classes, the physically and mentally unfit, the criminal types, and others who were considered as socially undesirable (Garland, 1985, cited in Webster, 2007: 14). In the USA and Europe, those of non-white background came under this last category. The result was a move towards forced sterilization and genocide, both of which were used in Nazi Germany. However, such sterilization programmes were also widely supported in the USA as a 'solution' to its 'race problem', in which the 'negro' especially was seen as contaminating its 'high mental qualities' (Rentoul, 1906, cited in Black, 2003: 208–209). In 1924, the US state of Virginia implemented the Racial Integrity Act, which made marriage between white and non-white people illegal. Three years later, in 1927, again in Virginia, the Supreme Court's case of *Buck* v. *Bell* upheld the practice of mandatory sterilization (of black African-American woman Carrie Buck), stating that it was in the interest of the state to promote the purity of the white race in America (Pinder, 2011: 140).

Today such forms of 'genetically based racism' (Parrott et al., 2005: 3) have gained new popularity, especially following the Human Genome Project, which ran from October 1990 to April 2003 in the USA, although with input from an international body of scientists (Bonham et al., 2005). This is one of the most notable human genetic research projects whose publicly stated aim was to identify, for health and life insurance purposes, the genes associated with diseases. The project stated that it sought to prove once and for all that biological races did not exist. However, the project actually became known for adding weight to previously discounted claims about racial inferiority. As a consequence, it was used to strengthen racism, so much so that it has been described by some as having been used as a form of 'genetic colonialism' (Dodson and Williamson, 1999, cited in McCann-Mortimer, Auggoustinos and LeCouteur, 2004: 412). Even UNESCO's International Bioethics Committee in 1996 argued that its findings could be 'misappropriated for racist ends by those seeking whatever scientific support they could find to legitimate discriminatory beliefs' (Gannett, 2001, cited in McCann-Mortimer et al., 2004: 412).

ACTIVITY

Consider at least two instances where you have been in the presence of racism. At its core, did this racism use biological or social explanations?

THE SOCIAL CONSTRUCTION OF RACE

One legacy of 'scientific' understanding is that it presents the term 'race' and racial differences between humans as neutral, natural and scientific. This is evidenced by the way in which race is a taken-for-granted notion, assumed by all those who use it to be unproblematic, clear and unambiguous (Rattansi, 2003: 241). However, many social scientists have come to regard the concept of 'race', as well as its use more generally, as highly problematic. Those who take this view argue that race is a socially and historically defined concept. Thus, it is socially constructed (Pilkington, 2003: 11). **Social constructionist** approaches, such as those presented by the Chicago School (discussed later in this book), emphasize the socially constructed nature of social life. As Berger and Luckmann (1966: 61) state: 'Society is a human product. Society is an objective reality. Man is a social product.' It follows, then, that race-thinking is a habit; a learned attitude passed on from one generation to another. This, however, does not detract from the important point that, although there is no such thing as races, which (genetic) scientific analysis in the modern era has proved, being perceived to be of a particular racial type (as defined in the work of previous centuries) continues to ensure that being of a particular race is considered significant. It brings either disadvantage or advantage. Race is considered to be significant, and so it becomes significant (Pilkington, 2003: 15).

Usually black and minority ethnic groups experience negative outcomes of various racialized processes. However, attempts have been made to harness race and its significance in more self-affirming and positive ways. This was true of the **Black power** movement. Emerging originally in 1950s USA, and later popularized by various political movements in the 1960s, the term 'Black power' refers to the political and ideological revolutionary movement which sought to take a more active role in achieving civil rights, given that previous methods, such as those advocated by Martin Luther King Jr, were seen to be making little progress (Valeri, 2003b: 31). The Black power movement sought to redefine the term 'black', associating it instead with more positive meanings, as seen in the use of the common phrase of this time, 'black is beautiful'. Many of its supporters went further, using **Afro-centrism**, or the development and centring of African history and culture, to try to 'correct' previously held negative views about those of African descent. One way of doing so was by 'escaping the universality of Eurocentrics', along with making Africa the centre of its subjects' cultural universe (Valeri, 2003a: 6–7). The idea of Black power was key to pro-black movements and collectives, such as the Black Panther Party. The idea of the Black power movement was not only to achieve civil rights, but also to raise the self-esteem and self-reliance of its members (Garner, 2010: 30). The movement also advocated the use of political action based on opposition, and violent opposition if necessary, to what was considered to be the existing power structure, which held whiteness as dominant. The movement was significant not least because it was the first time that white populations had their whiteness and its ensuing privileges challenged (Valeri, 2003b: 31). This explained the violent responses as well as other pre-emptive measures taken by white populations and state authorities when faced with movements which used Black power as its guiding principle – such as influential figures being killed or imprisoned (Garner, 2010: 30).

Most social scientists agree that race is something that is socially constructed as opposed to being naturally given. However, there is some dispute as to the status and continued use of the term. Many see race as 'a crude biological concept which is sociologically meaningless' (Rex, 1986, quoted in Bagley, Young and Scully, 1992: 71). In this sense, use of the term 'reflects and perpetuates the belief that the human species consists of separate races' and therefore 'can deflect attention from cultural and religious aspects' of identity (Runnymede Trust, 2000: 6). Miles (1989: 75) argues that if we continue to use the term, it gives greater credibility to the idea of natural racial-types. Hence, many social scientists have rejected the term. To demonstrate this, they have either highlighted its 'contested character' (Mason, 2000: 8) by not using it altogether or by using it in inverted commas. However, in calling for the term to be completely 'banished', Pilkington (2003: 17) makes the point that as the inverted commas approach becomes routinized it is likely to lose its impact. One advance on this problem has been offered by Miles (1989), who argues that we should replace the term 'race' with that of 'racialization' in order to highlight the 'Other-defining process', which uses both alleged and real biological characteristics. In acknowledging the socially constructed nature of 'race', the term 'racialization' is used to refer to those social relations where racial meanings are found (Moore, 2003: 273). It is a preferred term as it recognizes the socially constructed nature of race (as opposed to it being a natural fact), without detracting from its social significance. Most importantly, the term also considers power and its relationship to racial categories.

Alternatively, Mason (1994, cited in Pilkington, 2003: 17) argues that race does not refer to categories (even socially defined ones) but to a social relationship – a social relationship that 'presumes the existence of racism' which, for Mason, means ideas and beliefs 'which emphasise the social and cultural relevance of biologically rooted characteristics'. It is this definition, Mason argues, that should alternatively be used in sociological debates. Doing so would avoid reifying the concept because it would highlight that there are actually no races, just the existence of a social relationship, which we refer to as 'race' (Pilkington, 2003: 17). Understanding race as a social relationship allows the recognition of how it 'remains a legitimate concept for sociological analysis because social actors treat it as real and organise their lives and exclusionary practices by references to it' (Mason, 2000: 7). Thus, although there are no such things as races, 'large numbers of people behave as if there are' and it is this that we social scientists must examine (Mason, 2000: 8). Regardless, we can agree that 'race has become a social fact: a self-evident characteristic of human identity and character' (Downing and Husband, 2005: 2). For this reason, the use, meaning and impact of race warrants social scientific attention.

During the 1960s, largely given that it was a core idea of the Black power movement, there emerged support for the view that there existed one essential Black identity that was core to all those of any black race. **Essentialism** holds that it is possible to identify the essence – that is, the truth or reality that lies behind a phenomenon. In terms of race, essentialism refers to the widely held assumption that humans possess indispensable innate and inherent characteristics which classify their true nature (McLaughlin, 2001: 109). However, it has since been argued that such polarized or singular concepts of race are problematic and insufficient to describe the complexity of social relationships and identities of particular groups, especially given that 'having a non-white skin colour does not indicate a related uniform experience' (Britton, 1999: 152). Consequently, a strong anti-essentialist critique emerged, notably by Stuart Hall (1996), who argued that the essentialist notion of a core black identity (and hence any essentialized identity) should not be viewed in terms of an essential black nature, or any other essentializing guarantee. Instead, Hall developed the concept of 'new ethnicities', arguing that we should move away from the conceptual autonomy of race, end the essential black subject, and dismantle the simple distinction of white oppressor/black oppressed. Race therefore becomes a linguistics categorization, constituted outside a pre-social biologically determined 'nature'.

One result of this was for preferences to develop for the use of alternative terms, such as culture and ethnicity. The use of terms outside 'race' brings the advantage of being able to widen the discussion to consider other non-typically raced groups who fall outside the traditional black–white confines but whose experiences are no less racially significant, especially in more recent times of xeno-racist and new popular racist thinking (Fekete, 2001; Kundnani, 2001; Sivanandan, 2006). For instance, consider the insightful body of work on 'browning' as an identification and **discrimination** process that draws on ethnic, cultural, racial and religious features (Bhattacharyya, 2008; Burman, 2010; Lugo-Lugo and Bloodsworth-Lugo, 2010; Meer and Modood, 2010; Semati, 2010). Here, discrimination refers to the act of unequal treatment of a person(s) because of (real or imagined) views held about their (perceived) group membership. In terms of race, this often refers to membership of racial, ethnic, religious or national groups. Discrimination is often linked to prejudice, although they do not have to occur together. For instance, one can have prejudicial views but not act on these (thus not be discriminatory). Consider, for example, business negotiations or those who fear receiving penalties for discriminatory behaviour (Healey, 2012: 31). **Prejudice** is a related term that refers to the tendency of an individual to think about others in negative, emotionally loaded ways. Prejudice often appears in instances where there is competition between groups, as it is then used to justify tactics within that competition as well as the privileged status of the winning group (Healey, 2012: 23).

For more modern social science observers, however, race is not only socially constructed, but is done so via a power relationship in society, where being white equals privilege and superiority, and being black equals disadvantage and discrimination. This is maintained and perpetuated due to the dominance of ethnocentric and Eurocentric ideology and power structures. Here, **ethnocentrism** refers to the ways in which members of one ethnic group privilege their group above all others, in particular using their own set of ideals and values to judge others. Often this involves using positive terms to define themselves and derogatory ones to describe others (Melotti, 2003b: 103). The term **Eurocentrism**, which is derived from ethnocentrism, uses Europe as an inevitable and natural reference point for measuring ethnic groups and allocating privilege (Harrison, 2003: 107). Racially based concepts are therefore socio-politically loaded concepts in that their meanings and usage are based on ideas that are developed, maintained and passed on in social human interaction through dialectical and behavioural processes. This is supported not least by the vast amount of work which also disproved the dated ideas from the Enlightenment period around the so-called problematic nature of black people, such as them having poor IQ levels, a proneness to violent behaviour, being untrustworthy, sexually promiscuous, and so on. However, these crude, offensive and outdated ideas continue to dominate and show themselves in a variety of discriminatory practices and attitudes. In suggesting reasons for this, many have pointed to the deeply embedded racism and discriminatory practices of wider society and institutions within that society, practices that are both intentional and unintentional. Thus a combination of the persistence of inaccurate stereotypes and a power imbalance means that racism continues to exist and perpetuate itself in the attitudes, beliefs and very real practices of social processes.

DOES RACE *REALLY* MATTER?

In the words of Cornell West (1993), 'race matters' because it has mattered so much in the lives of millions of people. Race is not a harmless classification system. Race determines status and rights at every level of our lives. One significant way in which race matters is in terms of racism. **Racism** uses race to distinguish and separate groups of people, with the influential group using political, economic and social power to control and exploit other groups. However, Mason (2000: 9) argues that, more recently, the term has problematically been used in more loose ways, for instance to express disapproval of patriotic fervour and in response to ignorance about another's culture. Nevertheless, there is agreement that racism is used as a tool to preserve the power of the dominant group. Although racism can be directed at any racial group, the numbers and types of documented cases has led to it now commonly being taken to refer to the victimization experienced by black and minority ethnic groups at the hands of the white majority. Indeed, bell hooks goes further and refers to this type of racism as 'white supremacist thinking … the invisible and visible glue that keeps white folks connected irrespective of many other differences' (hooks, 2013: 3).

There are many types of racism, although all have very similar motivations, patterns and outcomes. Garner (2010) provides a good discussion of these, but for now it is useful to identify some prominent types of racism. These include:

- **Eco-racism** – this refers to the specific reasoning given for hostility towards migrant communities. This type of racism is presented in ecological terms, using claims about migration causing environmental damage as a reason for racially discriminatory attitudes. For example, population increases lead to the greater use of central heating systems that consume more oil and increase atmospheric pollution. It is argued that using the cover of environmental concern attempts to present the eco-racist as neutral (Braham and Valeri, 2003: 82–83).

- Ideological racism – a belief system which is embedded in culture. Members of that culture are taught stereotypes and negative emotions about other groups. For instance, consider the racist belief system used to justify slavery in the American South, which was absorbed by each new generation of southern whites (Healey, 2012: 32).

- Institutional racism – first coined by Stokely Carmichael and Charles V. Hamilton in 1967, this refers to the overt and covert 'predication of decisions and policies in considerations of race for the purpose of *subordinating* a racial group and maintaining control over that group' (Carmichael and Hamilton, 1967, reproduced in Cashmore and Jennings, 2001: 112). The term was later popularized following the inquiry into the murder of Stephen Lawrence (Macpherson, 1999), which emphasized more strongly the role played by the organizational culture's routine institutional practices and structures.

The impact of racism varies. Often it shapes the everyday routines and lives of victims in terms of access to places and spaces or to goods and services. For some, though, the impact goes beyond social limitations. Some victims of racism also go on to experience serious mental health issues. Here, for instance, Williams and Williams-Morris (2010) found that racism in societal institutions in particular negatively impacted on access to resources which limited the socioeconomic mobility and poor living conditions of those experiencing racism. In addition, victims of racism who accepted negative cultural stereotypes also suffered from poor self-evaluation. The impact of racism here thus adversely affected mental health and had a deleterious effect on psychological well-being (Williams and Williams-Morris, 2010: 243). This is supported by other research – see, for example, Landrinel and Klonoff, 1996; Larson, Gillies, Howard and Coffin, 2007; Williams, Neighbors and Jackson, 2003.

There are also other serious impacts of racism: for instance, global slavery; lynching, attacks by the Ku Klux Klan, Jim Crow and segregation in the USA; apartheid in South Africa; the pursuit of Aryan supremacism and the Final Solution in Nazi Germany; and the genocide in Rwanda. These examples indicate that, for some, race is indeed a matter of life or death. Black and minority ethnic experience of the terror emerging from white domination sets the norm as it is accepted and largely goes unchallenged by white-majority mainstream society – even those not participating or actively consenting to such terror. This is because the mainstream's lack of challenge inadvertently maintains and perpetuates racial inequality for social, political and economic reasons of self-interest.

ACTIVITY

bell hooks (1992) talks about 'white terror' and its power. Consider the ways in which whiteness has been used (if at all) to exert control over others. Is hooks's argument valid today?

In contemporary society, the racialized unequal treatment of black and minority ethnic groups remains rife, although it often presents itself in more masked and reworked forms. However, people of black and minority ethnic background continue to be seen as 'flawed psychologically, morally and socially', not only as individuals, but in terms of their cultures and family life, and indeed every aspect of their lives (Owusu-Bempah and Howitt, 2000: 95). One result is that they are more readily labelled as deviants. The term **'black deviance'** refers to the process by which individuals come to be socially constructed as deviants or in some cases criminal, and where particular reference is made to race, ethnicity, religion or nationality to do this. For example, consider the focus in more recent times of media images, lay stereotypes and even political commentary on strict Asian parents who force their young daughters into arranged marriages; the parasitical nature of work-shy Irish travellers; and the hordes of bogus asylum seekers who are a drain on the county's welfare resources. The imagery of the black and minority ethnic dangerous 'other' also serves to create images of white victims. This is then used to justify further discriminatory attitudes and behaviour (Patel and Tyrer, 2011: 24). For instance, consider the presentation of Romanian and Bulgarian migrants in the lead-up to the free movement transition controls from 1 January 2014[2] and the ensuing attempts to severely restrict their numbers. A number of news organizations, such as the UK's *Daily Mail*, covered the event in depth, and, it can be argued, fuelled feelings of panic, fear, anger and hatred. For instance, look at the *Daily Mail*'s coverage of this news story in the run-up to the free movement of Bulgarian and Romanian migrants (see Image 2.1): the use of a rather downtrodden and shabby looking elderly lady who appears unable to contribute to the economy, against the backdrop of a typically British institution, visually evokes nationalistic emotions of fear and anger. The accompanying narrative is highlighted in parts with shading and bold text, to emphasize the key points of threat, which, the article suggests, runs across all the key areas of society. The message in this visually and textually xeno-racist article is that 'they' are a threat to 'us' and must be stopped, if only to protect all that is British.

Image 2.1 Romanian and Bulgarian free movement in the EU caused particular panic in newspapers such as the UK's *Daily Mail*. Courtesy of the *Daily Mail*, London.

Here we had a moral panic which made direct links between the UK's decline and the 'influx' of migrants. Migrants are imagined as having a predisposition to over-breeding (having lots of babies); causing overpopulation, which leads to a drain on the NHS, housing and education services; participating in 'welfare scrounging' and criminal behaviour; as well as importing a problematic culture into the country. Indeed, it has been argued that so severe and blurred is the immigration–refugee–asylum moral panic that in recent times all non-white people, regardless of whether they are British, a tourist, labouring migrant, or whatever, are being constructed within a wider framework of an asylum hysteria (Garner, 2007; McGhee, 2005).

A number of Human Rights Acts offer protection from many racially discrimina-tory practices. On an international level, this includes a number of measures introduced to protect people from the most dangerous consequences of racism, such as murder, genocide and enslavement. Examples of legislation include:

- Convention on the Prevention and Punishment of Crime of Genocide (1948)

- Supplement Convention on the Abolition of Slavery and the Slave Trade (1956)

- United Nations Declaration of the Elimination of All Forms of Racial Discrimination (1963)

- Universal Declaration of Human Rights (1948)

- International Covenant on Civil and Political Rights (1966)

- European Convention on Human Rights (1950)

- American Convention on Human Rights (1978)

- African Charter on Human and People's Rights (1986)

In the UK, such rights are absolute under the Human Rights Act (1998), and give us rights and freedoms that might not be covered by discrimination legislation, such as the Race Relations [Amendments] Act (2000). In terms of race matters, human rights refer to issues around safety, dignity, society and our private life. It is about the right to equal treatment and freedom from discrimination on (perceived) grounds of race, religion, ethnicity and nationality: 'People have the right not to be treated differently because of race, religion, sex, political views or any other status, unless this can be justified objectively. Everyone must have equal access to Convention rights, whatever their status' (Human Rights Act, 1998, article 14). However, in reality, violations of these Acts occur on a regular basis. For instance, consider the case of Jean Charles de Menezes, shot in 2005 in London's Stockwell tube station, or any other of the numer-ous cases where black and minority ethnic people experience enhanced victimization by the state (such as stop and search, deaths in custody, over-sentencing), as well as the rising numbers of recorded racist victimizations. Of interest is a body of literature which has found that some black and minority ethnic groups not only fail to report racism, but consider racism to be an inevitable part of their everyday norm. For example, in their study of the perceptions of prejudice by members of the Pakistani population in Northern Ireland (UK), Donnan and O'Brien (1998: 204–205) found that their respondents felt that racist experiences were a 'normal' and expected part of being a member of the black and minority ethnic (migrant) population living in a white majority society. However, although such views were sometimes shared by the younger members of this ethnic group, not all were so readily accepting of the 'normalization' view.

Not only does race *really* matter in society, but it should also matter to social scientists. Of particular value here, especially in highlighting the relationship between power and racially based injustice (victimhood), is the approach taken by **critical criminology**. Considering itself to be a radical alternative to mainstream criminology, this approach argues that attention must be paid to the determining contexts of social conflict rather than causation factors (Chadwick and Scraton, 2001: 70). As such, the relationship between knowledge and power must be considered (see Foucault, 1980). In particular, critical criminological thought draws our attention to the exploitation and victimization of the powerless, by the powerful, controlling and oppressive state (Scott and Marshall, 2005: 124). In terms of race, it considers the ways in which black and minority ethnic groups have particularly been subjected to discriminatory practices by a criminal justice system and other powerful organizations and institutions that evade accountability.

Case study: Online racism following Nina Davuluri's crowning as Miss America 2014

Nina Davuluri was crowned Miss America in 2014 and became the first Indian American woman to win the title. Davuluri is the daughter of Indian immigrants from Vijayawada in Andhra Pradesh (India). She was born in Syracuse, New York, and grew up in Oklahoma and Michigan. Having previously won the title of Miss New York, Davuluri received a mass of online racist and xenophobic abuse, largely via the popular social media platform Twitter, immediately after she won the Miss America 2014 title:

'And the Arab wins Miss America. Classic' – @Granvil_Colt

'Ummm wtf? Have we forgotten 9/11?' – @anthonytkr,

'How the f*** does a foreigner win miss America? She is a Arab!' – @jakeamick5

(Tweets cited in *The Times of India*, 16 September 2013)

The online abuse[3] targeted at Davuluri had centred on her Indian background and what soon became a reimagined shift to a 'Muslim' and 'Arab' heritage. This repositioning served to satisfy a type of anti-Muslim hostility that is framed by the xenophobic sentiments of white-American post-9/11 hatred. Tweets emerged which referred to Davuluri as 'a terrorist', claiming that her win was a victory for Al Qaeda (Broderick, 2013, cited in Cisneros and Nakayama, 2015: 108).

The powerfully explicit 'racial, national and gendered dimensions of the Miss America Pageant' acted as an 'ideal' platform for the festering of the cyber-hate received by Davuluri in that it allowed for the 'old racisms' to present themselves within what is often referred to as a post-race era (Cisneros and Nakayama, 2015: 109). Despite the presence of previous non-white winners,[4] alongside the insistence that we are now living in a post-race era, evident not least in America by the election of Barack Obama, the first black African-American president, the Miss America Pageant nevertheless remains framed by a wider project that seeks to reinforce the imagined racial and gendered logics of the American national identity: the beautiful, feminine and white woman. Of course it is a naturally occurring phenomenon, so the logic goes, given that non-white women are vulgar and sexually deviant (see Chapter 6). Thus the whiteness and national identity ideals (in other words, American-ness) of the Miss America Pageant remain a narrative of racial nationalism, white supremacy and anti-black (or, in 2014, heightened anti-Muslim) hatred.

The use of social media to exhibit such racist ideology was powerful, in part because of the blurred lines between hate speech and freedom of expression when in cyberspace, as well the opportunities for invisibility that are provided when online. Social media also offers a ready means of being able to communicate to large audiences instantly and in real time. In combination, this makes it easy for expressions of hate to spread rapidly and remain unregulated. Cyberspace also allows for older racial logics, that is racialized rationales of inferiority, to be used as a source and expression of abuse. For instance, tweets in the Davuluri case which objected to her being crowned Miss America drew heavily on a number of stereotypes that were characteristic of 'old' race logics about white supremacy, biological/cultural essentialism and exclusion (Cisneros and Nakayama, 2015: 113). Davuluri was 'brown', not only in her biological features, but also in her cultural expression of this difference, this being demonstrated in her self-selected talent performance of a Bollywood fusion dance. By that 'brown' fact alone, she was perceived as being unable to hold the Miss America title – a view held by many of those who sent abusive tweets.

ACTIVITY

What does Nina Davuluri's crowning as Miss America 2014 tell us about how we use racialized labels to determine a national identity?

CONCLUDING THOUGHTS

The discussion in this chapter has considered in more detail the ways in which 'race' is socially constructed and, from this, how it is then used to discriminate against some populations. The development of race ideology, and in particular its biological, essentialist and cultural roots, has been highlighted to enable a fuller appreciation of how the idea of separate and fixed races, along with the notion of a natural order of races, continues to dominate social relationships. Within this context, the chapter notes the importance of examining and challenging such racialized constructions and the ensuing experiences of racism. The online racism directed at Nina Davuluri, the 2014 Miss America title holder, is discussed to highlight some of the issues covered in the chapter. The key question raised in the chapter centres on identifying the continued development, application and impact of race markers in what is often referred to as a post-race society.

MAIN POINTS

- Scientific racism was used to present ideas about white superiority and black inferiority.

- Race is socially constructed as it is politically and historically defined.

- Race matters because it allows patterns of racism, in particular the power to control and exploit.

- There are different types of racism, including eco-racism, ideological racism and institutional racism.

STUDY QUESTIONS

1. How has race been used in the past? How does this differ from its use in contemporary society?

2. To what extent is race socially constructed?

3. If there is no such thing as race, why does society behave as if there is?

4. What is the source of racism?

FURTHER READING

Carmichael, Stokely and Hamilton, Charles V. (1967) 'Black power: The politics of liberation in America', in E. Cashmore and J. Jennings (eds.), *Racism: Essential Readings*. London: Sage. pp. 111–121.
Dyer, Richard (1997) *White*. London: Routledge.
Fekete, Liz (2001) 'The emergence of xeno-racism', *Race and Class*, 43(2): 23–40.

REFERENCES

African Charter on Human and People's Rights (1986).
American Convention on Human Rights (1978).

Bagley, Christopher, Young, Loretta and Scully, Anne (1992) *International and Transracial Adoptions: A Mental Health Perspective*. Aldershot: Avebury.

Berger, Peter and Luckmann, Thomas (1966) *The Social Construction of Reality: A Treatise in the Sociology of Knowledge*. New York: Doubleday.

Bhattacharyya, Gargi (2008) *Dangerous Brown Men: Exploiting Sex, Violence and Feminism in the War on Terror*. London: Zed Books.

Black, Edwin (2003) *War Against the Weak: Eugenics and America's Campaign to Create a Master Race*. New York: Thunder's Mouth Press.

Bonham, Vence L., Warshauer-Baker, Esther and Collins, Francis S. (2005) 'Race and ethnicity in the genome era: The complexity of the constructs', *American Psychologist*, 60(1): 9–15.

Braham, Peter and Valeri, Mauro (2003) 'Eco-racism', in G. Bolaffi, R. Bracalenti, P. Braham and S. Gindro (eds.), *Dictionary of Race, Ethnicity and Culture*. London: Sage. pp. 82–84.

Britton, Nadia J. (1999) 'Racialized identity and the term black', in S. Roseniel and J. Seymour (eds.), *Practising Identities: Power and Resistance*. London: Macmillan. pp. 134–154.

Burman, Jenny (2010) 'Suspects in the city: Browning the "not-quite" Canadian citizen', *Cultural Studies*, 24(2): 200–213.

Chadwick, Kathryn and Scraton, Phil (2001) 'Critical criminology', in E. McLaughlin and J. Muncie (eds.), *The Sage Dictionary of Criminology*, London: Sage. pp. 70–72.

Cisneros, David J. and Nakayama, Thomas K. (2015) 'New media, old racisms: Twitter, Miss America, and cultural logics of race', *Journal of International and Intercultural Communication*, 8(2): 108–127.

Convention on the Prevention and Punishment of Crime of Genocide (1948).

Donnan, Hastings and O'Brien, Mairead (1998) '"Because you stick out, you stand out": Perceptions of prejudice among Northern Ireland's Pakistanis', in P. Hainsworth (ed.), *Divided Society: Ethnic Minorities and Racism in Northern Ireland*. London: Pluto Press. pp. 197–262.

Downing, John and Husband, Charles (2005) *Representing 'Race': Racisms, Ethnicities and Media*. London: Sage.

Ely, Peter and Denney, David (1987) *Social Work in a Multi Racial Society*. Aldershot: Gower.

European Convention on Human Rights (1950).

Foucault, Michel (1980) *Power/Knowledge: Selected Interviews and Other Writings, 1972–1977*. Edited by Colin Gordon. Brighton: Harvester Wheatsheaf.

Garner, Steve (2007) *Whiteness: An Introduction*. Abingdon: Routledge.

Garner, Steve (2010) *Racisms: An Introduction*. London: Sage.

General Assembly of Virginia (1924) *Racial Integrity Act 1924*. Washington, DC: The Government Printing Office.

Hall, Stuart (1996) 'New ethnicities', in D. Morley and K. Chen (eds.), *Stuart Hall: Critical Dialogues in Cultural Studies*, London: Routledge. pp. 441–449.

Harrison, Gualtiero (2003) 'Eurocentrism', in G. Bolaffi, R. Bracalenti, P. Braham and S. Gindro (eds.), *Dictionary of Race, Ethnicity and Culture*. London: Sage. pp. 107–109.

Healey, Joseph F. (2012) *Diversity and Society: Race, Ethnicity and Gender*. Newbury Park, CA: Pine Forge Press.

Herrnstein, Richard J. and Murray, Charles (1994) *The Bell Curve: Intelligence and Class Structure in American Life*. New York: The Free Press.

hooks, bell (1992) *Black Looks: Race and Representation*. Boston, MA: South End Press.

hooks, bell (2013) *Writing Beyond Race: Living Theory and Practice*. New York: Routledge.

Home Office (1998) *Human Rights Act 1998*. London: The Stationery Office.

Home Office (2000) *Race Relations [Amendments] Act 2000*. London: The Stationery Office.

Jensen, Robert (2011) 'Whiteness', in S.M. Caliendo and C.D. McIlwain (eds.), *The Routledge Companion to Race and Ethnicity*. Abingdon: Routledge. pp. 21–28.

Knox, Robert (1850) *Races of Man*. Philadelphia, PA: Lea and Blanchard.

Kundnani, Arun (2001) 'In a foreign land: The new popular racism', *Race and Class*, 43(2): 41–60.

Landrinel, Hope and Klonoff, Elizabeth A. (1996) 'The schedule of racist events: A measure of racial discrimination and a study of its negative physical and mental health consequences', *Journal of Black Psychology*, 22(2): 144–168.

Larson, Ann, Gillies, Marisa, Howard, Peter J. and Coffin, Juli (2007) 'It's enough to make you sick: The impact of racism on the health of Aboriginal Australians', *Australian and New Zealand Journal of Public Health*, 31(4): 322–329.

Long, Edward (1774) *History of Jamaica*. London: T. Lowndes and Son.

Lugo-Lugo, Carmen R. and Bloodsworth-Lugo, Mary K. (2010) '465° from September 11: Citizenship, immigration, same-sex marriage and the browning of terror', *Cultural Studies*, 24(2): 234–255.

Macpherson, William (1999) *The Stephen Lawrence Inquiry*. Cm. 4262-1. London: Home Office (www.archive.official-documents.co.uk/document/cm42/4262/4262.htm).

Mason, David (2000) *Race and Ethnicity in Modern Britain*. Second Edition. Oxford: Oxford University Press.

McCann-Mortimer, Patricia, Auggoustinos, Martha and LeCouteur, Amanda (2004) '"Race" and the human genome project: Constructions of scientific legitimacy', *Discourse and Society*, 15(4): 409–432.

McGhee, Derek (2005) *Intolerant Britain? Hate, Citizenship and Difference*. Maidenhead: Open University Press.

McLaughlin, Eugene (2001) 'Essentialism', in E. McLaughlin and J. Muncie (eds.), *The Sage Dictionary of Criminology*. London: Sage. p. 109.

Meer, Nasar and Modood, Tariq (2010) 'Analysing the growing scepticism towards the idea of Islamaphobia', *Arches Quarterly*, 24(7): 116–126.

Melotti, Umberto (2003a) 'Colonialism', in G. Bolaffi, R. Bracalenti, P. Braham and S. Gindro (eds.), *Dictionary of Race, Ethnicity and Culture*. London: Sage. pp. 39–40.

Melotti, Umberto (2003b) 'Ethnocentrism', in G. Bolaffi, R. Bracalenti, P. Braham and S. Gindro (eds.), *Dictionary of Race, Ethnicity and Culture*. London: Sage. p. 108.

Miles, Robert (1989) *Racism*. London: Routledge.

Moore, Robert (2003) 'Racialization', in G. Bolaffi, R. Bracalenti, P. Braham and S. Gindro (eds.), *Dictionary of Race, Ethnicity and Culture*. London: Sage. pp. 273–274.

Mukhopadhyay, Carol (2011) 'Race', in S.M. Caliendo and C.D. McIlwain (eds.), *The Routledge Companion to Race and Ethnicity*. Abingdon: Routledge. pp. 203–207.

Owusu-Bempah, Kwame and Howitt, Dennis (2000) *Psychology Beyond Western Perspectives*. Leicester: The British Psychological Society.

Parrott, Roxanne, Silk, Karri, Dollow, Megan, Krieger, Janice L., Harris, Tina M. and Condit, Celeste (2005) 'Development and validation of tools to assess genetic discrimination and genetically based racism', *Journal of the National Medical Association*, 97(7): 1–11.

Patel, Tina G. and Tyrer, David (2011) *Race, Crime and Resistance*. London: Sage.

Pilkington, Andrew (2003) *Racial Disadvantage and Ethnic Diversity in Britain*. Basingstoke: Palgrave Macmillan.

Pinder, Sherrow O. (2011) 'Eugenics', in S.M. Caliendo and C.D. McIlwain (eds.), *The Routledge Companion to Race and Ethnicity*. Abingdon: Routledge. pp. 138–141.

Rattansi, Ali (2003) 'Race', in G. Bolaffi, R. Bracalenti, P. Braham and S. Gindro (eds.), *Dictionary of Race, Ethnicity and Culture*. London: Sage. pp. 239–245.

Runnymede Trust (2000) *The Future of Multi-Ethnic Britain*. London: Runnymede Trust.

Scott, John and Marshall, Gordon (2005) 'Criminology, critical', *Oxford Dictionary of Criminology*. Oxford: Oxford University Press. p. 124.

Semati, Mehdi (2010) 'Islamaphobia, culture and race in the age of Empire', *Cultural Studies*, 24(2): 256–275.

Sivanandan, Ambalavaner (2006) 'Race, terror and civil society', *Race and Class*, 47(1): 1–8.

Supplement Convention on the Abolition of Slavery and the Slave Trade (1956).

The Times of India (2013) 'Racist tweets mar sweet moment for Nina Davuluri, first Miss America of Indian origin', *The Times of India*, 16 September 2013 (http://timesofindia.indiatimes.com/nri/us-canada-news/Racist-tweets-mar-sweet-moment-for-Nina-Davuluri-first-Miss-America-of-Indian-origin/articleshow/22631169.cms).

Tizard, Barbara and Phoenix, Ann (2002) *Black, White or Mixed-Race? Race and Racism in the Lives of Young People of Mixed Parentage*. London: Routledge.

United Nations General Assembly (1963) *United Nations Declaration of the Elimination of All Forms of Racial Discrimination* (1963). New York: United Nations.

United Nations General Assembly (1948) *Universal Declaration of Human Rights 1948*. New York: United Nations.

United Nations General Assembly (1966) *International Covenant on Civil and Political Rights 1966*. New York: United Nations.

Valeri, Mauro (2003a) 'Afrocentrism', in G. Bolaffi, R. Bracalenti, P. Braham and S. Gindro (eds.), *Dictionary of Race, Ethnicity and Culture*. London: Sage. pp. 6–7.

Valeri, Mauro (2003b) 'Black', in G. Bolaffi, R. Bracalenti, P. Braham and S. Gindro (eds.), *Dictionary of Race, Ethnicity and Culture*. London: Sage. pp. 31–33.

Webster, Colin (2007) *Understanding Race and Crime*. Maidenhead: McGraw-Hill/Open University Press.

West, Cornell (1993) *Race Matters*. Boston, MA: Beacon Press.

Williams, David R., Neighbors, Harold W. and Jackson, James S. (2003) 'Racial/ethnic discrimination and health: Findings from community studies', *American Journal of Public Health*, 93(2): 200–208.

Williams, David R. and Williams-Morris, Ruth (2010) 'Racism and mental health: The African American experience', *Ethnicity and Health*, 5(3–4): 243–268.

NOTES

1. This was the series of so-called medical experiments (now referred to as medical torture) on concentration camp prisoners, mainly Jews (including Jewish children) from across Europe, as well as some Romani people, Soviets and disabled Germans. Typically, the experiments resulted in death, disfigurement or being left with a permanent disability.

2. From 1 January 2014 Bulgarians and Romanians were given the freedom to live and work in EU Member States. This brought them in line with the citizens of all other Member States (except Croatians, who will be subject to transitional controls until 2020).

3. For further examples of the tweets Davuluri received, see Cisneros and Nakayama (2015).

4. This includes (the first and only) Jewish winner Bess Myerson in 1945 and (the first) African-American winner Vanessa Williams in 1984, whose wins were incidentally used to satisfy a wider 'race' agenda (Banet-Weiser, 1999, cited in Cisneros and Nakayama, 2015: 112). However, the total number of non-white winners remains significantly low.

3

UNDERSTANDING SOCIETY

INTRODUCTION

This chapter will provide a discussion on the definition, role and function of society. It will especially focus on the formation of contemporary society, marking out in particular new and distinct features. The reader will develop an understanding of how we think about society and the significance of social relationships, norms and values in our everyday lives. The theory and concepts covered in the chapter will include: apartheid; assimilations; Chicago School; community; culture; denizen; social exclusion; social norms; and symbolic interactionism. The case study described in the chapter is the Alphaville gated community in Brazil. The key question raised in the chapter is: How powerful are 'rules' in society, and why do we usually obey them?

KEY TERMS

- Apartheid

- Assimilation

- Bicultural

- Chicago School

- Community

- Culture

- Denizen

- Diaspora

- Environmental racism

- Globalization

- Marginalization

- Modernity

- Multiculturalism

- Social divisions

- Social norms

- Super-diversity

- Symbolic interactionism

WHAT IS SOCIETY?

Society is relatively absent as an object in that it cannot be described in fixed and certain ways. Rather, it is an assemblage of social actions and interaction, which become framed by changing individual meanings. Thus, the concept of 'society' is social – indeed, it is significantly social! The emphasis on its significance was well illustrated in the sociological backlash against the British ex-prime minister Margaret Thatcher, who, in 1987, had declared that 'there is no such thing as society'. Thatcher's comment sought to emphasize the responsibility of 'individual men and individual women' who make free choices and thus (should) take some responsibility for themselves. In doing so she sought to make Britain move away from dependency and towards self-reliance. Thatcher's comment, though, was heavily criticized for its lack of appreciation for the role that society plays in the construction of individuals' lives, especially in terms of the various networks of power that are located within the structures of society. For instance, it is argued that Thatcher lacked an appreciation of how not everyone was equally able to make free choices. However, Thatcher's comment reignited both lay and sociological interest in the existence and processes involved in the construction of society.

Today, although sociologists still cannot agree on a universal definition and social theory of society, there is general agreement that it exists and that it is important. Society is important not least because it shapes our lives. At its most basic, society defines who we are and what we can do. As Campbell (1981: 3) simply put it: 'Human life is unthinkable outside society. Individuals cannot exist in complete and permanent isolation. ... [Man] is a social being.' Society also needs individuals and groups, who in turn shape the formation, boundaries and content of a given society. Thus, the relationship between society and the individual(s) is not a mutually exclusive one. Rather, they are bound up in myriad and complex ways. Although there is no universally agreed definition of society, discussions have identified the following elements as significant in the existence of society:

- A sovereign social entity (with a nation-state organizing the rights and duties of members);

- Use of a citizenship status (for entitlements and expectations);

- Existence of a collective consciousness (over and above the individual);

- Meaningful networked relationships and mutual dependence;

- The creation of inclusionary (and exclusionary) boundaries to define belonging;

- Existence of various social systems and institutions (for resources and services);

- A common cultural identity (real or imagined);

- A shared material identity (via the use of national symbols, flags, customs and traditions).

Debates have also produced a common understanding of society which is readily used and accepted as a given, in lay talk at least. This refers to 'a group of people who share a common culture, occupy a particular territorial area, and feel themselves to constitute a unified and distinct entity' (Scott and Marshall, 2005: 622). In this sense, the idea of collectives, or community, is important. A **community** is a term which is often used to refer to a particular set of social relationships based on elements that its members perceive themselves to have in common. Communities are considered to be one of the basic components of society (Hoey, 2007: 399). Giddens (1993) argues that communities have important curative remedies for various social ills. Indeed, Zygmunt Bauman (2001: 3) goes further and argues that, although never actually achievable, the utopian ideal of community nevertheless motivates us to continually seek it out, an effort which, in itself, has important bonding functions. However, this bonding (*or* inclusion) inevitably brings with it exclusionary measures: in order to have an 'us', there needs to be an (undesirable) 'them' from which the first group can separate and distinguish themselves. Members of a community must, according to Sigmund Freud, give up individual desires and powers. Only when individual interests are subsumed into those of the community collective can civilized communal life become possible (Freud, 1961: 41). Sociologically, it has been recognized that there are real communities as well as imagined ones. Similarly, there are more general collectives (or communities) in which, it is assumed, there is one unitary common belief, for instance, when we speak of 'capitalist society' or 'Western society'.

In sharing a unitary common belief, culture is considered to be a significant part of what bonds members of a society together. **Culture** is used to describe all non-biological aspects in human society that are socially transmitted, such as shared customs, values and beliefs which characterize a given social group and which are often passed down from one generation to the next (Gindro, 2003: 61). Members of society not only learn 'culture', but must also internalize it. It is argued that the concepts of culture and society are so inextricably bound up with one another that neither can meaningfully exist without the other (Punch et al., 2013: 21). Following the Second World War, the concept of culture took a specific conceptual turn, when it was presented as a preferential term over 'race', partly to avoid legitimizing many of the biologically based practices that had been carried out under conceptualizations of 'race'. However, culture as a concept has been attacked as adopting the problematic heritage of 'race', namely its biologically and essentially based assumptions about specific population groups, as well as placing European (white) culture in a normative – thus higher and more privileged – position.

Society in recent times has come to be more complex, with traditional geographical boundaries being widened or removed altogether. Indeed, modern society is considered to be so fragmented that some have questioned whether a unified cultural (norms and values) system actually exists (Punch et al., 2013: 21). In addition, it is now possible for a society to form in situations where members (may) have no physical contact with one another. Take, for instance, the case of online communities and the very meaningful bonds felt by its members, who in many ways can very much be considered to be a real community (Haythornwaite, 2007; Raacke and Bonds-Raacke, 2008; Ren et al., 2012). Communities in cyberspace have grown rapidly and have transformed the modern world. Cyberspace, by which I mean the internet, new media and social networking sites, allows us to connect on a global scale in real time. This connectivity is significant, especially given that it can be argued that the markers of a traditional society, namely its norms, values, cultural transmission, and so on, also feature in a virtual society. Therefore, for some, an online virtual society may offer the same, if not more, than (an)other non-virtual one. Such communities are able to mobilize successfully to make a significant impact on structural inequalities and in doing so change the social and political landscape of wider society. For example, consider the power of online protesting communities and their ability to mobilize and organize themselves globally using online social networking sites, Facebook, Twitter and YouTube, during the Arab Spring[1] of 2010–2011 (Cohen and Kennedy, 2013: 6).

There is also now a myriad of societies, some of which have shared commonalities as well as distinct differences. This has resulted more than ever in a state where we now have different types of society and varying sub-categories within them. This aspect of **modernity**, a term used to characterize the history of social relations from the end of the eighteenth century, a time which saw mass demographic and industrial revolutions, means that 'social relations are relatively impersonal, impermanent, varied and unpredictable' (Abercrombie and Warde, 1998: 6). For some, this feature of modernity is embraced and actively engaged in; for other, it causes feelings of fear, anxiety and insecurity. In a similar vein, it has also been argued that globalization has undermined the autonomy of traditional geographically defined societies (Scott and Marshall, 2005: 622). Thus, we can no longer take nationally defined societies, for example, 'British society' or 'American society', for granted. Waters (1995: 3) defines **globalization** as 'a social process in which the constraints of geography on social and cultural arrangements recede and in which people are becoming increasingly aware that they are receding'. There are various social and cultural developments that indicate active participation in globalization, such as use of the world wide web for communication, patterns of consumption and consumerism, sports events such as the Olympic Games, and world political systems (United Nations) (Scott and Marshall, 2005: 249).

It has been argued that the concept of society as once commonly 'embedded within notions of nation-state, citizenship and national society', can now be challenged, especially given that we have an increasingly borderless world (Urry, 2000: 5–6). In this sense, society is no longer (if it ever was at all) a self-functioning and self-reproducing entity. Thus, Urry argues, we should focus on the physical, imaginative and virtual movements that form social collectives. Mobilities, such as the travel of people, ideas, images, objects, and so on, are important in the development of contemporary social life in terms of how we experience time, space, dwelling and citizenship, and it is this 'post-societal phase' that we must come to appreciate and investigate (Urry, 2000: Preface). Given the contestations over the status of society, some have sought to replace the term 'society' with what they consider to be more accurate representations of the phenomenon. For instance, Marxist theoretician Louis Althusser (1918–1990) has suggested that the term 'social formation' be used instead. This refers to a combination of three interconnecting levels of relationships (economic, ideological and political) which are all significant in social formation (or entities more widely known as 'society').

Regardless of what we call 'it' or how we think about it, one point is constant – there is 'something' (which we currently refer to as 'society') that plays a huge role in who we are and how we experience life. For this reason alone, it is for sociology (and the 'sociological imagination') to investigate the social being and its environment.

As C. Wright Mills (1959: 6) noted:

> We have come to know that every individual lives, from one generation to
> the next, in some society; that he lives out a biography, and that he lives
> it out within some historical sequence. By the fact of his living he contrib-
> utes, however minutely, to the shaping of this society and to the course
> of its history, even as he is made by society and by its historical push and
> shove. The sociological imagination enables us to grasp history and bio-
> graphy and the relations between the two within society.

--------------------------------- **ACTIVITY** ---------------------------------

Recall your participation or belonging to a[ny] society. What was your role? What
were the rules and norms? Were you a full member of that society? If so, why and
how was this achieved? Now, consider when you were an outsider of a[ny] society.
Why did you not belong? Would you have changed your identity, beliefs and behaviour to belong to that society?

THE SIGNIFICANCE OF SOCIETY

There are various theories on the role and importance of society, both for the collective and the individual, and how we distinguish one society from another largely
depends on our motivations and value position (Billington, Hockey and Strawbridge,
1998: 20). Symbolic interactionism, a theoretical approach most commonly associated with Charles Cooley (1864–1929), William Isaac Thomas (1863–1947) and, in
particular, George Herbert Mead (1863–1931), has been presented as a way of
understanding the relationship between the individual and 'society'. Mead argued
that the perceptions and behaviour of individuals are influenced by their membership of social groups, or, as Mead called them, 'the generalized other' (Mead, 1995:
369). This membership is important as it shapes the individual's 'self' – the way in
which an individual is self-conscious and how they identify themselves. The individual's construction of 'self' demonstrates how they are 'becoming an organic
member of society … taking over the morals of that society and becoming an essential member of it' (Mead, 1995: 372). Erving Goffman (1922–1982) later added to
this when he argued that individuals have a variety of different 'roles' which they
'play' at different times, depending on the 'impression' that they seek to create, as
well as the different social groups to which they belong (Goffman, 1959).

Functionalist Emile Durkheim argues that society is an important reality which exists
beyond the individuals that compose it. We enter (as we are born into) an ongoing society, and then leave it (when we die). Thus, for Durkheim, society is more than the sum
of its parts (Macionis and Plummer, 2002: 84). Society has the power to shape individuals' thoughts and behaviour. Here, established structures, or what Durkheim calls social

facts – for example, cultural norms and religious belief – and **social norms** – a shared expectation of behaviour that is considered to be desirable for the well-being of a group's interest within a given setting – both have an objective reality and are internalized by members of society. This form of moral discipline serves to regulate individual behaviour and reinforce the collective rules of that society (Durkheim, 1982). This point is most powerfully argued in Durkheim's work on suicide, where he maintained that the least regulated members of society are those who suffer the highest rates of suicide (Durkheim, 1997b). For Durkheim, the patterns of 'social solidarity' that bonded and united traditional societies are different from those found in modern societies (Macionis and Plummer, 2002: 66). Modern societies impose far fewer restrictions on their individual members. However, Durkheim argued that this is not necessarily a good thing as 'modern freedom' brings with it the greater potential for 'anomie', this being a condition where society provides very little moral guidance to its individuals, resulting in disagreement between members over what are seen to be the appropriate norms and values for governing behaviour (Punch et al., 2013: 48).

The concerns of anomie can be witnessed in the work of the Chicago School, which studied relationships between members of a community residing in an American geographical 'zone', specifically looking at how environmental factors influenced human social interaction (bonds and behaviour). Although the theoretical tradition largely observed links between environmental factors and crime, its insight into the organization of human communities more generally is important for understanding society. The *concentric zone theory*, developed by Ernest Burgess (Park et al., 1925), argued that modern cities were made up of a series of five concentric circles expanding outwards from the centre (inner-city core). Each of the five zones contained communities which shared social status: at the centre was the business district, an area of low population; outside this was the 'zone in transition', an area marked by run-down housing, high population numbers and inward movement of immigrants, poverty and disease; next was the working-class zone; after that they middle-class zone; and finally the affluent suburbs. The 'zone in transition' was the area in which Chicago theorists were most interested, as it was this zone, they argued, that saw great flux and restlessness, with communal ties being largely absent. It was an area that was considered to be 'socially disorganized' (Park et al., 1925). This area was considered by the Chicago School to be a problem, or an area of concern for wider society. However, Durkheim (1997a) argued that society and all its elements, both positive and negative, have important 'functions' which contribute overall to the healthy survival and sense of belonging that is so essential to society. Durkheim gave the example of crime, which is often universally perceived to be a problem and harmful for society. However, Durkheim argued that when society's members recognize and respond to (criminal) acts, they are also reinforcing the boundaries of acceptable and unacceptable behaviour – they are defending the morality of that society.

Not everyone in society enjoys full membership benefits, or even full inclusion. This was clear in the work of the Chicago School. This is not least because of the tendency for human nature to want to increase its advantage. This tendency, alongside the historically developed structures of inequality, has resulted in some groups asserting power to gain advantage, control and benefit. This means that while some groups dominate, others become dominated, and consequently experience disadvantage in social, health and financial areas. Such experiences of inequality are common among members of a diaspora community. **Diaspora** refers to a particular type of journey when members of a community, often defined by national or ethnic affiliation, are usually forced to make a journey from their place of birth to a 'host' society, namely in instances of slavery, expulsion, indentured labour, persecution, political conflict, war, and so on. Diaspora communities, which consider themselves to have a shared history (whether this be a real or imagined one), never quite feel truly settled or accepted in their 'host' society once their journey is complete. This makes diaspora journeys essentially different from other types of community relocations or dispersals (Braham and Zargani, 2003: 73). Cohen (1997: 180) provides a good summary of the elements of diaspora communities:

1.   Dispersal from an original homeland (sometimes traumatically); or

2.   The migration from a homeland for reasons of work, trade, or colonization;

3.   The collective memory of a homeland;

4.   The idealization of the ancestral homeland;

5.   The development of a return movement;

6.   A strong ethnic consciousness and a sense of distinctiveness;

7.   A troubled relationship with host societies;

8.   A sense of solidarity with co-ethnics in other countries;

9.   The possibility of a distinctive creative life in pluralistic host societies.

It is important to recognize that because the concept of diaspora involves centralizing ethnicity or nationality, the concept has come under critique for its homogenizing and essentializing tendencies (Collyer, 2011: 132).

   Society is clearly full of **social divisions**, which are socially constructed based on the meanings we attach to the categories that mark them. In highlighting the importance of considering social divisions for our understanding of how society works, Payne (2000: 1) notes that:

> The *meanings* we bring to the label depends on the cultural significance we
> have learned to attach to them during our lives up to this moment. ... If we
> are to make coherent sense of our own lives, let alone understand what is
> going on in our society and why society as a whole operates as it does, the
> idea of 'social divisions' is one of the most useful and powerful tools available.

The categories that are used in the marking of social divisions may initially seem 'natural', not least because they are considered to have a biological basis. However, they are the outcomes of complex power relations, which are themselves based on advantage, status, resource access and privilege. Although some categories and ensuing social divisions can be strong and long-lasting, they are never fixed. They will vary according to space, time and context. This is due to their socially constructed nature. Similarly, social divisions can share some elements of a common identity, but remain uniquely different in other areas. Saying this, though, it has been argued that some categories and ensuing social divisions are sharper than others. Race is one such category. More importantly, these sharper divisions can have a very significant impact on the life chances of its members.

For Sibley (1995: ix), 'The human landscape can be read as a landscape of exclusion ... power is expressed in the monopolization of space and the relegation of weaker groups in society to less desirable environments...'. Hence it is not uncommon to find black and minority ethnic groups in less desirable areas, excluded on the social, psychological and geographical margins. For example, at its most extreme, consider the favelas in Brazil or shanty towns of India. Wacquant (2008: 240) notes how some places suffer disproportionately from 'territorial stigmatization' and become labelled as 'a lawless zone' or 'an outlaw estate', outside the common norm, where residents go on to become 'confined to a branded space' and have negative interactions with others, especially powerful others such as employers, the police and welfare officers (Wacquant, 2008: 171–174). Specialist public policy intervention measures have the effect of further stigmatizing and marginalizing residents of such areas (or urban ghettos) (Wacquant, 2008: 240). The **marginalization** of black and minority ethnic groups remains a common feature of contemporary society and, despite various anti-discrimination laws, it often acts as a basis for social segregation, which then contributes to other areas of disadvantage, such as low educational attainment, poor employment prospects and a concentration in deprived areas (Bracalenti and Braham, 2003: 174). The sociological study of inequality in society has therefore focused on the reasons for, the maintenance of, and the consequences emerging from inequality. This is discussed in the work on social stratification (how the structure of layers, or strata, emerge), social control (how the upper layers dominate and how inequality is maintained) and social conflict (the conditions under which inequality generates conflict) (Fulcher and Scott, 2007: 12–13).

MULTICULTURAL SOCIETY

The term **multiculturalism** has been used in a number of different ways: first, to refer to the demographic features of a given society; secondly, to refer to an ideological approach that recognizes and accepts racial, religious or cultural diversity; and thirdly, to refer to a set of state policies on governing a diverse society (Noor and Leong, 2013: 714). More recently, multiculturalism has been used within the context of debates about citizenship, patriotism and difference. In particular, the term has come to be synonymous with discussions about the anxiety emerging from high(er) levels of immigration and the (supposed) widening of cultural diversity. In examining such anxieties, Hage (2003: xii–2) uses the term 'paranoid nationalism' and the

figure of the 'white worrier' to represent the (young white South Australian's) feelings of marginalization emerging from Australian multiculturalism and immigration.
Consequently, multiculturalism in this context is presented as a condition, or an ill,
of society that needs to be carefully managed in order to avoid threats to social cohesion and national security (including the security of the nation's identity).

Inevitably, then, multiculturalism has been inextricably linked with ideals about
the rights and duties of 'legitimate citizenship'. The ideal of such citizenship is itself
linked to problematic constructions of desirability and undesirability of the 'racialized
other'. This was most forcefully illustrated with British immigration policy in
response to the 'threat' of postcolonial immigration in the post-war period. It was
this, and more specifically the notion of the postcolonial 'Black immigrant, enemy
within', that was the focus of Enoch Powell's now famous 'rivers of blood' speech
in April 1968. Such moral panics around multiculturalism, and in particular immigrant groups, have been a common feature of modern society, and was most
recently illustrated with the 'asylum problem', from which emerged panics about
supposed 'waves' of asylum seekers, many of which are bogus, who drain the country of its resources, pose a security problem, as well as dilute core elements of the
national identity. The metaphors of threat are commonly found in the mass media
and become embedded in the thinking of lay people, ranging from moderate forms
of cultural nationalism to more overt forms of xeno-racist views. A scan of any anti-
immigration right-wing media outlet illustrates this well. This deviant imagery has
been so widely generalized and accepted without question that it has led to the
portrayal of all those seen as falling outside the 'White host' category as 'bogus'.
McGhee (2005) argues that the disproportionate reaction and excessive use of
deterrence policies has led to the creation of a climate that is, in the words of
Sivanandan (2006), xeno-racist – a combination of racism and xenophobia that
produces a type of discrimination that is not colour-coded but seeks to treat the
Black postcolonial immigrant in the same way it does the White asylum seeker from
Eastern European countries.

It has also been suggested that although multiculturally sensitive polices may
claim to preserve and promote cultural diversity within a multicultural society, in
reality they could act as an obstacle to the embraced realization of a multicultural
society by failing to allow different groups to truly interact with one another. For
example, Western countries such as Britain and Sweden, which faced higher immigration flows during the 1970s, stated that they were keen to apply multicultural
embracement policies to help immigrant communities maintain the distinctiveness
of their own cultural identity. However, it has been argued that this approach
resulted in cultural divisions and social divisions (Callari Galli, 2003: 184).
Unsurprisingly, there has been a surge in the popularity for harsher immigration and
nationality laws. For example, consider Britain's 1981 Nationality Act and 2014
Immigration Act. Although the approaches underlining these laws differ, be they
based in defensive notions of nationality/security, or the pursuit of a diversity-
welcoming but unified national identity, or on motivations for securing citizens who
can most usefully contribute to the advancement of the nation, all these laws take

the starting point that culturally (racially) diverse populations are a 'social problem' for the 'host' nation unless they can prove otherwise. Thus they are 'illegitimate', and must prove themselves 'legitimate', for instance, by becoming assimilated into the 'host' nation.

Assimilation is often viewed as a process of gradual adaption that leads towards inclusion in the 'host' society and the disappearance of one's own cultural identity (or difference). This is often referred to as 'cultural assimilation'. Those in favour of cultural assimilation argue that integration methods rightly focus on cultural aspects and a 'thick' understanding of what creates national unity, which is considered vital for a harmonious and strong society (Michalowski, 2011: 750). Assimilation strategies are often pursued through specific integration policies which seek to make 'newcomers' citizens of the 'host' nation by establishing membership criteria and using methods of assessment, such as citizenship tests, to measure commitment and worthiness of prospective citizens, for instance those used in Austria, the UK, Germany, the Netherlands and the USA (Michalowski, 2011: 749). As an illustration, the American citizenship test draws heavily on notions of cultural assimilation (or 'naturalization'). In doing so, its key underlying principle is the eventual pursuit of becoming an American citizen, namely by learning the English language and all about American history, and to some degree accepting this as truth and adopting it as one's own narrative. It has been argued that as a political strategy in matters relating to migrant populations, assimilation seeks to keep the national culture homogeneous and thus in a position of relative power and authority (Zanfrini, 2003: 19). At times when assimilation policies have failed, the unwillingness or inability (due to stark differences) of newcomers has been blamed, as opposed to the forced elements of the assimilation process or the failure to recognize that some ethnic groups may want to retain some of their cultural identities and values. Denizen status has also been held up as one way in which individuals can prove themselves legitimate. Denizen is a term used to describe someone who is a foreign citizen with the legal status of a permanent resident (citizen), and who enjoys full social and economic rights as well as being well integrated into the 'host' country, but who refuses to give up their identification with and rights in their country of origin (Valeri, 2003: 67–68). There is no issue *per se* with the individual refusing to adopt the identity of the new 'host' country because they have in all other ways proven themselves a worthy citizen. They are therefore considered not to have been a drain on welfare resources or committed criminal behaviour.

In some cases, the multicultural status of a given society has come to be viewed in such problematic ways that policies of strict racial separation have been adopted. Apartheid is a regime which uses racial/ethnic lines to prevent the mixing of groups in areas such as housing, education, employment, medical care, political participation and even sexual relations. It was most strikingly used in South Africa following the general election of 1948, where new legislation legalized existing practice and separated the population into four groups ('black', 'white', 'coloured' and 'Indian', the latter two being further divided into several subcategories). In practice, the doctrine of apartheid in South Africa resulted in whites being allocated power with its black and minority ethnic populations experiencing disadvantage and inequality. Although officially abolished in 1990, it has been suggested that the legacy and impact of apartheid in South Africa continues to harm its black and minority ethnic groups.

Although problematized, multiculturalism is considered by some as positive for a progressive society. Berry (2000) argues that a true multicultural society sees all 'ethno-cultural' groups maintaining their cultural heritage and identity while also participating within wider society. For this to happen successfully, intercultural contact between members of that society must be under conditions where cultural difference is respected, and diversity accommodated in a fair and equitable way (Berry, 2000, cited in Sibley and Ward, 2013: 702). For example, Singapore has selected this path, and, it is argued, has successfully developed as a multicultural society. It has thrived economically as a small (and potentially vulnerable) island (see Noor and Leong, 2013). Although, to a degree, all societies are multicultural – an inevitable outcome of geographical movement throughout the ages – the term in the modern era is largely used to refer to the cohabitation of specific racial groups, namely those with recent heritage from nations in the ex-colonies and Eastern Europe, in countries where there is a homogeneous ethnic group of white (Western European) heritage. The term therefore incorporates considerations of how independently formed groups have for political, economic or social reasons come to cohabit a shared space or society.

However, some countries have consciously moved away from a multicultural status, instead presenting themselves as bicultural nations, despite having some degree of a multicultural demographic element. Bicultural, in this sense, requires two originally distinct cultures to co-exist on equal terms alongside each other, such as in Belgium, Switzerland and New Zealand. The latter considers itself to be more bicultural in light of its historical relationship between indigenous Maori and British colonizers. This is formalized in the country's Treaty of Waitangi (1840): 'The core vision involves a bicultural partnership arising from principles of *kawanatanga* (governorship by the Crown), *rangatiratanga* (tribal self-management), equality for all citizens, reasonable cooperation between the Crown and *iwi*/tribes, and redress of past injustices' (Byrnes, 2005, cited in Sibley and Ward, 2013: 701). It has been argued that in terms of social equality, patriotism and economic success, a treaty developed within a bicultural framework is more progressive than one developed within a multicultural framework, especially when the latter uses race-based interventions to try to reduce social inequalities (as is the case in the UK, for instance). However, in many societies a bicultural framework is not possible, and indeed even in New Zealand there are constant challenges and contestations (see Sibley and Ward, 2013).

ACTIVITY

What is the impact of socio-political narratives that choose to refer to multiculturalism when discussing population changes? Can multiculturalism ever be discussed outside race?

It is also worth noting that some commentators have argued that we are now living in a society that is 'super-diverse'. Super-diversity is an advance on the multicultural state. It is used to refer to a condition found in cities/countries, for instance, London (UK), which has recently (since the late 1990s) experienced rapid population changes, largely emerging from new levels and types of immigration flow, which have then contributed to the creation of varied and complex identities. However, although emerging from changes in immigration patterns, the super-diverse condition moves beyond the sole use of ethnicity as a marker of difference/similarity. This fact alone distinguishes it from multiculturalism. In describing a state where a given society has surpassed previous experiences of diversity, super-diversity is considered to be 'distinguished by a dynamic interplay of variables among an increased number of new, small and scattered, multiple-origin, transnationally connected, socio-economically differentiated and legally stratified immigrants who have arrived...' (Vertovec, 2007: 1024). Furthermore, Fanshawe and Sriskandarajah (2010) argue that super-diversity is especially strong in some societies, such as those found in Britain, because people are now more willing and able to express their identities. The discussion on super-diversity is still in its relative infancy. With this comes opportunity, but it would be interesting to see if this conceptualization of diversity becomes misappropriated by those who seek to curb (particular types of) immigration.

Case study: The Alphaville gated community in Brazil

Alphaville[2] is the name of a gated community on the outskirts of São Paulo (Brazil) which is marketed as a 'safe city'. The site is surrounded by high perimeter fences and guarded on a 24-hour basis by private security patrols, CCTV surveillance, intruder sensors and spotlights. Comprising over 20,000 residents all protected by over 1,000 private security officers, its residential entrance policy states that no residents with criminal records are accepted (Cohen and Kennedy, 2013: 167–168). With the promise of enhanced personal safety and secured property, it is unsurprising that it has proven very popular with São Paulo's wealthy middle-class population, who have flocked to Alphaville in their masses. The less wealthy members of São Paulo's population are also concerned about personal and property offences – especially given the well-known reality that poor people are more likely to be victims of crime. However, a number of highly publicized cases involving attacks on wealthy business people in São Paulo have resulted in heightened panics among the city's wealthier population, who have been able to act on fears and move to Alphaville, given their economically advantageous position.

Gated communities are attractive for a number of reasons: they potentially offer less residential turnover and thus more established population densities; they have higher standards of design and quality open space; and they have a greater sense of place and community (Grant, 2004: 1–3). However, the sociological literature on society, social relations and gated communities is less positive. For instance, it is argued that gated communities create an urban apartheid (Widgery, 1991), and bring

(Continued)

(Continued)

with them the danger of exerting 'socio-cultural control' on those considered undesirable within that given space (Coleman, 2007: 233–234). Gated communities that are only accessible with wealth are limited in terms of social and cultural diversity, and often result in a racial divide – with the poorer black and minority ethnic members of the population being denied access. As a form of spatial divide, gated communities echo the racist suburban separation practices of countries such as the USA and South Africa, whose ghettos and shanty towns ensure that black and minority ethnic populations are kept in disadvantaged social situations and continue to experience deprived conditions. In this sense, they are considered to be sites that sustain practices of environmental racism, given that its poorer black and minority ethnic population members are pushed to less desirable sites of urban neglect and decay.

────── ACTIVITY ──────

Do gated communities such as Alphaville actually serve to perpetuate and sustain racial divide in society – or is the issue more complex?

CONCLUDING THOUGHTS

This chapter has discussed key social elements of society, in particular a multicultural society. In looking at the socially constructed nature of society, the chapter has highlighted the continued significance of social relationships, norms and values in one's position and status in a given society. The impact of modern features, such as globalization and diaspora, along with the tendency for a Eurocentric racializing of immigration, has meant that not only are traditional boundaries being redrawn and enforced, but also there is a new way in which social divisions are emerging. A case study discussion of the Alphaville gated community in Brazil has highlighted the ways in which society can be artificially constructed, and then used to create an urban apartheid that exerts socio-cultural control on black and minority ethnic undesirable bodies. The chapter encourages a consideration of questions around the development and obeying of 'rules' in society.

MAIN POINTS

- The significance of real and imagined communities in society.
- The use of shared norms and values for the functioning of a healthy society.
- The socially constructed nature of society leads to social divisions.
- The limits of policy on multiculturalism and its use to present ideas about legitimate citizenship.

STUDY QUESTIONS

1. Why are community relations and bonds important in society?

2. To what extent is the term culture used as a synonym for race?

3. Is a truly multicultural society possible, or even desirable?

FURTHER READING

Billington, Rosamund, Hockey, Jenny and Strawbridge, Sheelagh (1998) *Exploring Self and Society*. Basingstoke: Palgrave Macmillan.

Cohen, Robin (1997) *Global Diasporas: An Introduction*. Seattle, WA: University of Washington Press.

Michalowski, Ines (2011) 'Required to assimilate? The content of citizenship tests in five countries', *Citizenship Studies*, 15(6–7): 749–768.

REFERENCES

Abercrombie, Nicholas and Warde, Alan, with Soothill, Keith, Urry, John and Walby, Sylvia (1998) *Contemporary British Society*. Second Edition. Cambridge: Polity Press.

Berry, John W. 'Socio-psychological costs and benefits of multiculturalism: A view from Canada', in J.W. Dacyl and C. Westin (eds.), *Governance and Cultural Diversity*, Stockholm: UNESCO & CIEFO, Stockhom University. pp. 297–354 .

Bracalenti, Raffaele and Braham, Peter (2003) 'Marginalization', in G. Bolaffi, R. Bracalenti, P. Braham and S. Gindro (eds.), *Dictionary of Race, Ethnicity and Culture*. London: Sage. pp. 174–175.

Braham, Peter and Zargani, Aldo (2003) 'Diaspora', in G. Bolaffi, R. Bracalenti, P. Braham and S. Gindro (eds.), *Dictionary of Race, Ethnicity and Culture*. London: Sage. pp. 73–76.

Callari Galli, Matilda (2003) 'Multiculturalism', in G. Bolaffi, R. Bracalenti, P. Braham and S. Gindro (eds.), *Dictionary of Race, Ethnicity and Culture*. London: Sage. pp. 183–187.

Campbell, Tom (1981) *Seven Theories of Human Society*. Oxford: Clarendon Press.

Cohen, Robin and Kennedy, Paul, with Perrier, Maud (2013) *Global Sociology*. Third Edition. Basingstoke: Palgrave Macmillan.

Coleman, Roy (2007) 'Surveillance in the city: Primary definition and urban spatial order', in S. Hier and J. Greenberg (eds.), *The Surveillance Studies Reader*. Maidenhead: Open University. pp. 231–244.

Collyer, M. (2011) 'Diaspora', in S.M. Caliendo and C.D. McIlwain (eds.), *The Routledge Companion to Race and Ethnicity*. Abingdon: Routledge. p. 132.

Durkheim, Emile (1982) *The Rules of Sociological Method*. Translated by W.D. Halls. New York: The Free Press.

Durkheim, Emile (1997a) [1893] *The Division of Labour in Society*. Translated by George Simpson. New York: The Free Press.

Durkheim, Emile (1997b) [1897] *Suicide: A Study in Sociology*. New York: The Free Press.

Fanshawe, Simon and Sriskandarajah, Dhananjayan (2010) *'You Can't Put Me in a Box': Super-diversity and the End of Identity*. London: Institute for Public Policy Research.

Freud, Sigmund (1961) *Civilisation and its Discontents*. Translated and edited by James Strachey. New York: W.W. Norton.

Fulcher, James and Scott, John (2007) *Sociology*. Third Edition. Oxford: Oxford University Press.

Giddens, Anthony (1993) *Sociology*. Second Edition. Oxford: Polity Press.

Gindro, Sandra (2003) 'Culture', in G. Bolaffi, R. Bracalenti, P. Braham and S. Gindro (eds.), *Dictionary of Race, Ethnicity and Culture*. London: Sage. pp. 61–65.

Goffman, Erving (1959) *The Presentation of Self in Everyday Life*. New York: Doubleday.

Grant, Jill (2004) *Why Planners are Ambivalent about Gated Communities*. Toronto: Canadian Institute of Planners.

Hage, Ghassan (2003) *Against Paranoid Nationalism: Searching for Hope in a Shrinking Society*. Sydney: Pluto Press.

Haythornwaite, Caroline (2007) 'Social networks and online community', in A. Joinson (ed.), *Oxford Handbook of Internet Psychology*. Oxford: Oxford University Press. pp. 122–137.

Hoey, Douglas (2007) 'Belonging: Community', in S. Matthewman, C.L.West-Newman and B. Curtis (eds.), *Being Sociological*. Basingstoke: Palgrave. pp. 399–419.

Home Office (1981) *The British Nationality Act 1981*. London: The Stationery Office.

Home Office (2014) *Immigration Act 2014*. London: The Stationery Office.

Macionis, John J. and Plummer, Ken (2002) *Sociology: A Global Introduction*. Second Edition. Harlow: Prentice Hall.

McGhee, Derek (2005) *Intolerant Britain? Hate, Citizenship and Difference*. Maidenhead: Open University Press.

Mead, George Herbert (1995) 'Self', in F. Anthias and M.P. Kelly (eds.), *Sociological Debates: Thinking about the Social*. Greenwich: Greenwich University Press. pp. 365–374.

Mills, C. Wright (1959) *The Sociological Imagination*. Oxford: Oxford University Press.

Noor, Noraini M. and Leong, Chan-Hoong (2013) 'Multiculturalism in Malaysia and Singapore: Contested models', *International Journal of Intercultural Studies*, 37(6): 714–726.

Park, Robert E., Burgess, Ernest W. and McKenzie, Roderick D. (eds.) (1925) *The City*. Chicago, IL: Chicago University Press.

Payne, Geoff (2000) 'An introduction to social divisions', in G. Payne (ed.), *Social Divisions*. Basingstoke: Palgrave. pp. 1–19.

Punch, Samantha, Marsh, Ian, Keating, Mike and Harden, Jeni (eds.) (2013) *Sociology: Making Sense of Society*. Fifth Edition. Harlow: Pearson.

Raacke, John and Bonds-Raacke, Jennifer (2008) 'My Space and Facebook: Applying the uses and gratifications theory to exploring friend-networking sites', *Cyberpsychology Behaviour*, 11(2): 169–174.

Ren, Yuquing, Harper, F. Maxwell, Drenner, Sara, Terveen, Loren, Kiesler, Sara, Riedl, John and Kraut, Robert E. (2012) 'Building member attachment in online communities: Applying theories of group identity and interpersonal bonds', *MIS Quarterly*, 36(3): 841–864.

Scott, John and Marshall, Gordon (2005) *Oxford Dictionary of Sociology*. Oxford: Oxford University Press.

Sibley, Chris G. and Ward, Colleen (2013) 'Measuring the preconditions for a successful multicultural society: A barometer test of New Zealand', *International Journal of Intercultural Studies*, 37: 700–713.

Sibley, David (1995) *Geographies of Exclusion*. London: Routledge.

Sivanandan, Ambalavaner (2006) 'Race, terror and civil society', *Race and Class*, 47(1): 1–8.

Urry, John (2000) *Sociology Beyond Societies*. London: Routledge.

Valeri, Mauro (2003) 'Denizen', in G. Bolaffi, R. Bracalenti, P. Braham and S. Gindro (eds.), *Dictionary of Race, Ethnicity and Culture*. London: Sage. pp. 67–69.

Vertovec, Steven (2007) 'Super-diversity and its implications', *Ethnic and Racial Studies*, 30(6): 1024–1054.

Waquant, Loic (2008) *Urban Outcasts*. Cambridge: Policy Press.

Waters, Malcom (1995) *Globalization*. Abingdon: Routledge.

Widgery, David (1991) *Some Lives! A GP's East End*. London: Sinclair-Stevenson.

Zanfrini, Laura (2003) 'Assimilation', in G. Bolaffi, R. Bracalenti, P. Braham and S. Gindro (eds.), *Dictionary of Race, Ethnicity and Culture*. London: Sage. pp. 19–22.

NOTES

1. The Arab Spring refers to a period from 2010 to 2013, where a series of strikes, demonstrations and uprisings against what was considered to be oppressive rule took place in Syria, Libya, Tunisia, Egypt, Bahrain, Yemen, Iraq, Jordan, Morocco and Algeria.
2. Ironically, Alphaville is the title of a famous French film made by Jean-Luc Godard in 1965, in which a futuristic city eventually ends up being run by a tyrannical surveillance system.

4

REPRESENTATIONS OF RACE

INTRODUCTION

This chapter will consider the key ways in which race and racial groups come to be represented and consumed, especially in matters relating to space, locality and society. In doing so, the reader will begin to appreciate and question the power of these representations and their stigmatic impact, as well as their use by the mass media, politicians and criminal justice authorities – namely, those considered to have a vested interest in generating fear, panic and concern about race and some racial groups. The chapter will draw on the theory and concepts of black deviance; browning; labelling; moral panics; stigma; and white victimhood. The case study in this chapter is Rochdale and the 'Asian sex gang'. The key question raised is: What is the impact of the media over-focusing on particular race issues?

KEY TERMS

- Black deviance

- Browning

- Caste

- Labelling

- Model minority

- Moral panics

- Stigma

- White victimhood

ATTITUDES ABOUT RACE ISSUES IN SOCIETY

Without knowing it, or even meaning to, we construct views and feelings about particular racial groups that we often act on. These views exist both on inter- and intra-racial levels. For example, consider those societies that have caste systems. Although caste classification systems are used in a number of African and Polynesian civilizations, it is most commonly associated with the political, religious and economic organization system in India. The term, which in India is derived from the word 'jati' meaning 'race', is used to organize and distinguish groups from one another as well as to prevent fraternization between groups (Canevacci, 2003: 35). For many who experience racialized processes of othering, there are very serious consequences of racialized views – for instance, see the insightful study of Blair, Judd and Chapleau (2004) on race and sentencing. In their British study, Heath, Rothon and Ali (2010) found that there is widespread prejudice among the white majority population, especially against less skilled migrants from culturally different societies. However, the authors go on to note that despite 'their experiences of hostility and discrimination, minorities exhibit high levels of attachment to Britain and have adopted identities as members of both British society and their minority group' (Heath et al., 2010: 205). In the main, though, views about racialized bodies continue to generate fear, anger, disgust and panic – in particular, 'moral panic'. A **moral panic** is a 'disproportionate and hostile social reaction to a condition, person or group identified as a threat to societal values' (Murji, 2001: 175). Goode and Ben-Yehunda (1994: 33–41) note that a moral panic is defined by at least five crucial elements:

1. Concern – a heightened and measurable level of concern over the behaviour of a certain group or category and the consequences that that behaviour is seen to cause for the rest of the society.

2. Hostility – an increased level of hostility towards the group or category regarded as engaging in the behaviour in question.

3. Consensus – a substantial or widespread agreement or consensus that the threat is real, serious, and caused by the wrongdoing group members and their behaviour.

4. Disproportionality – a sense felt by the majority of the society that a more sizeable number of individuals are engaged in the behaviour in question than is actually the case, and that the threat, danger, or damage said to be caused by the behaviour is far more substantial than is actually likely to be the case in reality.

5. Volatility – a moral panic is volatile and can erupt suddenly (although it may lie dormant or latent for long periods of time, and may reappear from time to time), and as such tend to be fairly limited temporally.

―――――――――――――――― **ACTIVITY** ――――――――――――――――

Using an example of a racialized moral panic, consider the presence of these five elements.

―――

Cohen (1972, cited in Goode and Ben-Yehunda, 1994: 24–29) argues that there are five societal segments involved in the expression of a moral panic:

1. The press – who are responsible for the over-reporting of events, giving them exaggerated attention, distortion, and stereotyping.

2. The public – who hold some latent potential to react to a given issue.

3. Law enforcement bodies – whose control actions demonstrate that a moral panic is taking place and that the society is said to be faced with a 'clear and present danger' that needs to be sharply attended to.

4. Politicians and legislators – where members of Parliament (and like) take an immediate interest in the case, holding urgent meetings and sending summaries to the Home Secretary, often calling for immediate action on the case.

5. Action groups – who generate appeals and campaigns, to cope with the newly existing threat.

Cohen (1972) argues that in addition to these five elements, there are two other important elements that characterize a moral panic: the creation of 'folk devils' and the development of a 'disaster mentality'. A folk devil is the personification of evil. They are stripped of all favourable characteristics and imparted with exclusively and often exaggerated negative ones. The disaster analogy is used in moral panic cases to call for action to be taken, very much like those taken before, during and after a disaster, such as a hurricane or earthquake (Cohen, 1972, cited in Goode and Ben-Yehunda, 1994: 29).

A moral panic uses stereotypical media representations as a foundation for an over-reaction, which then leads to increased demands for intensified social control. Stanley Cohen's (1972) work on moral panics involving the Mods and Rockers in the 1960s is considered key to an analysis of the concept. Later, Hall et al.'s (1978) work on 'muggings' (street crime) highlighted the significance of social variables, notably race, in the creation of a moral panic. In examining the media's role in racial-ized moral panics, Rosalind Yarde (The *Guardian*, 12 November 2001) highlights how the media use language and scaremongering tactics to present black and minor-ity ethnic people in particular as 'demons'. In the 1960s and 1970s, the media talked about 'floods' and 'tides' and 'deluges' of 'coloured' people who'd come to drain the host's national assistance. Tabloid papers like the *Daily Express* gave us a barrage of mixed metaphors that referred to the hordes of immigrants, which, it revealed, are 'flooding' the UK like 'ants from an ant hill'. Over the decades, plenty of stories on race continued to promote the same negative stereotypes over and over again. For instance, in 1982 the *Daily Mail* ran a front-page story headlined 'Black crime: the alarming figures'. The story focused on a new crime (mugging), which, although it constituted less than 1% of all serious recorded crime, became a major preoccupa-tion in society. One impact of this is that all those of immigrant heritage become criminalized – 'crimmigrant' bodies viewed with suspicion, hostility and subjected to a range of specialist surveillance and control measures (Aas, 2011).

More recently, racialized moral panics have appeared in America, Australia, Canada and Europe, in particular about asylum seekers. These groups come to be presented as a social problem. For example, in two separate studies, Bralo (1998) and Kaye (1998) found that the majority of the articles on asylum seeking and asylum seekers in their sample frame presented these groups in negative ways, often as deviant 'others' to be met with suspicion. In Europe especially, suspicion about asylum is 'sub-sumed under the immigration debate which in turn is framed by the general categories of race, race relations and ethnicity' (Cohen, 2002: xxii). Distinctions between immi-grants (old and new), economic migrants, tourists, refugees, asylum seekers become blurred. This blurring occurs most prominently and powerfully in media, political and public discourse. Doly, Kelly and Nettleton (1997) note how throughout Europe in the 1990s a hostile agenda, which demonized all immigrant bodies, emerged. These groups became presented as 'bogus', 'scammers', 'gypsies', 'welfare scroungers', 'job-stealers', and so on. Scanning of the tabloid press highlights just how common this vilification is. Carefully selected and emotionally powerful metaphors are often used in narratives involving these groups: such as how water is represented as *flood, wave, deluge, influx and pouring (into)*; the idea that refugees are more criminal and prone to violent behaviour; and the suggestion that refugees are *scroungers* and *beg-gars* (Cohen, 2002: xxiii–xxiv). This is matched with language that presents the 'host society' as a victim – at risk of job-loss; insufficient housing; strained educational, health and welfare resources; and crime (most notably, terrorism). The idea of white

victimhood is not new, but has appeared in many previous racialized events. For instance, consider the representation of white people during media reporting of the Brixton (UK) urban disturbances in 1995.[1] They were not only presented as the victims of **black deviance**, but also eventually as dignified and brave heroes (Malik, 2002: 88).

These bodies and others imagined to be like them then become the focus of blame for a whole series of other social anxieties (Welch and Schuster, 2005). For instance, consider the 'reimagination' of young people of South Asian and Muslim heritage during the urban disturbances in Oldham and Bradford (UK) in May 2001. Media and political commentary presented these groups as having caused violent disturbances due to their inevitable inability to assimilate into the host British culture and their tendency to violent behaviour more generally – views that were later exacerbated following the September 2001 terror attacks in America (Alexander, 2005: 199–200). What is interesting is that during these urban disturbances, very little, if any, mention was made of the demonstrations and antagonism that right-wing groups, such as the National Front and the British National Party, had been carrying out in these areas just prior to the disturbances, not to mention the years of discrimination and disadvantage (in housing, education and employment) faced by its black and minority ethnic population. Also of interest is the way in which the wider South Asian and Muslim community were being punished – a clear indication that they had shifted from the once popular image of being 'passive' to now being seen as an 'aggressive' threat (Goodey, 2001: 443). This was most evident in the publicly expressed narratives surrounding the (over)sentencing[2] of those individuals who had participated in the disturbances (Allen, 2003; McGhee, 2003). For instance, consider the then Home Secretary, David Blunkett's quote: 'Maniacs who were engaging in [the disturbances] are now whining about sentences they have been given. ... At last the courts are handing out sentences that are a genuine reprisal but also a message to the community' (David Blunkett, quoted in The *Guardian*, 6 September 2002).

In addition, there were also wider and newer practices of racial and religious demonization at play. This was illustrated in the embodiment of 'brown bodies' as a whole to present them as a new kind of deviant – one to be feared for their uncivilized, irrational, non-negotiable and violent culture. This occurred during the Oldham and Bradford disturbances, but more recently it has become more powerfully evident in the recent global terror-panics. Here, 'brown'/'**browning**' are labels that make reference to the specific positioning of this group within the spectrum of perceived ethnic deviance, as well as the racialization processes that are used in constructing this group as a particular type of deviant category (Patel, 2013: 35). However, 'browning' within the recent terror-panic context continues to powerfully 'relegitimise state racism' (Bhattacharyya, 2008: 75), as well as those views common in lay society. It does this by highlighting notions of 'brown difference' that are cultural, non-essential, and unlike past violence against other black and minority ethnic groups. In doing so, there is an attempt to move away from accusations of racism. Yet, in reality, 'browning' remains discriminatory as it continues to link a particular black and minority ethnic body with a particular set of negative social meanings (Bhattacharyya, 2008: 58).

ACTIVITY

Gather some examples of media news stories where a particular racial group is presented as a problem for society. Consider the following: (1) What is the image showing? (2) What emotions, feelings and views does it evoke (particularly for different audiences)? (3) What is the overt message of the image? (4) What is the covert (if any) message of the image (maybe linked to politics)? (5) What are the implications of these messages? (6) What would work on moral panics say about this image?

(MIS)REPRESENTING THE RACED BODY

In terms of racial representations, there are various institutional and structural forces at play. A key one is the media and entertainment industry. Black and minority ethnic groups are both under-represented and mis-represented in the mass media. In terms of the latter, it is argued that media representations and images of black and minority ethnic people reinforce negative stereotypes of the 'foreigner' who is unable or unwilling to change (assimilate) in order to fit in with ideas of white-Britishness or Englishness? Take, for example, the case of the British comedy programme *Mind Your Language*, aired on ITV in the 1970s. Set in an English-language school where there were Indian, Pakistani, Greek, Japanese, Turkish and Chinese students, the programme reinforced popular crude national stereotypes. The source of humour didn't just emerge from the students' own foreign background, with their accents, customs, clothes and the situations they would find themselves in, but also in their racial difference from the English teacher, the only racially neutral character (Malik, 2002: 96). Many films and television programmes have instead attempted to correct stereotypes by presenting more accurate portrayals of black and minority ethnic people and by covering the experiences of racism. For instance, consider Steven Spielberg's 1985 movie *The Color Purple* (based on the novel of the same name by Alice Walker), which shows the racism, poverty and sexism faced by African-American women in the early 1900s. Similarly, there is Steve McQueen's movie *12 Years a Slave* (2013) (an adaptation of the 1853 memoir, *12 Years a Slave* by Solomon Northup), which tells the story of a New-York-State-born free African-American man who was kidnapped and sold into slavery. However, we also now need to ask if all films written and produced by black and minority ethnic people themselves have corrected misrepresentations or if they have actually reinforced negative stereotypes, often in the name of humour. For instance, consider the portrayal of Asian Muslim men in *East is East* (1999, directed by Damien O'Donnell) as ignorant, homophobic, sexist, polygamous wife-beaters.

The mass media have selectively over-reported particular aspects of news or special-interest stories in order to generate concern or to support existing concern about black and minority ethnic groups. In this sense, it plays a powerful role in setting the agenda for political debate and public mood. One recent example is the preoccupation with the idea that the presence of both older, established and newer black and minority ethnic people of immigrant background poses a threat to the national identity of the 'host country'. Braham (2003: 254) notes how this was most powerfully illustrated with the Salman Rushdie Affair in 1989 following the publication of *The Satanic Verses*: 'In this coverage British Muslims appeared not merely as fundamentalists, intolerant of the views and rights of others, but as an undifferentiated mass of *outsiders* – that is alien to the British way of life.' This was illustrated with the news coverage of events surrounding and following the 9/11 attacks in September 2001, which ultimately led to discussions about British-born (or Canadian-born, American-born, Australian-born, and so on) Muslims being 'incompatible' with Britain's national identity and all that is seen to be entailed in the British way of life. It is argued that these bodies are not just seen as also evidencing the death of multiculturalism (Gilroy, 2006), a view popularized by the common use of terms such as 'homegrown terrorist' and 'the enemy within'. Even more, these 'hostile' bodies are presented as posing a danger to the security of the nation. This results in calls by the Government (and its allied state officials) to tighten membership of a particular notion of national identity and British patriotism. However, Gilroy (2005) argues that the construction of Britishness is problematic given that it is shaped by Britain's biased understanding of its own Empire and postcolonial history, and the tendency to view Britishhess through an 'airbrushed, nuanced and nostalgic filter' (Gilroy, 2005: 434–437).

Another area in which representations of the raced body are in abundance is within the criminal justice system. Of particular interest is the way in which actual crime carried out by some members of black and minority ethnic background is then re-presented to the public as typical and indicative of black and minority ethnic culture. A landmark study indicating the power and existence of such racialized criminal representations emerged in the 1972, with Gus John's study of Handsworth (a neighbourhood in Birmingham, in the UK). The study found that perceptions in Handsworth about race and crime were far more complex than the police's explanations that the growth of crime was due to the work of a 'hard core' group of 40 or 50 (black and minority ethnic) youngsters. Instead, John argued that the high crime rates and links to black and minority ethnic people amounted to three main issues: (1) the prevalence of rumours, fears and explanations of black and minority ethnic involvement in criminal activities; (2) a tendency by the police to blame the 'hard core' of young black and minority ethnic youth for 'giving the area a bad name'; and (3) deep resentment by older and younger black and minority ethnic people with their social position and the discrimination that they had to endure. However, notions of black and minority ethnic groups' predisposition to deviant/criminal behaviour maintained a foothold in public opinion. This was fuelled in the late 1970s with the muggings moral panic (Hall et al., 1978) and the attempts of various politicians, most notably Enoch Powell in the UK, to use small-scale urban disturbances to support calls for greater immigration control and, in some cases, the repatriation of foreign nationals. This period also saw highly problematic crime statistics and the unquestioning acceptance of police evidence, linking race to crime. In the 1980s, we saw the 'race riots' (such as those in Toxteth and Brixton, UK) which fuelled political and lay associations of race and crime. In the 1990s evidence about the severity of racist attitudes within the police force really began to emerge, with the case of Stephen Lawrence, for example, although there remained a refusal at institutional level and in some sectors of the lay public to seriously acknowledge problems of discrimination (Solomos, 1993). In the new millennium, we witnessed 9/11 and the panics about race and crime moving to a new level. A newer black and minority ethnic criminal type was created – the Islamic terrorist – leading to legislative changes as well as social panics about the 'enemy within'. Although a UK narrative, this is not so very different from that which has occurred in other white-majority countries.

Misrepresentations about black and minority ethnic people are often linked to immigration, in particular the idea of the 'immigrant imaginary' (Sayyid, 2004), and notions of the 'model minority'. The latter term is commonly used in the USA to describe those members of racial groups who are of recent immigrant heritage and who are considered to have achieved a high level of success in contemporary American society. On the face of it, the term appears to be an accolade due to its supposed praising nature (Cheryan and Bodenhausen, 2011: 173). However, a closer critical analysis of the term, its use and its context highlights how it relies on a set of Euro- or American-) centric principles and stereotypes about racial groups of recent immigrant heritage, which also renders invisible those who have not conformed to such centricity. The use of the term 'immigration' is itself automatically associated with the immigration to countries such as Britain of people whose origins lay in the New Commonwealth countries (namely former countries of the British Empire, such as India, Jamaica and Kenya). However, views about immigration and citizenship have in recent years taken 'an ethnic turn' (O'Nions, 1995). Consider, for example, how members of the Romany travelling community have persistently suffered discrimination and prejudice from the rest of society. For instance, in England and Wales, the Criminal Justice and Public Order Act (1994) contains provisions which reduce the number of authorized Traveller sites available in an attempt to discourage the nomadic way of life which has been central to the lives of many Travellers for hundreds of years. Exclusionary practices are aimed at forcing the Traveller community to abandon their culture and traditions. Stigmatizing attitudes seek to assign them with deviant labels, such as 'work-shy', 'criminal', or 'social parasite'.

Furthermore, McLaughlin (2005) uses the UK case of Stephen Lawrence to highlight how one particular newspaper (the *Daily Mail*) engaged in a process of making a certain type of blackness 'respectable'.[3] This was only possible by measuring it against an undesirable form of whiteness. Here, Doreen and Neville Lawrence, the parents of the murdered boy, were 'transformed into a couple of extraordinary moral authority and respectability and their son Stephen was idealized as an icon for Middle England. He was the gifted black schoolboy whose dream of becoming an architect had been brutally ended' (McLaughlin, 2005: 171). In comparison, the five white youths accused of the murder were described as 'racist savages', the 'pack of bigots', the 'gang of evil killers', the 'moronic thugs' 'overflowing with hatred' who were 'walking free and smirking at the thrill of getting away with it' (*Daily Mail* excerpts, cited in McLaughlin, 2005: 171). Alone, the Lawrence family could not be held up as black, desirable and respectable. This was only the case because they were held up against images of 'white psychopathological savagery that threatened all that Middle England stood for' (McLaughlin, 2005: 171). This sat well with the wider panics of the time that were also occurring around masses of lawless white masculine youth, who lacked the work ethic, had no respect for authority and were capable of extreme violence (McLaughlin, 2005: 180). This discourse also exceptionalized the Lawrence killing – the claim being that such racist violence is not carried out or sanctioned by white Middle England. James Rhodes (2011) notes a similar pattern in his consideration of BNP[4] support, whiteness and class.

Here, a **stigma** is defined as a 'sign of disgrace imposed upon certain identified individuals as a means of marking them out as different, deviant or criminal' (Muncie, 2001b: 292). It involves judgements about moral inferiority and character-istic flaws which not only need to be avoided at all costs, but also need to be controlled and ideally removed if society is to function successfully. The term is most commonly associated with Erving Goffman (1963). Goffman identified three types of stigma: (1) physical deformities; (2) character blemishes (such as dishonesty); and (3) the 'tribal' stigmas of race, nation and religion. In his earlier work, *The Presentation of Self in Everyday Life* (1959), Goffman used the metaphor of the theatrical stage to explain human identity construction. Goffman argues that in the presence of others individuals attempt to maintain a stable and positive image of 'self' by putting on a 'performance' – that is, they choose words, speech, mannerisms, posture, clothing, and so on, for 'impression management'. This is the 'front' region of the performance. This is the place where the performance is given and where indi-viduals generally conform to the particular roles expected of them. The 'back' region is where individuals prepare themselves or hide their true self from their audience. Linked to this, the term 'labelling' is a sociological approach to the understanding of crime and deviance. It refers to the social processes through which certain individuals come to be seen as problematic. Within such social processes, stereotyping, stigmati-zation and audience responses are considered to play significant roles (Muncie, 2001a: 159). Howard Becker (1963) argued that in order to understand deviance, we need to appreciate the role played by social audiences and their reactions to particu-lar people and what they consider to be their offending behaviour. Labelling has been criticized for its limited explanation of why it is that some behaviours come to be defined in a historical and political context as deviant, while others do not (Muncie, 2001a: 160). However, despite this, it allowed us to appreciate the role played by society in defining offending behaviour, as well as highlighting the significance of stigma, social reaction and control (Muncie, 2001a: 160).

In looking at immigration and stigmatization, in particular at attempts to de-stigmatize (or at least renegotiate negative labels), Ignatiev (1995) examines how Irish immigrants (Catholics) had once been an underclass in Ireland, barred from voting, running for office, or going into the law or the military. Catholic taxes went to the Protestant church and Catholic orphans were brought up as Protestants. When the first wave of immigration began, America did not offer much immediate relief. For instance, in the American South, Irish workers were sometimes hired for work that was deemed to be too dangerous for risking a slave's life. However, Ignatiev

(1995) argues that white Irish workers used race to distance themselves from the black slaves. In doing so, they ensured themselves a better spot in society. This, Ignatiev proposes, is why the Irish, who had a long tradition of opposing slavery at home, never rose to the abolitionist cause, and in fact became virulent racists. The sharper the distinction between whites and blacks, the safer they were. According to this analysis, white identity means nothing but the privilege of *not* being black.

THE POWER TO DEFINE RACE

The use of a racialized othering process allows stigmatizing racial labels to be attached to bodies. However, it also allows for whiteness to be used as a non-raced norm. This brings with it assumed authority, power and control that self-perpetuates, given that those in power ensure that their position of privilege is maintained. As critical thinkers, we need to ask questions like 'when did white become the colour of Europeans?' and 'when did this become denoted not only as non-deviant, but also as a norm against which all else is measured?' Clearly, whiteness is also a socially constructed, multifaceted and fluid identity. However, it is positioned within a particular position of authority within the nexus of power relations that has been discussed in this book.

Within the mass media and entertainment industry there is an abundance of positive white imagery. Further, these positive images often echo the myth of the colonial saviour, or even the white messiah who is seen to be rescuing black and minority ethnic subjects from their plight. This fiction presents whiteness (and virtually always maleness) as benevolent and selfless, and black and minority ethnic people as a social problem or in need of uplift and direction. For instance, there is the film *Blood Diamond* (2006), where a racist white Rhodesian mercenary rescues a black Sierra Leonese and his son from black villains (Lacy and Ono, 2011: 13); or *Dangerous Minds* (1995), in which a white middle-class female teacher teaches a group of disruptive and deviant Hispanic American inner-city high school students; or *The Blind Side* (2009), where a white woman and her family take an orphaned African-American boy into their home and teach him valuable life lessons and help him to excel in football. Ultimately, such representations impose cultural imperialism, where the non-white/black and minority ethnic subjects support the white subjects' journey into fulfilment, admiration and success. The non-white/black and minority ethnic subjects remain invalid and unable to cope without the(ir) white saviour.

Studies using a thematic examination of how black and minority ethnic people are presented and how this influences attitudes in lay society have shown the power of language and imagery. For example, consider the Toxteth (UK) disturbances in 1981 and the selective visual presentations, which were largely of the 'rioters' armed with 'weapons' and the police in positions of bravery and defence. It is worth mentioning that no pictures of or references to the heavy-handed policing or white looters were given in the news reports. Indeed, information about some of these aspects only emerged in the wider public arena years after the disturbances. There was no analysis about police harassment, such as the use of CS gas, discriminatory urban policing methods and a racist stop and search method applied both before and during the disturbances. These representational strategies were echoed many years later in the 1995 Brixton (UK) disturbances, where television news channels again organized their reports around a series of racially biased formulaic structures:

1. Images of the riots ('gangs or predominantly black youths took to the street').

2. Police efforts to manage the chaos.

3. An emotive case study of an injured policeman and the (white) man who had rescued him. Here other white people were not only depicted as heroes but also as victims (the injured policeman was interviewed from his hospital bed).

4. The Home Secretary's (Michael Howard) visit to Brixton the next day.

5. The views of Sir Paul Condon that 'no civilized country can tolerate that'.

6. Brixton's 'troubled past' and regeneration programmes for the area.

It has been noted that all this occurred within a framework that made no attempt whatsoever to humanize Wayne Douglas, the man who had died in police custody and whose case is said to have contributed to the protests leading up to the disturbances (Malik, 2002: 88).

These formulaic structures were also present in the more recent case of Hurricane Katrina, which hit the New Orleans area of the USA in 2005. Given its supposed pride in being a nation of immigrants and having a 'melting-pot' society, what was interesting about the US news reporting was the ways in which it made specific, yet subtle representations of 'black otherness' (by which we read non-American), and in particular its invention of mass 'black criminality'. First, in the early days of the hurricane aftermath, news media coverage and political-speak commonly referred to its (predominantly black African-American) survivors as 'refugees' – a term which seemed displaced, not least because these survivors were American citizens whose experiences had occurred while they were well within their country's geographical borders (Sommers et al., 2006). The use of the term 'refugee' evokes negative feelings of 'foreign otherness' whose presence causes *us* more harm and threat. In comparison, using the more accurate term 'survivor' would have evoked feelings of heroism, strength and courage – qualities which the surviving individuals (and, more specifically, their racial heritage) were not deemed worthy of within the context of American race relations and nationalism.

Secondly, there was the printing of two photographs taken by two different photographers, each with a different accompanying caption. Both photographs showed survivors in water with groceries that they had taken from stores. One photograph featured a young black African-American man, and the caption read: 'A young man *walks* through chest-deep flood water after *looting* a grocery store' (emphasis added). The second photograph, featured two white people, and the caption read: 'Two *residents wade* through chest-deep water after *finding* bread and soda from a local grocery store' (emphasis added). Race and racialized language clearly played a role in assigning status to what appeared to be subjects in a very similar situation (Sommers et al., 2006). The media's racialized framing of Katrina not only demonized 'black looters', presenting them as 'subhuman savages', but absolved white officials of their own failures (Lacy and Haspel, 2011: 21–24). The practice of black demonization and white absolving is commonplace in times of uncertainty (Patel, 2013).

ACTIVITY

Bowling and Phillips (2002) argue that negative racialization processes are also intertwined with religion, ethnicity, culture and nationhood. This means that not all those referred to as 'white' can escape problematic portrayals – for instance, the Irish, Maltese, Russians and Jews have all at one time or another been thought of as a problem for the social order of England (2002: 77). Can you think of recent examples to support or contradict Bowling and Phillips's argument?

There has been some considerable work done in recent years to challenge the negative portrayal of black and minority ethnic groups, and similarly the position of privilege that whiteness holds. It is argued here that critical analysis must consider the racist underpinnings of State policies on immigration and citizenship, as well as in other areas, such as employment, housing and crime control. Such an analysis would highlight the continued existence of racist practices and offer a more informed analysis of race matters. Here *critical race theory* would be especially useful. This theory emerged in the mid-1970s, in the USA, primarily as a number of lawyers, activists and legal scholars realized that the advances of the 1960s US Civil Rights era had not only stalled, but were in many respects being rolled back. The critical race movement seeks to study and transform the relationship between race, racism and power (Delgado and Stefancic, 2001: 2–3). Wider examinations of those institutions which hold the power to define (and go on to regularly define) race should undertake a level of examination which would, first, involve a critical analysis of why the State responds to race matters in the way it does, especially those involving people of particular black and minority ethnic background. For example, the State's view of the Oldham and Bradford disturbances (discussed earlier) was to explain it with a view that the Christian and Islamic faiths were so different that there was a 'clash of cultures', which led to 'self-segregation' and 'parallel lives', largely on the latter's part (Cantle, 2001; Denham, 2002).

Secondly, this analysis must also take into account the use of notions of white victimhood, via a deconstruction of Western whiteness as the norm, especially in cases where a white rationale is used to justify discriminatory attitudes and behaviour. For example, consider the backlash of discriminatory behaviour against British Asian Muslims following 9/11. This is rooted in the idea that white is the norm against which everything else is not only measured, but is unable to be equal to or superior than. As Dyer argues, 'in other words, whites are not of a race, they're just the human race' (Dyer, 1997: 3). Here, the idea that black people have culture, and a problematic one at that, and that white people have civilization is perpetuated and it is this perpetuation that needs to be challenged and changed (Khan, 1979, cited in Ely and Denney, 1987: 12). But the question is how these ideas can be challenged, especially when ideas of white norm and even hierarchical ideas about white supremacy are so embedded in societal attitudes. Here, whiteness needs to be questioned and dislodged from its central and advantageous position. Its invisibility needs to be questioned in lay thought, political debates and even media messages (Dyer, 1997). Dyer sees the norms of obsessive self-control, rationality, order and repression of emotions as white qualities. This also then creates the norms of black and minority ethnic others as sensual, vivacious and of childish disorder.

Case study: Rochdale and the 'Asian sex gang'

In May 2012, forty-seven young girls were identified as victims of child sexual exploitation. The case centred on the town of Rochdale (UK), and coverage soon became embodied within a racialized narrative, largely because it involved white victims and offenders who were either of British Pakistani or Afghan background and of Muslim faith. Media coverage of the case talked about 'grooming' and the offenders' use of drugs, alcohol, bribery and violence as a way of carrying out the child sexual exploitation. The violent and abusive nature of the case is not denied.[5] The offenders were guilty of carrying out some of the most terrible behaviour against some of society's most vulnerable members. Like many child sexual exploitation cases, the Rochdale case was about power, violence and gender. It had the hallmarks of hundreds of other child sexual exploitation cases around the world: the abuse of vulnerable young girls whose lives were already disorganized and disadvantaged in that a number of the Rochdale victims were from care homes, and thus identified as easy targets by manipulative men who used their power and status (many were business owners with financial stability, as well as being physically strong and emotionally tactical), to groom girls and carry out the abuse over a length of time.

However, what is interesting is the way in which the Rochdale case very early on became presented as a racialized crime, largely by being interpreted through a 'cultural repertoire', which led to the extensive use of racial bias: the Pakistani hyper-sexualized predator targeting the ultimate victim – young white girls (Miah, 2015: 54–55). This narrative was also illustrated by the move away from the term 'child sexual exploitation' towards that of 'Asian sex gangs'. Indeed, the use of the term 'Asian' in coverage of the case – a term which has traditionally been used to refer to all those of South Asian (Indian, Pakistani and Bangladeshi) heritage – had the immediate effect of widening the group to which the 'grooming stigma' could be applied. The result was the creation of a new type of racial crime threat (Cockbain, 2013: 22). The image and explanation presented by observers and 'experts' was that this new particular type of crime was symptomatic of a supposed restrictive Asian culture, and its practice of arranged marriages, which saw young men of Pakistani heritage having a pent-up sexual frustration and lack of respect for females, especially white females. For example, consider some of the comments made about the case, such as that by former Home Secretary Jack Straw, who said:

> ...there is a specific problem which involves Pakistani heritage men ... who target vulnerable young white girls. ... These young men are in a western society, in any event, they act like any other young men, they're fizzing and popping with testosterone, they want some outlet for that, but Pakistani heritage girls are off-limits and they are expected to marry a Pakistani girl from Pakistan, typically. (Cited on the BBC, 2011)

As Cockbain (2013: 26) notes, the notion that child sexual exploitation is the only outlet for sexual release is highly problematic and does nothing to help us understand the real complexity of such abuse. In addition, of course, 'Asians, like whites or blacks, do not commit [these] offences *because* they are Asian, white or black', and to suggest this brings the danger of presenting every Asian man as a 'groomer-in-waiting' (Cockbain, 2013: 30).

The Rochdale case and its construction of new folk devils, the 'Asian sex gangs', was possible because it drew on racist foundations and anti-Muslim hostility that was already prevalent in the UK, and more specifically in towns such as Rochdale.[6] This hostility was based on wider preoccupations with a clash of distinctly opposite cultures, failed multiculturalism, problems of mass immigration, problematic family formations (arranged and forced marriages), and the encroaching threat of Sharia Law. These factors were presented as the direct cause of Rochdale's child sexual exploitation and 'Asian grooming' (Cockbain, 2013: 26).

ACTIVITY

An analysis of data, such as that provided by Cockbain (2013), has found that child sexual exploitation is *not* a uniquely Asian threat. Why, then, do people in positions of power and authority continue to present it as such? What are the implications of these racialized constructions for victims of such abuse?

CONCLUDING THOUGHTS

This chapter has discussed the variety of ways in which race is used as a marker to distinguish bodies, and how this racialized representation then comes to be consumed in narratives of identity, rights and citizenship in society. It has been highlighted that racialized representations are heavily influenced by the mass media, the political schedule and criminal justice authorities. These influences are extremely powerful, not least because of their already established position of power and authority, which emerges from them being predominantly white (male and middle-class) establishments. This power structure draws on the deep-rooted hostility against members of black and minority ethnic populations that is embedded into aspects of lay society. This all serves to create fear and panic about particular racialized groups, and ultimately limit their life chances. In using the case of Rochdale and the 'Asian sex gang', it is argued that some groups over others will always fall foul of being racially defined and used to support the lay (white world) view that some races are biologically and/or culturally predisposed to problematic behaviour.

MAIN POINTS

- Racialized moral panics often present its folk devils as a social problem.

- Browning has been used to discriminate against certain black and minority ethnic groups, while at the same time moving away from accusations of racism.

- The mass media play a key role in setting the race agenda and directing public opinion.

- Critical race theory has been significant in addressing the relationship between race, racism and power.

STUDY QUESTIONS

1. To what extent can the 'model minority' ever be an actuality?

2. How and why are some black and minority ethnic groups able to de-stigmatize themselves and move away from a racially based deviant label?

3. Who or what has the power to define race?

4. Is critical race theory still relevant for contemporary analysis into race and racism?

FURTHER READING

Burdsey, Daniel (2011) 'Strangers on the shore? Racialized representation, identity and in/visibilities of whiteness at the English seaside', *Cultural Sociology* [Online], 30 June 2011, pp. 1–16.

Malik, Sirita (2002) *Representing Black Britain: Black and Asian Images on Television*. London: Sage.

McLaughlin, Eugene (2005) 'Recovering blackness/repudiating whiteness: The *Daily Mail's* construction of the five white suspects accused of the racist murder of Stephen Lawrence', in K. Murji and J. Solomos (eds.), *Racialization: Studies in Theory and Practice*. Oxford: Oxford University Press. pp. 163–183.

REFERENCES

Aas, Katja Franko (2011) '"Crimmigrant" bodies and bona fida travelers: Surveillance, citizenship and global governance', *Theoretical Criminology*, 15(3): 331–346.

Alexander, Claire (2005) 'Embodying violence: "Riots", dis/order and the private lives of "the Asian Gang"', in C. Alexander and C. Knowles (eds.), *Making Race Matter: Bodies, Space and Identity*. Basingstoke: Palgrave Macmillan. pp. 199–217.

Allen, Chris (2003) *Fair Justice: The Bradford Disturbances, the Sentencing and the Impact*. London: Forum Against Islamaphobia and Racism.

BBC (2011) 'Jack Straw: Some white girls are "easy meat" for abuse', *BBC News Online*, 8 January 2011 (www.bbc.co.uk/news/uk-england-derbyshire-12141603).

Becker, Howard (1963) *Outsiders: Studies in the Sociology of Deviance*. New York: The Free Press.

Bhattacharyya, Gargi (2008) *Dangerous Brown Men: Exploiting Sex, Violence and Feminism in the War on Terror*. London: Zed Books.

Blair, Irene V., Judd, Charles M. and Chapleau, Kristine M. (2004) 'The influence of Afrocentric facial features in criminal sentencing', *Psychological Science*, 15(10): 674–679.

Bowling, Benjamin and Phillips, Coretta (2002) *Racism, Crime and Justice*. Harlow: Pearson.

Braham, Peter (2003) 'Race and the Media', in G. Bolaffi, R. Bracalenti, P. Braham and S. Gindro (eds.), *Dictionary of Race, Ethnicity and Culture*. London: Sage. pp. 252–255.

Bralo, Zrinka (1998) (Un)cool Britannia: Discourse Analysis of Construction of Refugees in the UK Press. Unpublished Master's Thesis. Department of Social Psychology, London School of Economics and Political Science.

Canevacci, Massimo (2003) 'Caste', in G. Bolaffi, R. Bracalenti, P. Braham and S. Gindro (eds.), *Dictionary of Race, Ethnicity and Culture*. London: Sage. p. 35.

Cantle, Ted (2001) *Community Cohesion: A Report of the Independent Review Team*. London: Home Office.

Cheryan, Sapna and Bodenhausen, Galen (2011) 'Model minority', in S.M. Caliendo and C.D. McIlwain (eds.), *The Routledge Companion to Race and Ethnicity*. Abingdon: Routledge. pp. 173–176.

Cockbain, Ella (2013) 'Grooming and the "Asian sex gang predator": The construction of a racial crime threat', *Race and Class*, 54(4): 22–32.

Cohen, Stanley (1972) *Folk Devils and Moral Panics*. London: MacGibbon and Kee.

Cohen, Stanley (2002) *Folk Devils and Moral Panics*. Fourth Edition. Abingdon: Routledge.

Delgado, Richard and Stefancic, Jean (2001) *Critical Race Theory: An Introduction*. New York: New York University Press.

Denham, John (2002) *Building Cohesive Communities: A Report of the Ministerial Group on Public Order and Community Cohesion*. London: Home Office.

Doly, Daniele, Kelly, Lynette and Nettleton, Clive (1997) *Refugees in Europe: The Hostile New Agenda*. London: Minorities Rights Group.

Dyer, Richard (1997) *White*. London: Routledge.

Ely, Peter and Denney, David (1987) *Social Work in a Multi-Racial Society*. Aldershot: Gower.

Gilroy, Paul (2005) 'Multiculture, double consciousness and the "war on terror"', *Patterns of Prejudice*, 39(4): 431–443.

Gilroy, Paul (2006) 'Multiculture in times of war: An inaugural lecture given at the London School of Economics', *Critical Quarterly*, 28(4): 27–45.

Goffman, Erving (1959) *The Presentation of Self in Everyday Life*. New York: Doubleday.

Goffman, Erving (1963) *Stigma*. Englewood Cliffs, NJ: Prentice-Hall.

Goode, Erich and Ben-Yehunda, Nachman (1994) *Moral Panics: The Social Construction of Deviance*. Oxford: Blackwell Publishing.

Goodey, Jo (2001) 'The criminalization of British Asian youth: Research from Bradford and Sheffield', *Journal of Youth Studies*, 4(4): 429–450.

Hall, Stuart, Critcher, Chas, Jefferson, Tony, Clarke, John N. and Roberts, Brian (1978) *Policing the Crisis*. London: Macmillan.

Heath, Anthony, Rothon, Catherine and Ali, Sundas (2010) 'Identity and public opinion', in A. Bloch and J. Solomos (eds.), *Race and Ethnicity in the 21st Century*. Basingstoke: Palgrave Macmillan. pp. 186–208.

Home Office (1994) *Criminal Justice and Public Order Act 1994*. London: The Stationery Office.

Ignatiev, Noel (1995) *How the Irish Became White*. Abingdon: Routledge.

John, Gus (1972) *Race and the Inner City*. London: Runnymede Trust.

Kaye, Ron (1998) 'Redefining refugee: The UK media portrayal of asylum seekers', in K. Koser and H. Lutz (eds.), *The New Migration in Europe: Social Constructions and Social Realities*. London: Macmillan. pp. 163–182.

Lacy, Michael G. and Haspel, Kathleen C. (2011) 'Apocalypse: The media's framing of Black looters, shooter, and brutes in hurricane Katrina's aftermath', in M.G. Lacy and K.A. Ono (eds.), *Critical Rhetorics of Race*. New York: New York University Press. pp. 21–46.

Lacy, Michael G. and Ono, K.A. (eds.) (2011) 'Introduction', in M.G. Lacy and K.A. Ono (eds.), *Critical Rhetorics of Race*. New York: New York University Press. pp. 1–20

McGhee, Derek (2003) 'Moving to "our" common ground: A critical examination of community cohesion discourse in 21st century Britain', *Sociological Review*, 51(3): 383–411.

Miah, Shamim (2015) 'The groomers and the question of race', *Identity Papers: A Journal of British and Irish Studies*, 1(1): 54–66.

Muncie, John (2001a) 'Labelling', in E. McLaughlin and J. Muncie (eds.), *The Sage Dictionary of Criminology*. London: Sage. pp. 159–160.

Muncie, John (2001b) 'Stigma', in E. McLaughlin and J. Muncie (eds.), *The Sage Dictionary of Criminology*. London: Sage. pp. 292–293.

Murji, Karim (2001) 'Moral panic', in E. McLaughlin and J. Muncie (eds.), *The Sage Dictionary of Criminology*. London: Sage. pp. 175–177.

O'Nions, Helen (1995) 'The Marginalisation of Gypsies', *Web Journal of Current Legal Issues*, 5 March 2015 (http://webjcli.ncl.ac.uk/articles3/onions3.html).

ONS (2011) *UK Census of 2011*. London: Office for National Statistics.

Patel, Tina G. (2013) 'Ethnic deviant labels within the "war on terror" context: Excusing white deviance', *Ethnicity and Race in a Changing World*, 4(1): 34–50.

Rhodes, James (2011) '"It's not just them, it's whites as well": Whiteness, class and BNP support', *Sociology*, 45(1): 102–117.

Rushdie, Salman (1988) *The Satanic Verses*. London: Vintage.

Sayyid, Salman (2004) 'Slippery people: The immigrant imaginary and the grammar of colours', in I. Law, D. Phillips and L. Turney (eds.), *Institutional Racism in Higher Education*. Stoke-on-Trent: Trentham Books. pp. 149–160.

Solomos, John (1993) *Race and Racism in Britain*. Basingstoke: Palgrave Macmillan.

Sommers, Samuel R., Apfelbaum, Evan P., Dukes, Kristin, N., Toosi, Negin and Wang, Elsie J. (2006) 'Race and media coverage of Hurricane Katrina: Analysis, implications, and future research questions', *Analyses of Social Issues and Public Policy*, 6(1): 39–55.

The *Guardian* (2001) 'Demons of the day', The *Guardian*, 12 November 2001. Reported by: Rosalind Yarde.

The *Guardian* (2002) 'Anger at Blunkett's "whining maniacs" attack', The *Guardian*, 6 September 2002. Reported by: Alan Tarvis.

The *Guardian* (2003) 'Anger as court's stance on riot upheld', The *Guardian*, 31 January 2003. Reported by: Vikram Dodd.

Welch, Michael and Schuster, Liza (2005) 'Detention of asylum seekers in the UK and US: Deciphering noisy and quiet constructions', in C. Critcher (ed.), *Moral Panics and the Media*. Maidenhead: Open University Press. pp. 162–174.

NOTES

1. These events were triggered by the death in police custody of Wayne Douglas. It is significant that no attempt was made to contextualize this (unexplained) death (in police custody) during the urban disturbances. Rather, attention focused on his criminal and violent past (Malik, 2002: 88).

2. For example, consider the four-year (later cut to three years) sentence given to Parveez Najeib, who was captured on video making a throwing motion, although no actual missile was visible (The *Guardian*, 31 January 2003).

3. The *Daily Mail* is a British daily newspaper which is well known for its anti-immigration views and its tendency to publish dubious stories about black and minority ethnic populations.

4. The BNP stands for British National Party, a far-right political party in the UK.

5. Given the distressing sexually abusive nature of this case, specific details of the abuse have been purposely omitted.

6. Rochdale is a market town located in Greater Manchester, UK. According to the 2011 UK Census, 22,265 people identified themselves as being British and of Pakistani heritage, with 29,426 followers of Islam, compared to 128,186 observers of Christianity (ONS, 2011). For a variety of reasons, racial tension has been prominent in Rochdale, and it is a town often racially stigmatized.

5

IDENTITY AND THE PLACE OF RACE

INTRODUCTION

This chapter will consider the ways in which race is embedded in notions of identity, space and citizenship. By reading this chapter, you will be able to appreciate how social groups are formed and identified along racial lines, and how notions of citizenship are actually informed by ideas about desirability/undesirability. The theory and concepts covered in the chapter include: cultural capital; globalization; heterophobia; hybrid identity; and mixophobia. The case study in the chapter concerns immigration and the 'Life in the UK' test – also known as the British citizenship test. The key question raised is: How are identities negotiated according to raced spaces?

KEY TERMS

- Cultural capital

- Differentiated universalism

- Essentialist perspective

- Ethnic cleansing

- Heterophobia

- Hybrid identity

- Mixed race

- Mixophobia

- Nation

- Nationalism

- Nation-state

RACIAL BOUNDARIES, IDENTITY AND SOCIETY

In reality, we all have a biologically mixed race and socially multi-racial background. Hence, none of us should lay claim to a fixed racialized (pure) identity or a given space. Indeed, it is important to recognize that somewhere along all our genealogical histories, some sort of racial 'mixing' has occurred. A world which has seen such vast levels of movement has inevitably ensured this. However, some individuals continue to fix 'race' firmly to a given space, often as a way of validating belonging to an identity or geographical space, and usually to maintain a position of privilege over others. For many, though, attaching bodies to a given space reinforces identity (or at least one's pursuit of an identity). For example, consider notions of American-ness, especially within the context of the 'American dream'. In his analysis of the American identity, Madriaga (2005) argues that whiteness is tightly intermingled with the processes of American national identification. In utilizing Cohen's (1985) model of community, which is itself derived from Turner's (1969) work, Madriaga argues that a public face of the American dream symbolizes a sense of 'us' that binds together all Americans regardless of ethnic and racial difference. However, in private, there are diverging interpretations and tensions, which ultimately reveal the ethnic and racial differences dividing 'us'. This indicates that although individuals may be divided by race and ethnicity, at the same time, they can still identify themselves as American. It is exactly within such contexts that we can draw on the work of Caroline Knowles (2003).

In examining constructions of racialized spaces, Knowles (2003: 78) highlights the need to explore the spatial dimensions of race making. This is because by understanding the spatiality of race, we are able to learn things about race which we cannot know by other means. Once we understand how race making takes place through space, we can then begin to appreciate that:

1. Race and ethnicity become attached by a number of social mechanisms, including stories, to physical space and territory.

2. Space is also etched by time, so that a racialized past and a racialized present confront each other.

3. The relationship between race and space is not just about difference *per se*, but about the inevitable forms of contestation and struggles over space (which that difference brings). (Knowles, 2003: 78–79)

Knowles (2003: 1) notes that 'intricately woven into the social landscapes in which we live, race is all around us; a part of who we are and how we operate ... it is part of the way the world operates'. We use ideas and assumptions about 'race' to predict the behaviour of others, to label people, and to allocate privilege or disadvantage. We also, though, do so within the context of space, or at least perceived notions of space, which is itself based upon historical notions, stereotypical ideas and the allocation of (perceived) rights. In doing so, it is used in overt and covert ways essentially to determine the life experiences of individuals. In addition to this, we should recognize the significance of globalization and its 'profound effects on culture and society' (Castles, 2000: 133). In terms of race and national identity, globalization means the international mobility of populations, so we are encountering in higher volumes and quicker than ever before new knowledge and experience about different communities, as well as creating challenges to the idea of singular and static national and cultural identities (Castles, 2000: 133).

In looking at the development of a racialized identity within a given sense of space, it is necessary to consider how a number of key elements are important. Both biological and cultural elements are in a constant state of being defined, negotiated and renegotiated – they are therefore socially constructed. This is at odds with the **essentialist perspective** on racial identity. This is the view that there is one clear and authentic set of 'black characteristics' which are unique to all black people and which do not alter across time (Ballis Lal, 1999: 56). According to this 'identity essentialism' model, not only does 'one facet of a person, such as race ... "trump" all other conceptions of selfhood' but 'it also determines experiences and life chances' (Ballis Lal, 1999: 56–57). This perspective also 'emphasises the benefits of knowing who you are as a consequence of either biological descent or socially constructed attributes such as race, and of participation in collectivities organised around an essentialist identity' (Ballis Lal, 1999: 57). The model also aligns itself alongside the value of utilizing the specific **cultural capital** offered by the racial community. Introduced by Pierre Bourdieu (1986), the term 'cultural capital' refers to non-financial assets which are used to advance mobility – often away from disadvantaged positions. Forms of cultural capital include various types of attitudes, knowledge and experience, such as those within education, religious guidance, language skills, and so on, and research has found cultural capital to be extremely useful for the advancement of disadvantaged black and minority ethnic groups, especially for black and minority ethnic women in education (Banks, 2009).

The essentialist model has commonly been used in debates about **mixed race** individuals' pursuit of a black racial identity. This term refers to those individuals who are visibly identified as embodying two or more racial or ethnic groupings (Spencer, 2006: 222). Although a common term that has come to replace more derogatory ones (such as 'half-caste' and 'half-breed'), it is nevertheless conceptually flawed given that it suggests that pure races exist. In reporting the findings of a small study and reflecting upon his own experiences as a social worker of Black heritage, Small (1991: 65) argues that 'the black experience is unique', and that a denial of one's true unique 'blackness' causes serious identity conflict and an inability to deal with the racism that these population groups will inevitably face from both black and white communities, both of which will make them feel as if they do not belong to one or the other. For mixed race individuals, then, the black identity must be lived and realized in order for them to survive in the racist society that we live in. As Small (1986: 88) states: 'If a healthy personality is to be formed, the psychic image of the child must merge with the reality of what the child actually is. That is to say, if the child is black (reality), he or she must first recognize and accept that he or she has a black psychic image.'

These essentialist views are at odds with social constructionist research examining the lives of mixed race populations in contemporary society. For instance, Kathleen Hall (1995) collected several stories given by second-generation British-Sikh teenagers growing up in Leeds (UK). Hall used this group to illustrate how cultural identity formation is an ongoing process. Hall (1995: 246) found that the British-Sikh teenagers' construction and negotiation of alternative ways of being a British-Sikh teenager in modern UK was based on 'a compromise' which had been the result of them having negotiated a mixed-race identity and, more specifically, multiple forms of a racialized identity that were available to them in their homes and communities. Thus, the British-Sikh teenagers 'act and react, fashioning their identities creatively, within the ambiguous space in between their British and Sikh selves' (1995: 258). In this sense, it is argued that an essentialized view of racial identity is limited. Rather, a socially constructed view of a multi-racial identity is more accurately representative of our histories, as well as being more specifically suited to the needs and existence of a growing body of people who do not see the value of racial essentialism, for instance those who consider themselves as owning a more flexible, diverse multi-racial identity, those children of mixed parentage and the second- and third-generation children of immigrants. These groups, in particular, are seen to negotiate themselves a flexible multi-racial identity, despite constant attempts to stigmatize and problematize them. For example, Ali (2005) undertook an empirical study into mixed race identities, and found that a number of ideas about mixed race people continue to dominate. This is the idea that mixed race people have 'bad blood'; that they belong to 'feckless families'; and emerge as racially confused individuals, marked out by labels such as 'coconuts and bounty bars' (Ali, 2005: 3–9). Additionally, Alibhai-Brown (2001: 118) argues that although problematized, many mixed raced individuals feel that 'one of the most pernicious effects of living in a racially divided and unequal society is that all sides conspire to rob you of your own individuality'.

It must also be recognized that such multi-racial and mixed race identities bring with them a different set of flexible and diverse meanings for the owner. This is linked to the notion of a **hybrid identity**. There is still much debate over what constitutes a hybrid identity, but in terms of recent race and society discussions, the idea of a hybrid identity is commonly used to refer to the creation of a new space, identity or state of being, following the cultural mix of a diasporized community with the 'host' society. Diverse 'hybrid identities' are 'positioned as an antidote to essentialism' and for this reason have some importance: 'Hybridity is a further acknowledgement of the complex multi-faceted nature of human identity, and particularly of the fact that different identities are uniquely melded together within individual biographies' (Downing and Husband, 2005: 18). Such identities are viewed as complex ways of being, as well as recognizing the equally complex routes of construction borne out of racializing processes. However, the historical development of the term 'hybrid' and the negative connotations in which it is bound are often viewed as problematic: 'In colonial discourse, hybridity is a term of abuse for those who are products of miscegenation, mixed-breeds. It is imbued in nineteenth-century eugenicist and scientific-racist thought' (Young, 1995, cited in Meredith, 1998: 1). Thus, although hybridity can be viewed as an advancement on essentialist racializing of identity, the problem which it itself creates must be addressed. It is suggested, therefore, that usage of hybrid identity theorization needs to go beyond its traditional scientifically racist and problematizing thinking. This is because such a traditional view of a hybrid racial identity, brings with it recognition of a new non-essential racial identity. However, it also brings the danger of still being tied to notions of an essentialized racial space located in between polarized (black and white) ones – it therefore creates a new essentialized racial category.

------------------------------ **ACTIVITY** ------------------------------

Does the growing number of individuals identifying themselves as 'mixed race' indicate a post-racial future?

MULTICULTURALISM AND THE NATION

It is important to recognize that multicultural societies are not a recent phenomenon of the post-war world. So much so that no society can truly claim to be made up of a 'pure' or homogeneous population (Punch et al., 2013: 282). As Lévi-Strass (1994: 424) noted: '…each society is multicultural and over centuries has arrived at its own original synthesis … the result of a mishmash, borrowings, mixtures that have occurred, though at different rates, ever since the beginning of time'. Indeed, multicultural societies were in existence long before the European expansion of the fifteenth century onwards (Hall, 2000: 212). More recently, multiculturalism has come to be conceived very differently from one country to another, depending on its local and national political culture and history (Modood, 1997: 4). For example, the recent state of multiculturalism, witnessed in Europe especially, has emerged from a variety of voluntary and involuntary movements, such as labour migration, refuge and asylum seeking, forced transportation (slavery), family reunification, and so on. Modood (1997: 1) notes that the recent movement of populations to Europe from its former colonies has resulted in a type of multiculturalism that is qualitatively different from the lives and experiences of existing populations, including other minority populations that already characterize some Western European countries. Current debates about multiculturalism focus on its 'challenges', especially to the nation's security and citizenship. **Nation** refers to 'a historical community, more or less institutionally complete, occupying a given territory or homeland sharing a distinct language and culture' (Kymlicka, 1996: 11). Often people in a nation 'have a feeling of belonging together on the basis of shared language, culture, traditions and history' (Castles, 2000: 133). In this sense, a nation is very much like an ethnic community whose sense of belonging is considered significant by its members.

Linked to this is the concept of the **nation-state**. This refers to a process of 'ethno-cultural homogenization of the population', usually achieved through schools, religious institutions such as the church, and national service, all of which play a role in transmitting a common language and culture. In some case, ethno-cultural homogenization can also see institutions engaging in **ethnic cleansing** in order to achieve positive outcomes for an ethnic in-group (Castles, 2000: 133–134). Ethnic cleansing refers to aggressive warlike conduct (including rape, torture and mass murder) against civilians on the basis of race, religion, ethnicity or nationality (Gindro, 2003: 90). As Kymlicka (1996: 11) notes, it is possible for a country to contain more than one nation, in which case it can be referred to as a 'multination state', with the smaller cultures in particular forming 'national minorities', such as in the USA, Canada and Australia. Significantly, though, Kymlicka argues that citizens of a multination state do not necessarily exclude themselves from membership of a common collective (1996: 13).

Those who differ racially from the 'host' nation are often perceived as 'immigrants', and illegal ones at that. This is problematic not only because it is an inaccurate status, but more so because of the negative context within which immigration has come to be viewed. In examining views about race and immigration in Britain, Craig (2007, cited in Law, 2010: 119) notes how racialized 'immigrants have been characterised as "cunning", "loathsome", "unprincipled" and likely to "swamp" British culture'. A quick scan of the international press on any given day illustrates the staunch fear and hatred with which immigrants have come to be universally viewed. Thus we have often seen government policy imposing strong racially defined immigration restrictions for those seeking to enter the country, as well as having weak protection from racial discrimination for those already in the country (Law, 2010: 120). For example, consider Britain's tightening of the entry criteria via the 1971 Immigration Act[1] and its recent use of the 'citizenship test' as a way of marking out those considered (relatively) worthy of being allowed to be in the country (this is discussed later in this chapter). Such restrictions are also evident in the American, Canadian and Australian citizenship tests, all of which are considered by critics to be unfair and discriminatory towards certain black and minority ethnic groups.

Earlier (between the 1960s and 1970s) British conceptualizations of multiculturalism saw it as 'a vaguely western political ideal ... which valorized the incidence of harmonious cultural differences in the social' (Hesse, 2000: 1). However, the term soon (from the mid-1980s) came to represent racial and ethnically marked differences, and a range of fears emerging from these differences about the nation's future. In some instances there is evidence of multiculturalism having been met with some element of fear – whether this be fear about a supposed religious threat, such as that seen in 1840–1922 with the Irish migrants in Britain; or about employment opportunities for the 'host' population, such as that seen in 1870–1940 with the Italians in France; or about challenges to the nation's aspirations, such as that seen in 1870–1940 with the Polish in Germany (Lucassen, 2005). More recently, there have been newer fears (or newer subjects of fears) which echo the old fears. For example, consider the anti-Muslim hostility in Australia, prominent especially around fears of its dominance over the country's Christian heritage; or the hostility faced by Romanian and Bulgarian migrant workers who in January 2014 were allowed to work without restrictions across the European Union.

This means that debates about multiculturalism have largely been based on it being viewed as an undesirable state that creates conflict. For instance, a study by Plaut et al. (2011) found that the 'inclusive' ideology of multiculturalism is not perceived by the white population as actually inclusive or relevant to themselves. This may, the authors argue, partly account for their lower support for diversity efforts in education and work settings (Plaut et al., 2011: 337). Similarly, cultural diversity is often perceived as a problem, with particular groups especially being subject to hostility, as seen in Dandy and Pe-Pua's (2010) study of attitudes to multiculturalism, immigration and cultural diversity in Australia. It is of little surprise, then, to see how this has resulted in agendas that seek to manage diversity – taken here as meaning managing the diversity of 'Others'. Castles (2000) highlights three common models here[2] (see Table 5.1). However, current debates about multiculturalism have focused on notions of a unified difference. In Britain, for instance, the last two governments have spent much time and effort in promoting this in their idea of a *new Britain*, which is to be achieved via very particular types of British citizenship and a British national identity (Driver and Martell, 2002, cited in McGhee, 2005: 163). This in part has emerged from the backlash against multiculturalism, as illustrated in British Prime Minister David Cameron's comment that state-sponsored multiculturalism has failed (David Cameron, 5 February 2011). The vision for a 'new Britain' is to be achieved through instituting **differentiated universalism**. Within the context of multiculturalism and difference, differentiated universalism is the idea that boundaries of cultural difference still exist, but that they become flexible and open to change. The intention is for a 'shared commonality' or a 'collective citizenship' to be developed.

Table 5.1 Three models for 'managing diversity'

Model	Principles	Used in
Differential exclusion	Immigrants, who are seen as ethnic minorities, are incorporated into certain areas of society (labour), but are denied access to others (citizenship and political participation).	Austria Germany Switzerland
Assimilation Aka: Integration	A policy that incorporates migrants into society through a one-sided process of adaption which requires them to give up their group identity, finally seeing them absorbed into the dominant culture.	Australia Britain Canada France The Netherlands USA
Pluralism	The acceptance of immigrant populations as ethnic communities who remain distinguishable from the majority population, but who should be granted equal rights (although often expected to conform to some key shared values).	Australia Canada USA

(Castles, 2000: 134–140)

It is claimed that to help develop this, there should be a move away from restrictive terminology. For example, Singh (2007: 1) has argued that the term 'multiculturalism' is seriously outdated, suited more to the 1960s, and that a new term should be used in its place. This would be 'shared futures' – a term which seeks to emphasize the significance of a collective future consciousness, despite having a history based on difference. More specifically, Castles (2000: 134) calls for a new notion of 'multicultural citizenship', which would be based on 'a system of rights and obligations which protects the integrity of the individual while recognizing that individuality is formed in a variety of social and cultural contexts'. In this sense, there are echoes of 'universalism'. Castles argues that migration and globalization 'make it necessary to work out new modes of inclusion for "the citizen that does not belong"' (Castles, 2000: 188), and in calling for such new citizenship, Castles marks out four key principles that should be included:

1. Taking equality of citizenship rights (including before the law) as a starting-point.

2. Recognizing that formal equality of rights can sometimes mask and legitimize disadvantage and discrimination. Multicultural citizenship must therefore accept group differences as legitimate.

3. Establishing mechanisms for group representation and participation.

4. Differential treatment for people with different characteristics, needs and wants (Castles, 2000: 144–145).

Castles argues that such new citizenship should ensure delivery of formal access to citizenship, for example by being able to get a passport of the country of residence, and also delivery of substantial citizenship, for example equal chances of participation in society, such as in politics and employment (Castles, 2000: 192).

However, as many critics have noted, there is great difficulty in achieving a new citizenship ideal when the echoes of a colonial past continue to dog every element of contemporary society. For instance, consider the persistence of heterophobic and mixophobic ideas within ideals of the 'desirable' and 'undesirable' citizen and/or society. **Heterophobia** refers to attitudes which racially reject others, but not on the basis of biological differences. Rather, the source of the rejection emerges from a fear of perceptions about what the presence of the racialized 'other' will bring, such as mixed race relationships, cultural differences, and so on. **Mixophobia** refers to an unconditional and irrational fear of race mixture. In order to legitimize views of the 'racial harm' of others, those harbouring mixophobic views tend to demonize racialized others as deviants from a natural order and biological norm. This is coupled with an extreme defence of racial purity, which is assumed to have lasted from time immemorial (Bracalenti, 2003: 182).

--- **ACTIVITY** ---

Blaut (1992: 289) once observed that we now seem to have 'a lot of racism but very few racists'. What does Blaut mean by this comment? To what extent is this comment a valid claim to make?

NATIONALISM, RACE AND CITIZENSHIP

In talking about the historical knowledge used by people in defining themselves and their identity, Harris and Sim (2000: 7) note that there are two types of history, a 'real history' and an 'imagined history'. Whether it is real or imagined, the ethnic, cultural and racialized history of the individual also shapes the way in which they view themselves, their place in society and their settlement on a racial identity. As has been argued by many over the years, to know where you are going in life, you have to know where you came from. In other words, in order to find a 'route' in life you are comfortable with, you have to know about your 'roots'. The content of such 'historical stuff' would include knowledge and/or experience of migration, oppression and struggle, war and conflict, economic development, traditional customs, religious beliefs and folklore, political governance, notable figures, and so on. Elements of one's history are selectively drawn upon and utilized by the individual in the negotiation of a racial identity. In addition, though, elements of the individual's history are also used by social others as a basis for their creation of assumptions, ideas and stereotypes, which they then go on to use in their racializing of the individual. The individual then takes these labels on board in their negotiation process, redefines them, and presents more accurately fitting labels in their place.

In the struggle for fitting and secure racial labels, there has been resurgence in nationalism in recent years. **Nationalism** refers to a sense of 'deep comradeship' by members of a national group (Cohen and Kennedy, 2013: 378). Members of a national group believe in unity based on shared history and destiny, common beliefs, and practices of rituals designed to preserve and celebrate one's national identity. The concept of nationalism and one's national identity is significant, given that individuals tend to identify more with their nation than with any other grouping (Haralambos and Holborn, 2013: 206). In arguing that a nation is 'an imagined political community', Anderson (1983, cited in Haralambos and Holborn, 2013: 207) insists we treat 'racism' and 'nationalism' as separate and different concepts. The first is based on 'dreams of external contamination' by people who have fixed, biological characteristics, and the second does not consider people to invariably belong to a particular group, given that they can be a member of a nation, but not become part of a different race. However, Anderson has been heavily criticized for his failure to consider the common historical origin of both racism and nationalism, and in particular the use of racism by Europeans to exploit non-Europeans. Robert Miles, for example, argues that racism and nationalism both lay claim to the existence of a natural division on which order (and hierarchy) emerges (Miles, 1989, cited in Haralambos and Holborn, 2013: 207).

The location of a fitting national identity can be a difficult task for some individuals, especially if we take the case of the black minority ethnic person living in a geographical location where there is a white majority, such as in Europe or the USA. For example, Barn (2001: 60) notes how:

> ...the issue of identity for children from a minority ethnic background living in a country such as Britain is particularly poignant. The negotiation and assertion of a black identity becomes a daily struggle in a country which is largely incongruous with one's self-image. Britain's credentials as a predominantly white, Christian country with a history of slavery and colonialism, and continuing racial disadvantage and discrimination play a significant role.

Clearly, ideas about nationhood are regularly 'defined in an exclusive relationship of difference' (Weedon, 2004: 20). A key marker of such difference is that of race. Within this British context, this means that for the black and minority ethnic person their presence in Britain has not only been viewed as 'problematic, temporary and conditional', but also as damaging to notions of true Britishness (Alibhai-Brown, 1999: 3). However, some argue that in more recent times there have been important shifts in notions of national identity. For instance, in his work on British Asians and the development of national identity, Pilkington (2002) argued that in the past cultural racism had excluded many black and minority ethnic groups from a British identity, but in more recent times these groups have come to challenge this exclusion by creating a more fitting and inclusive national identity, for instance through the use of a hyphenated reference label, such as 'British-Asian' (Pilkington, 2002).

In asking questions about the content of a national identity, Homi Bhaba challenges what he refers to as the 'cultural basis' of a national identity, in particular, the construction of its meanings and symbols, and their sources of legitimacy (Bhaba, 1990, cited in Jackson and Penrose, 1993: 11). Similarly, Philip Cohen's 'perversions of inheritance' notes how ideas about 'race' and 'nation' are actually rooted in shared common myths about biological descent, which are themselves often created in the 'racist imagination' (Cohen, 1988, cited in Jackson and Penrose, 1993: 11). This 'imagination' is of little surprise given that the nation has more widely been seen as 'an imagined political community … *imagined* because the members of even the smallest nation will never know most of their fellow members, meet them, or ever hear of them, yet in the minds of each lives the image of their communion' (Anderson, 1991: 6). Indeed, as Castles highlights in his discussion of citizenship, nationality and migration, when the 'migrant has always been the "Other" of the nation', we should recognize that they are especially susceptible to processes of exclusion, even though they are actually a part of society (as a worker, tax-payer, and so on) (Castles, 2000: 187).

Although 'race' and 'nation' are both concepts that are (politically and) socially constructed, and utilized largely for the purposes of power, control and rule of one group over another, they are often seen by those unable or unwilling to think critically about them as taken-for-granted and fixed entities. More so because for many they are seen as inter-connected – both historically and for future determination. This brings into consideration the argument that Britishness and whiteness are inextricably intertwined. It certainly appears so when we consider recent government politics (of both New Labour and later the Conservative–Liberal Democrat Coalition). For instance, consider the British New Labour party politician Gordon Brown's obsession with Britishness – Brown's 'British jobs for British people' promise in 2007, which was matched with a crackdown on migrant workers.[3] Such an obsession, though, is not new. For example, the following is part of a speech that was made in 1989, during calls to allow British passport[4] holders from Hong Kong to settle in Britain, where the Conservative Member of Parliament (MP) John Townend said:

The fact that the Hong Kong Chinese are very hardworking and hold British passports does not make them British. If millions of Chinese come to the UK, they would not integrate and become yellow Englishmen ... this possibility should make us consider what has already happened to this green and pleasant land – first as a result of waves of coloured immigrants and then by the pernicious doctrine of multi-culturalism ... the British people were never consulted as to whether they would change from being a homogeneous society to a multiracial society. If they had been, I am sure that a resounding majority would have voted to keep Britain an English-speaking white country. (John Townend, cited in Miles, 1990: 148)

Clearly, dominant notions of 'true' Britishness (or in this particular case 'Englishness') are still based on racial terms, and very much based on notions of difference and ideas of who is included (and excluded) from its category. This is recognized by Modood, Beishon and Virdee (1994: 108), who noted that many Caribbean youths found that their colour is an 'obstacle to their being accepted as British'. Similarly, a 2005 study of black and minority ethnic people in Britain found that although the majority considered themselves to be 'fully' or 'mainly' British, 22% of the black sample said that they did not feel at all British; 60% of black respondents and 54% of Asian respondents had experienced racist name calling or verbal abuse, with 24% and 18% respectively having experienced racist physical attacks or harassment. As a result of such racial intolerance and exclusion, some of the sample had considered leaving Britain (ICH Research, 2005, cited in Fulcher and Scott, 2007: 223).

Jackson and Penrose (1993: 2) argue that 'race' and 'nation' are categories that need first to be deconstructed in order to redress human divisiveness and inequalities: '...if we can learn how specific constructions have empowered particular categories, we can disempower them, or appropriate their intrinsic power, to achieve more equitable ends'. Such a deconstruction would involve removing the ambiguity of meaning and any replacement euphemistic language that surrounds the terms 'race' and 'nation'. Jackson and Penrose (1993: 9) argue that this is especially important given that 'the nation-state is a crucial locus for the articulation of racist ideologies, because of the extent to which it embodies the idea of "race" and legitimizes it through the granting or withholding of citizenship, the right to enter and remain within a country, and a host of other entitlements'.

ACTIVITY

Taylor (1991) argues that in England nationalism is regarded as a vulgar sentiment. However, where such sentiments are expressed by English people themselves, they are presented in a more palatable and polite language of patriotism. Do you agree?

Case study: Immigration and the 'Life in the UK' test

In recent years UK politics has been dominated by talk about 'community cohesion' and 'managed migration', which has resulted in a strict tightening of border controls, largely via immigration policy (Kundnani, 2007: 129). Garner (2007) argues that asylum seekers and immigrant workers have especially experienced a tightened grip. These two separate categories have become blurred into one singular category of undesirable other, or what he calls the 'asylumgration' blur (Garner, 2007: 136). Within a post-race era, not only has this blurring become acceptably normal in the mainstream, but in addition, because of the over-focus on community integration and national (anti-terror) security, the blurring has been presented in simplistic racialized terms. As Kundnani notes, the language used in policies such as the White Paper *Secure Borders, Safe Haven: Integration with Diversity in Modern Britain* (Home Office, 2002), mirrors the 'war on terror' with the 'war on asylum' (Kundnani, 2007: 136). For instance, the White Paper's Foreword, provided by then Home Secretary, David Blunkett MP, states: 'Having an clear, workable and robust nationality and asylum system is the pre-requisite to building the security and trust that is needed' (Home Office, 2002: 4).Thus, from the view of lay society across the UK, asylum seekers, immigrants and terrorists are one and the same, and subsequently all are seen as hostile and a threat to space. Asylum seekers and immigrants regularly face hostility on the basis that they are considered to be a threat to society – as invaders of space, with unfair access to resources, who spread disease, and have questionable sexual morality, and so on (Garner, 2007: 146–147). Garner notes that it is not surprising that of the voters in the 2004 Irish referendum, many had voted for increased immigration restrictions because of reported negative feelings towards immigrants, namely that 36% felt that the country was being exploited by immigrants and a further 27% saying that they felt there were too many immigrants. Garner also notes how there is a range of common views held about immigration and asylum in Britain, namely that Britain is a soft touch; that there are too many of them; that the majority of them are not genuine and pose a threat to British culture and to the British economy; and that they are treated well to the detriment of 'legitimate' British people.

Racial classifications enter the scene here when we consider (as discussed in earlier sections of this book) that images of immigration and asylum seeking are coloured – quite literally! This, as Garner (2007: 154) notes, means that discussions on asylum seeking and immigration in Britain become intertwined with ideas about racial purity, integration and the idea of home. Black and minority ethnic populations are readily seen as asylum seekers/refugees or immigrants – others who are not of 'this' place, and who are thus unwanted in 'this' space. Crude cultural (and offensively inaccurate) characteristics are applied to them and used to defend discriminatory and exclusionary behaviour (Kundnani, 2007). Interestingly, this also occurs when black and minority ethnic populations do have legal citizenship status. Take, for example, the description of African Americans in the aftermath of Hurricane Katrina in 2005 who were described as refugees by various news organizations. This description was not only inaccurate, but highly offensive given that the term implies that the victims were people from outside the American borders. Black and minority ethnic populations continually have their citizenship status challenged. It is unsurprising, then, that they often suffer disproportionately from special tests and measures, which, although they appear to be a fair test that determines whether an(y) individual can become a citizen or not, are actually, by design, inadequate and flawed. One such test is the 'Life in the UK' test – also commonly known as the 'British citizenship test'. The 45-minute (24-question) test was introduced in November 2005 across the UK. Anyone seeking to become a British citizen is required to pass the test by correctly answering at least 75% of the questions – although retaking the test until a pass is achieved is possible. In talking about the test, the Home Office stated that it sought to create a more meaningful way of becoming a British citizen in order to help integration and have a collective set of British values and traditions (BBC News Online, 1 November 2005). Based on information contained in the *Official Handbook for the Life in the UK Test* (2013),[5] the following is a selection of some of the (multiple choice) questions included in the test:

- Where are the Geordie, Cockney and Scouse dialects spoken?
- When did Sir Francis Drake's ship the 'Golden Hind' first circumnavigate the globe?
- What is Christmas pudding made from?
- What was the nationality of Anne of Cleves, the wife of Henry VIII?
- Is it expected that women should stay at home and not work?
- Are there charities which may help people who cannot afford to pay for a vet?
- When were films first shown publicly in the UK?

Although the test is still in use, it has been widely criticized for being a tool for controlling immigration via its ethnically exclusive and Eurocentric roots, as opposed to offering an equitable opportunity for all immigrants. In addition, the crudeness of the test's questions and the relative insignificance of information gleaned from answers render the test problematic in terms of its ability to actually prepare immigrants for life as a British citizen. Citizenship tests in general are questioned for what is considered by some to be their 'intention or effect of raising hurdles' for its candidates (Joppke, 2010: 7) because immediately there is a barrier for those immigrants whose first language is not English. In addition, citizenship tests may in reality be concerned with measuring moral judgement and psychological attitude, rather than knowledge and acceptance of history, values and traditions (Joppke, 2010: 21). The problem with this is that, ultimately, they may seek to 'try to control one's freedom of thought and freedom of conscience' (Orgad, 2010: 21). Etzioni (2007: 353) argues that citizenship tests are often used as a way of controlling immigration, evidenced not least by how, first, 'it is almost exclusively immigrants or their children who are subject to these tests', and, secondly, citizenship exams have historically been used in line with given attitudes about immigration.

ACTIVITY

Answer the 'Life in the UK' questions above. How did you do? Are you 'British enough'? What is the value of such a test in measuring national identity, pride and belonging?

CONCLUDING THOUGHTS

This chapter has discussed the embedding of race in notions of identity, space and citizenship. There has been a consideration of how group formation is influenced by race. This is then used to determine idealistic and practical access to citizenship status, and its associated rights. The social construction of a national identity has also been examined, with a consideration of the significance and power of its imagined roots. The 'Life in the UK' test and its relationship with immigration has been used as a case study to illustrate how racialized tools are used to regulate and control the movements of racialized populations in legal and socially palatable ways. The chapter has invited a consideration of questions about how we (are able to) negotiate identity within spaces and contexts that are marked out as racially significant.

MAIN POINTS

- Any individual's claim to having a single and essential racial identity is highly problematic.

- Racial identification is intrinsically linked to local, national and global politics.

- The notion of collective citizenship, via managed migration, shared culture and a unified common national identity, is used to mask racialized order.

STUDY QUESTIONS

1. Compare and contrast essentialist perspectives and social constructionist approaches to racial identity.

2. Why do racialized identities persist within what can be described as a local-global era?

3. Is a single national identity possible?

FURTHER READING

Cornell, Stephen and Hartman, Douglas (1998) *Ethnicity and Race: Making Identities in a Changing World*. London and Thousand Oaks, CA: Sage. Chapter 5 'Case Studies in Identity Construction'.

Kalra, Virinder S., Kaur, Ramindeer and Hutnyk, John (2005) *Diaspora and Hybridity*. London: Sage.

REFERENCES

Ali, Suki (2005) *Mixed-Race, Post-Race: Gender, New Ethnicities and Cultural Practices*. Oxford: Berg.

Alibhai-Brown, Yasmin (1999) *True Colours: Public Attitude to Multiculturalism and the Role of the Government*. London: Institute for Public Policy Research.

Alibhai-Brown, Yasmin (2001) *Mixed Feelings: The Complex Lives of Mixed-Race Britons*. London: The Women's Press.

Anderson, Benedict (1991) *Imagined Communities*. London: Verso.

Ballis Lal, Barbara (1999) 'Why the fuss? The real and the symbolic significance of trans-racial and intercountry adoptions', in P. Morgan (ed.), *Adoption: The Continuing Debate*. London: Civitas – Institute for the Study of Civil Society.

Banks, Cerri A. (2009) *Black Women Undergraduates: Cultural Capital and College Success*. New York: Peter Long.

Barn, Ravinder (2001) *Black Youth on the Margins: A Research Review*. York: Joseph Rowntree Foundation.

BBC News Online (2005) 'New UK citizenship testing starts', *BBC News Online*, 1 November 2005 (http://news.bbc.co.uk/1/hi/uk_politics/4391710.stm).

Blaut, James M. (1992) 'The theory of Cultural Racism', *Antipode*, 24: 289–299.

Bourdieu, Pierre (1986) 'The forms of capital', in J.G. Richardson (ed.), *Handbook of Theory and Research for the Sociology of Education*. New York: Greenwood Press. pp. 241–258.

Bracalenti, Massimo (2003) 'Mixophobia', in G. Bolaffi, R. Bracalenti, P. Braham and S. Gindro (eds.), *Dictionary of Race, Ethnicity and Culture*. London: Sage. pp. 182–183.

Cameron, David (2011) Speech on radicalization and Islamic extremism. Munich, Germany, 5 February 2011.

Castles, Peter (2000) *Ethnicity and Globalization*. London: Sage.

Cohen, Anthony P. (1985) *The Symbolic Construction of Community*. London: Ellis Harwood/Tavistock.

Cohen, Robin and Kennedy, Paul, with Perrier, Maud (2013) *Global Sociology*. Third Edition. Basingstoke: Palgrave Macmillan.

Dandy, Justine and Pe-Pua, Rogelia (2010) 'Attitudes to multiculturalism, immigration and cultural diversity: Comparison of dominant and non-dominant groups in three Australian States', *International Journal of Intercultural Relations*, 34: 34–46.

Downing, John D.H. and Husband, Charles (2005) *Representing 'Race': Racisms, Ethnicities and Media*. London: Sage.

Etzioni, Amitai (2007) 'Citizenship tests: A comparative, communitarian perspective', *The Political Quarterly*, 78(3): 353–363.

Fulcher, James and Scott, John (2007) *Sociology*. Third Edition. Oxford: Oxford University Press.

Garner, Steve (2007) *Whiteness: An Introduction*. Abingdon: Routledge.

Gindro, Sandra (2003) 'Ethnic cleansing', in G. Bolaffi, R. Bracalenti, P. Braham and S. Gindro (eds.), *Dictionary of Race, Ethnicity and Culture*. London: Sage. p. 90.

Hall, Kathleen (1995) '"There's a time to act English and a time to act Indian": The politics of identity among British Sikh teenagers', in S. Stephens (ed.), *Children and the Politics of Culture*. Chichester and Princeton, NJ: Princeton University Press. pp. 243–264.

Hall, Stuart (2000) 'Conclusion: The multi-cultural question', in B. Hesse (ed.), *Un/ Settled Multiculturalisms: Diaspora, Entanglements, Transruptions*. London: Zed Books. pp. 210–241.

Haralambos, Michael and Holborn, Martin, with Chapman, Steve and Moore, Stephen (2013) *Sociology: Themes and Perspectives*. Eighth Edition. London: Collins.

Harris, David and Sim, Jeremiah (2000) 'An empirical look at the social construction of race: The case of mixed-race adults'. Paper presented at the American Sociological Conference, Michigan.

Hesse, Barnor (2000) 'Introduction', in B. Hesse (ed.), *Un/Settled Multiculturalisms: Diaspora, Entanglements, Transruptions*. London: Zed Books. pp. 1–30.

Home Office (1971) *Immigration Act 1971*. London: HMSO.

Home Office (2002) *Secure Borders, Safe Haven: Integration with Diversity in Modern Britain*. London: HMSO.

Jackson, Peter and Penrose, Jan (1993) 'Introduction: Placing "Race" and Nation', in P. Jackson and J. Penrose (eds.), *Constructions of Race, Place and Nation*. London: University College London Press. pp. 1–26.

Joppke, Christian (2010) 'Five concerns about citizenship tests', in R. Bauböck and C. Joppke (eds.), *How Liberal are Citizenship Tests?* San Domenico di Fiesole, Italy: Robert Schuman Centre for Advanced Studies. pp. 1–4.

Knowles, Caroline (2003) *Race and Social Analysis*. London: Sage.

Kundnani, Arun (2007) *The End of Tolerance*. London: Pluto Press.

Kymlicka, Will (1996) *Multicultural Citizenship*. Oxford: Oxford University Press.

Law, Ian (2010) *Racism and Ethnicity: Global Debates, Dilemmas, Directions*. Harlow: Longman.

Lévi-Strauss, Claude (1994) 'Anthropology, race and politics: A conversation with Didier Eribon', in R. Borofsky (ed.), *Assessing Anthropology*. New York: McGraw-Hill. pp. 420–426.

Lucassen, Leo (2005) *The Immigrant Threat: The Integration of Old and New Migrants in Western Europe since 1850*. Urbana, IL: University of Illinois Press.

Madriaga, Manuel (2005) 'Understanding the symbolic idea of the American dream and its relationship with the category of "whiteness"', *Sociological Research Online*, 30th September 2005 (www.socresonline.org.uk/10/3/madriaga.html).

McGhee, Derek (2005) *Intolerant Britain? Hate, Citizenship and Difference*. Maidenhead: Open University Press/McGraw-Hill.

Meredith, Paul (1998) 'Hybridity in the third space: Rethinking bi-cultural politics in Aotearoa/New Zealand'. Paper presented at the Te Oru Rangahau Maori Research and Development Conference, Massey.

Miles, Robert (1990) 'Racism, ideology and disadvantage', *Social Studies Review*, 5(4): 148–151.

Modood, Tariq (1997) 'Introduction: The politics of multiculturalism in the new Europe', in T. Modood and P. Werbner (eds.), *The Politics of Multiculturalism in the New Europe: Racism, Identity and Community*. London: Zed Books. pp. 1–25.

Modood, Tariq, Beishon, Sharon and Virdee, Satnam (1994) *Changing Ethnic Identities*. London: Policy Studies Institute.

Orgad, Liav (2010) 'Five liberal concerns about citizenship tests', in R. Bauböck and C. Joppke (eds.), *How Liberal are Citizenship Tests?* San Domenico di Fiesole, Italy: Robert Schuman Centre for Advanced Studies. pp. 21–24.

Pilkington, Andrew (2002) 'Cultural representations and changing ethnic identities in a global age', in M. Holborn and M. Haralambos (eds.), *Developments in Sociology*. Volume 18. Ormskirk: Causeway Press.

Plaut, Victoria C., Garnett, Flannery G., Buffardi, Laura E. and Sanchez-Burks, Jeffrey (2011) '"What about me?" Perceptions of exclusion and whites' reactions to multiculturalism', *Journal of Personality and Social Psychology*, 101(2): 337–353.

Punch, Samantha, Marsh, Ian, Keating, Mike and Harden, Jeni (eds.) (2013) *Sociology: Making Sense of Society*. Fifth Edition. Harlow: Pearson.

Singh, Darra (2007) *Not Speaking English is the Single Biggest Barrier to Successful Integration*. London: Commission on Integration and Community Cohesion.

Small, John (1986) 'Transracial placements: Conflicts and contradictions', in S. Ahmed, J. Cheetham and J. Small (eds.), *Social Work with Black Children and their Families*. London: Batsford.

Small, John (1991) 'Ethnic and racial identity in adoption within the United Kingdom', *Adoption and Fostering*, 15(4): 61–69.

Spencer, Stephen (2006) *Race and Ethnicity: Culture, Identity and Representation*. Abingdon: Routledge.

Taylor, Peter (1991) 'The English and their Englishness: A curiously mysterious, elusive and little understood people', *Scottish Geographical Magazine*, 107: 146–161.

Torpey, John (1999) *Invention of the Passport: Surveillance, Citizenship and the State*. Cambridge: Cambridge University Press.

Turner, Victor (1969) *The Ritual Process: Structure and Anti-Structure*. Ithaca, NY: Cornell University Press.

Weedon, Chris (2004) *Identity and Cultures: Narratives of Difference and Belonging*. Maidenhead: Open University Press/McGraw-Hill.

NOTES

1. The 1971 Immigration Act contained provisions and restrictions that favoured the immigration of those people who came from 'white' Commonwealth countries, such as Australia, South Africa and Canada.
2. Castles (2000: 135) notes that no one country fits these models in singular, linear or exact ways. Rather, settlement (which is in itself flexible and constantly being revised) is an evolutionary and ambivalent process.
3. Although David Cameron, the leader of the Opposition Conservative Party, soon pointed out that such a policy was illegal under European Union law.
4. The British passport was first made available to all British nationals in 1858. Thus, Torpey (1999: 9) notes: it 'signalled the dawn of a new era in human affairs, in which individual states and the international state system as a whole successfully monopolized the legitimate authority to permit movement within and across their jurisdictions'.
5. Currently in its third edition, this guide is available from the Stationery Office, London.

6

THE OTHER 'ISMs'

INTRODUCTION

This chapter demonstrates how an analysis of race in contemporary society cannot be undertaken in isolation from other social variables. In doing so, it highlights the complex and varied nature of race issues in a society that also draws boundaries around gender, sexuality, age, class, geography and the urban environment. The chapter draws distinctions and evidences the multifarious nature of identities in society and the measurement of these against racial categories. The theory and concepts covered will include: Black feminist critique; critical race theory; intersectionality; postcolonial theory; and underclass. The case study in the chapter concerns the media's reporting of the 2012 gang rape of Jyoti Singh Pandey in Delhi (India). The key question raised is: How is a raced hierarchy influenced by other social variables?

KEY TERMS

- Anti-Semitism

- Black feminist critique

- Critical race theory

- Everyday racism

- Exoticism

- Infibulation

- Intersectionality

- Orientalism

- Postcolonial theory

- Scapegoating

- Underclass

ORDINARY AND EVERYDAY RACISM

Social scientists use the term 'micro-aggression' to refer to those instances where 'race' is significant in an event. This is a sudden, stunning or dispiriting transaction that negatively marks the days of black and minority ethnic people. They can be unconscious or conscious small acts, but they are perpetrated on the basis of stereotypes about race (and sometimes gender, age, class, sexuality, and so on). Sometimes, though, events are not 'micro' at all, and this is what **critical race theory** examines. Largely influenced by European philosophers such as Antonio Gramsci and Jacques Derrida, and radical figures/groups, such as Frederick Douglas, W.E.B. DuBois, Cesar Chavez, Martin Luther King, the Black Panther Movement and the Chicago movements of the 1960s and early 1970s, critical race theory is interested in the relationship between power and the construction of social roles as well as the unseen, largely invisible collection of patterns and habits that make up patriarchy and other types of domination, especially in matters relating to race (Delgado and Stefancic, 2001: 4). In practical terms, the theory is driven by a desire to redress historic wrongs. However, the theory has often been criticized for its sympathetic understanding of nationalism and group empowerment (Delgado and Stefancic, 2001: 5). Despite this, the movement emerging from the theory has splintered. For example, there now exist an *Asian American jurisprudence* and the *Latino-critical contingent*, which both study migration theory and policy, and language rights and discrimination based on accent or national origin; the *American Indian group*, which addresses indigenous people's rights, sovereignty and land claims; the *queer-crit interest group* and the *British Asian Movement*, which both have interests in identity and representation.

Based on the view that racism in dangerously 'ordinary' and that it weaves into every aspect of what is considered to be a (social, material and economic) system of 'white-over-colour' society, there are several key arguments in relation to critical race theory. These include the suggestion that the 'ordinariness' of racism makes it difficult to cure or even address. The theory suggests that 'interest convergence', also known as 'material determinism', means that because racism advances the interests of white elites (materially) and working-class people (psychically), large segments of society have little incentive to eradicate it. The theory acknowledges a social construction thesis and the idea that race is a product of social thought and relations. This means that there is 'differential racialization' and varied consequences for different black and minority ethnic groups. Critical race theory advocates the idea of 'a unique voice of colour' which holds that because of their different histories and experiences of oppression, different black groups may be able to communicate to their white counterparts matters that the whites are unlikely to know. In other words, minority status brings with it presumed competence to speak about race and racism (Delgado and Stefancic, 2001: 8–9). In more recent times, the concern of critical race theory is a belief in the need to still address what they call Eurocentric standards in a variety of areas, such as crime, justice and victim's rights, but also more generally in terms of identity issues, media presentations on what is desirable and undesirable, education, and global politics in immigration, space, place and nationality (Delgado and Stefancic, 2001:132).

Critical race theorists would also have a concern with the real-life and damaging effects on black and minority ethnic populations following the failures of institutions and systems that should treat all members of society equally – if not at least on a humanitarian basis. For example, take the case of Hurricane Katrina, which hit the Gulf Coast of America in August 2005. When Katrina fell on New Orleans it was members of the black African-American community, especially its poor, female population, who suffered disproportionately (Healey, 2012: 16). First, given that they were located in poorer neighbourhoods with limited access to resources, such as transport, they were unable to escape the city when news of Katrina's approach was broadcast. Secondly, there was a significant failure in the American government's pre-storm evacuation plan and the aftermath relief system. In the first instance, the Mayor of New Orleans, Ray Nagin, was criticized for having failed to use available transport to evacuate those without transport, which is a requirement under the State of Louisiana's evacuation plans. After the hurricane, Mayor Nagin and other government officials had also failed to arrange for survivors to be supplied with basic needs, such as food, water and shelter, which was later followed by claims that, as a result, several citizens had needlessly died.

It is important to recognize that racism as a daily routine, known as '**everyday racism**', is a common feature of society. It includes verbal violence, for example written and spoken statements, hate-fuelled speech, xenophobic rhetoric and insulting slogans and graffiti as well as physical violence, namely assault and murder (Andrisani, 2011: 132). Everyday racism can be carried out by lay members of the public, but is also commonplace among politicians (as discussed in other chapters), the entertainment industry and in the sporting arena:

- In 2015, the entertainment and fashion presenter Giuliana Rancic said of mixed-race artist Zendaya Coleman, who had attended the American Oscars ceremony with her hair styled in dreadlocks, that Zendaya's hair must smell 'like patchouli ... or weed'. Rancic's comment is especially interesting given that a few months earlier she had described Kyle Jenner, a (white) celebrity who had worn her hair in locks, as 'edgy'.

- In May 2013, Tiger Woods' opponent Sergio Garcia, while on stage at the Golfing European Tour's gala players' awards dinner, stated 'We will have him round every night. ... We will serve fried chicken.'

The nature and impact of 'everyday racism' has been well documented and in many ways its reality is starting to reach public consciousness. However, it can be suggested that we have now reached a stage where racism is extra-ordinary. This means that it has become more than an uncomfortable but acceptable expression of racist views. Rather, racism today has come to be normalized and expected. Indeed, for some, challenging racism is considered unusual. Consider, for instance, the 2009 broadcast on Australian national television of a Jackson Five parody group, Jackson Jive, whose blacked-up faces were challenged by a clearly shocked and disgusted Harry Connick Jr, one of the celebrity judges. Indeed, it was Connick who was later criticized by the Australian (white) public for over-reacting and failing to understand that in Australia this sort of thing is funny (and normal), as illustrated by the host of the show's response:

> I noticed that when we had the Jackson Jive on ... and it didn't occur to me till afterwards, I think we may have offended you with that act. ... I know that to your countrymen, that's an insult to have a blackface routine like that on the show, so I do apologise.

So the suggestion (or rationale) is that in the USA blacked-up faces are offensive, but in Australia it's just 'good clean fun'!

It has been argued that 'everyday racism' is also interlinked with classism, namely prejudice or discrimination on the basis of social class (usually to benefit the upper class at the expense of the lower class). One illustration of this can be found in debates which talk about a supposed subhuman category, or an '**underclass**' of people, a term which was used in sociological theorization as early as the eighteenth century (McLaughlin, 2001: 310). In rediscovering and popularizing the term, Charles Murray (1984, 1990) used it to refer to those populations in the USA and Britain who had poor educational attainment; high levels of single (mother) parenthood and absent fathers; voluntary unemployment; welfare dependency; increased drug dependency; increased engagement in violent crime; and a lack of morals as they choose to be in their situation (which specifically distinguished them from 'the deserving poor') (Phoenix, 2003: 324). In *The Emerging British Underclass* (1990), Murray used metaphors of 'plague' and 'disease' in his discussion of the underclass to argue that, as a group firmly established in the USA, they would soon be a sizeable feature of British society, given that these 'underclass' characteristics are transmitted from one generation to the next.[1] Murray argued that these 'illegitimate' features are also overwhelmingly found in black populations, which he argued was a normal feature of black culture. Murray's conceptualization of the underclass is seen as overly individualistic and racist as well as being overly simplistic in its ability to explain the significance of structural inequalities. Despite this, though, we often see media coverage focusing disproportionately on the criminal and deviant behaviour of people who are often viewed as being of such a background. They are regularly described in dehumanized ways and as being 'feckless', for instance media headlines have included: 'Stop giving benefits and this feckless underclass will stop breeding' (*Daily Express*, 16 February 2009), and 'How can rewarding the feckless and punishing the hardworking be the right way to support families?' (*Daily Mail*, 19 August 2014). Politicians have also harboured such views, for instance, in the aftermath of the August 2011 'riots' in England then Justice Secretary Kenneth Clarke said: 'Our feral underclass is too big, has been growing, and needs to be diminished' (Clarke, quoted in *The Telegraph*, 4 October 2011). However, as Rhodes (2011) notes following his study of BNP[2] support in England, there are also subdividing categories of whiteness which are largely defined by class distinctions and notions of respectability and responsibility. These groups are often marked out with specific negative labels, such as 'white trash' – their very existence is seen to threaten not only social order but also the symbolic superiority of whiteness (Wray, 2006: 2).

INTERSECTIONAL DYNAMICS

The **Black feminist critique** argues that both gender and ethnicity are sites of inequality. Here, sexism, class oppression and racism are inextricably bound together, and forms of feminism that strive to overcome sexism and class oppression, but which ignore race, can discriminate against many people, including women, through racial bias. This perspective argues that black women experience a different and more intense kind of oppression in comparison to their white counterparts. As hooks (1995: 79) notes, black women are oppressed by white patriarchy, by sexist black men and by racist white women. They point to the emergence of Black feminism after earlier movements led by white middle-class women failed, as they saw it, to cater for their needs, as they largely ignored oppression based on race and class. Patricia Hill-Collins (2000: 35) considers Black feminism to include women who theorize the experiences and ideas shared by ordinary black women that provide a unique angle of vision on self, community and society. Black feminists contend that the liberation of black women entails freedom for all people, since it would require the end of racism, sexism and class oppression (Moody-Ramirez and Dates, 2014: 38). In addition, hooks (2013: 37) notes that women, who are ultimately the hands-on workers of race matters, should be careful that they do not continue to 'teach white supremacist thought and practice' and thus maintain its system of domination. Rather, all women working towards equality and anti-oppressive practices need to ground their efforts in 'true sisterhood' and 'female solidarity', which will ultimately challenge what hooks calls the 'imperialist white supremacist capitalist patriarchy' (2013: 38).

It was Anna Julia Cooper who, writing in 1892, can be credited as one of the leading pioneers of race theory, especially in relation to black feminist thought and the concept of **intersectionality**. Cooper argued that there were different outcomes when different structures of inequality (such as race, class and gender) existed (Law, 2010: 55). In looking specifically at the intersections of race, gender and class in terms of black women in the USA, Patricia Hill-Collins (2000) argued that such intersections are important determinants of the outcomes of experiences, and that it is insufficient to consider any one variable in isolation. It is argued that variables need to be seen as interlocking and mutually reinforcing, given that they form a 'matrix of domination' (Healey, 2012: 14). For Hill-Collins (2000, 2005, cited in Cohen and Kennedy, 2013: 167), the 'matrix of domination' comprises four components:

1. Structural: Slow-changing systems of law, politics and economics influence life-chance.

2. Disciplinary: Bureaucracies set rules and routines, and in doing so they organize and control social behaviour, as well as define what counts as 'knowledge'.

3. Hegemonic: The cultural realm, specifically language, imagery, school syllabus, mass media, and so on, shapes consciousness and persuades people to accept them and the prevailing distribution of power as legitimate.

4. Interpersonal: A distribution and reinforcing of authority in the everyday interpersonal relations of family, community and workplace.

In order to resist any 'matrix', Hill-Collins argued that individuals need to pursue self-determining possibilities (Cohen and Kennedy, 2013: 167). Many academics, including Angela Davis (1980), bell hooks (1982) and Fiona Williams (1989), have developed work on intersectionality, but it is Kimberlé Crenshaw (1989, 1995) who has highlighted the significance of these intersectional elements, especially in relation to the differences between structural and political agendas, or what she calls *structural intersectionality* and *political intersectionality* (1995: 358–359).[3] It is important to note that intersectionality applies to all individuals, as we all have multiple identities which vary according to the context (or situation) in which we find ourselves – hence the use of the term 'situational identity' (Yuval-Davis, 2009, and Anthias, 2005, cited in Cohen and Kennedy, 2013: 167).

These approaches are also concerned with causes that help to empower black and minority ethnic women who experience marginalization and limited choice.

For instance, recent causes have focused on anti-infibulation campaigns. Gindro (2003b: 147) provides a useful outline of **infibulation**: the practice 'refers to the mutilation of the female genital apparatus by the reduction of the lower orifice of the vagina, usually with the added practice of the extirpation of the clitoris, the small labia and most of the large labia. The two sides of the vulva are sewn together, leaving only an orifice in the lower part to allow the flow of urine and of menstrual blood.' Gindro (2003b) notes how infibulation has cultural ritual significance, most prominently in East Africa, where it is seen as a way of preventing sexual promiscuity, which also brings with it upholding a woman's reputation and her family's honour. Feminists and campaigners have argued against the practice, highlighting also its medical risks. However, because other forms of ritual mutilation, such as circumcision, are allowed to continue in some faiths and cultures, the struggle to end female infibulation has to date been unsuccessful.

The approaches to the study of intersectional identities has especially been critical of feminist legal theory and what is seen as its non-representative and essentializing tendencies, given that it is made up of mostly white, heterosexual and socioeconomically privileged women who consider there to be gender universality and thus claim to speak for all women, which inadvertently encourages unconscious racism (Harris, 2000: 263).[4] The idea that there are differences within the female community actively challenges the essentializing notion of 'sisterhood' that the cause relies on so heavily. Thus, the different levels of subordination and oppression experienced by different types of women – or, to be more precise, their racially specific nature – comes to be ignored and inadvertently maintained by mainstream feminist approaches (Anthias and Yuval-Davis, 1993: 97). As Harris (2000: 271) notes: '… feminist essentialism represents not just an insult to black women, but a broken promise – the promise to listen to women's stories, the promise of feminist method'. Mainstream 'white' feminism is therefore considered as racist, given that it ignores the racial oppression and anti-racist struggle of black women. As Anthias and Yuval-Davis (1993: 101) note:

> Black women are not only oppressed by men and institutionalized forms of sexism in the state but also by white (both men and women) and by institutionalized racism. The blindness to race (and the consequent invisibility of Black women) and the failure to take a strong stance against racism are seen as the products of the endemic racism of white feminism.

There are, in fact, great differences between the experiences, needs and concerns of women whose other (racial) identities differ from one another. Angela Harris (2000) uses the issue of rape as a case in point, arguing that for black and minority ethnic women it brings 'unique ambivalence'. Harris argues that rape for black and minority ethnic women equals a type of vulnerability to the act itself, as well as a lack of legal protection that is radically different from their white counterparts – unsurprising given that during slavery and colonialism black and minority ethnic women have been regularly subjected to rape, sexual abuse and harassment by their white employers/masters. This was often with the knowledge of their white female employers/mistresses, and a consequence of a belief system that viewed black and minority ethnic women as naturally sexually promiscuous, and in this sense unable to be a victim of rape. As Harris (2000: 270) notes: '"Rape" was something that only happened to white women; what happened to black women was simply life.' This has come to create a situation where sexual violence against black and minority ethnic women is ignored, and even today, in an era of enhanced legal protection, it has not reached the level of recognition that it has for white women. At the same time, black and minority ethnic women simultaneously acknowledge that black and minority ethnic men are also violently victimized or 'terrorized' both by white men and women, for instance via disproportionate sentencing and a susceptibility to false allegations (Harris, 2000: 270–271). Again, the sexually deviant mythical images of black and minority ethnic men make them especially vulnerable. The systematic and institutionalized violence that black minority ethnic men experience therefore acts as a form of 'racial castration', a means by which the 'threat' (of their potential ability to compete for resources) can be curtailed and controlled.

It is also important to recognize that 'Black' within Black feminist concerns should not be taken as another essentializing category. Different categories of women who fall within the black and minority ethnic category have different needs and concerns depending on very specific histories and oppressive experiences. For instance, the concerns of South Asian Muslim women differ from those of the black African-Caribbean woman. It is true that both categories are constructed in problematic ways and as socially deviant, and it is also true that both have experienced oppression linked to colonial rule. However, in recent times, the specific types of attack and racial discrimination handed out to each group has varied significantly. Thus, although there are some bonding ties that can collectively unite these groups, there are also specific issues that divide them.

ACTIVITY

Anthias and Yuval-Davies (1993: 104) argue that a black gendered identity is not a homogeneous one. Collect evidence to support and disprove this claim.

THE ROLE OF RACE, GENDER AND CLASS IN CONSTRUCTIONS OF THE OTHER

During the American era of post-slavery, Southern segregation and northward migration, some liberation was made accessible and indeed obtained by the black African-American population. However, it is argued that the female members of this population group remained disproportionately vulnerable, not only within the wider white majority society, but also within the black African-American community (Healey, 2012: 151). In terms of the latter, it was commonplace for African-American women to become housewives, often having left the workforce. This was because it was believed that a working African-American woman was too reminiscent of her slave role (Gutman, 1976, cited in Healey, 2012: 151). Ironically, this view continued even into the American civil rights and Black Power movements. This is not surprising given that they were male-dominated movements, which considered their African-American women to be supporters of men rather than equal partners in liberation. This is especially problematic given that women too were involved in liberation and equality struggles, yet were denied leadership roles or decision-making positions (Healey, 2012: 190).

Postcolonialism refers to the socio-political and cultural space that developed in the period following colonization (Spencer, 2006: 134). **Postcolonial theory** is concerned with examining the continued racialized experiences of pre-colonized subjects. Particular strands of postcolonial theory, similar to feminist theory, have an interest in how black and minority ethnic women come to be presented as a particular type of (Oriental) 'other', with their unique experience of continued dual colonization by racial (imperial) and patriarchal domination (Spencer, 2006: 125). Here, the use of **exoticism** has been commonplace in the construction of 'other' colonial women. Exoticism refers to the ways in which Western culture understands the fascination given to distinct cultures, usually by artists and scholars, but increasingly by lay members of society in general. Exoticism has been seen by some as evidencing an evolutionary movement, given that it represents the ability of Western culture to have a positive interest in other countries and cultures. However, this has been critiqued on the basis that often that interest is in reality superficial and selective, and that it continues to constitute a form of racism (Gindro, 2003a: 112–113).

ACTIVITY

Does racialized exoticism still exist in contemporary society? Can one argue that such exotic images are now being reclaimed by black and minority ethnic women as a way of overcoming oppression? Draw on evidence and examples to validate your points.

Such constructions have ultimately rendered the 'other' colonial woman as powerless – they are mute, vulnerable and a subject of the Western man's sexual gaze – as well as being a measure against which freedom is granted for her Western female counterpart. For instance, consider representations of the veil and hijab, which are seen through the Western gaze as symbols of oppression. Interestingly though, historical Western perceptions of those who wear these garments has often presented wearers as a tease, who use the veil to indicate sexual availability. Thus, veiled bodies are seen as active invitations for the desire of its wearers to have sexual liberation. The coming together of notions of cultural liberation and sexual liberation further represents a conquest challenge for the Western male gaze. The Western male gaze especially used this rationale to justify sexual desire as well as its conquest and rule over the 'enslaved' woman's supposed 'backwards' and 'oppressive' culture.[5]

It is argued that there remains a strong echo of the imperialist gaze in contemporary society. In more recent times, though, the veiled body has come to largely represent fear and hostility, albeit still within the notion of oppressive cultures. As Spencer (2006: 126) notes, veils and hijabs have come to act as a 'visual cue to bolster claims of the "alarming" rise in Islamic militancy'. Therefore, although still the object of 'the gaze', the veiled body is today considered to be less an exotic body. In addition, Franks (2000: 923–924) notes that when the wearer of the veil or the hijab is white, they become subjected to a form of 'racism by proxy' – a hate gaze where they are seen as 'race traitors' to their natural (white) superiority. In contrast, other groups have remained strongly within the traditional exotic image, and in doing so have continued to act as a source of postcolonial sexual fantasy and rule for white Western men. For instance, consider the sex tourism industry, and specifically the case of East Asian brides. Often termed 'mail order brides', women from Asian countries such as the Philippines[6] are seen as attractive to Western men, largely for their assumed obedience and subservience (Stone, 2004).[7] This is their illusionary appeal and with this they are considered to be non-threatening. In addition, they are considered to bring with them a desire to 'please' their Western husbands, which consequently means a ready willingness to fulfil the Western-woman image by fully integrating themselves into their new Western lives, for instance, learning the language, dressing in non-traditional clothing, and so on. However, within these white male Western desires are echoes of **Orientalism**. This refers to the depiction, emerging from European colonial domination, of Asian women as alluring sources of fascination, particularly in terms of their sexuality (Rattansi, 2003: 212). As Edward Said (1978) notes, Orientalism acts as a form of institutionalized power and systematic control over those viewed through its lens. This is illustrated by the ways in which the Orient and its subjects (including its 'mail order brides') have come to be governed in conformity with the West's representations of the Orient, as opposed to the realities of the Orient in itself (Rattansi, 2003: 213).

As Ali (2005: 156–157) notes, it is important that we recognize the different ways in which particular gendered and racial types become associated with different types of sexuality, for example the black male as a sexual predator, the black woman as animalistic and insatiable, the sexually expert South Asian woman, the feminized South Asian man, the submissive Pacific Rim Asian woman, the sexually mysterious and cruel Pacific Rim Asian man, and the lascivious and dangerous Arab man. Hunter (2005: 1) highlights that there are also different stereotypes and treatments reserved for people of darker skin tone, something that Hunter refers to as 'colourism', which is actually practised by 'whites and people of color alike'. Colourism refers to instances when those physical features and skin tones which are associated more closely to whiteness, namely light skin, straight noses, straight hair, and so on, assign their owner assumed positive traits and privileges. Colourism is especially prominent among women, and has been increasingly associated with sexuality. For instance, Hunter (2005: 7) notes: 'There are many familiar images such as the black Mammy (loyal servant), and the black Jezebel (whore), and their Mexican American counterparts – the deeply religious, pious, Mexican American mother, and the 'hot tamale' promiscuous, Mexican or Mexican American woman'.

Hunter goes on to argue that what these racialized, colourized and gendered stereotypes do is serve to label particular racial groups as particular types of subordinate subject (Hunter, 2005: 7). Ali (2005) notes how there is also diversity of stereotyping and thus (more favourable) treatment for those whose 'mixedness', for instance of mixed racial heritage status, is visible, as is the case for those whose skin colour is considered less extreme, such as light-skinned black women. This is because such women are seen as still being able to satisfy Western white male sexual desire and colonial fantasy 'safely' away from the (supposed) animalistic, dangerous and diseased/infectious character of their darker-skinned counterparts (hooks, 1992, cited in Ali, 2005: 160).

Bhattacharayya (2008: 87–88) also reminds us of the sexual stereotypes about 'the black man and his mythical penis', which actually indicated 'the insecurities of the powerful'. Boskin (1986, cited in Moody-Ramirez and Dates, 2014: 17) also notes how the use of the 'Coon', 'Jim Crow' and 'Sambo' images in America, especially as objects of laughter, also sought to strip the black African-American male of masculinity, dignity and self-respect – qualities that would otherwise present him as a sexual competitor, warrior and economic adversary. In her analysis of Muslim men and the processes of deviant labelling within the context of the 'war on terror', Bhattacharayya (2008) argues that there is a difference in the popularized, racialized mythologies about 'the dangerous black man' from that of 'the dangerous Muslim man'. However, similar processes of racist, gendered and sexualized imagery have been used against the Muslim man, who has come to embody 'a dangerous hyper-masculinity and a mutilated deviation from proper manhood ... portrayed as impenetrable, secretive, enmeshed in an alien culture that inhabits the secret places if an unsuspecting host society. Their masculinity is regarded as excessive and dysfunctional, too absolute in the internalisation of restraint, too refusing of desire or of malleability, too literal in their understanding of the ideal masculinity' (Bhattacharayya, 2008: 89).[8] Consider, for instance, the representation of Arab and Muslim men, especially as being subjects of either security threats (in particular, terrorist behaviour) or as oppressors (of women) who are primitive and hypersexual. In terms of the few instances when racialized bodies are presented more favourably, they are given Eurocentric features – for example, consider Disney's animated movie, *Aladdin* (1992). Although of Arabic background, Aladdin can only be presented as 'good' if he has European features and an American accent. In addition, his status as 'a good Arab' only becomes palatable with the backdrop of what is described in the opening as a 'barbaric homeland' where 'bad Arabs' are given exaggerated accents and characteristics. These stereotypes and resultant attitudes are commonplace in media and entertainment sources.

Often such groups are subject to '**scapegoating**'. This refers to the ways in which an innocent person or group is held responsible for wider social and economic problems, such as crime, unemployment, housing shortages, and so on. It is not uncommon for racial and ethnic groups to be scapegoated, especially in Western societies such as those found in America, Australia and Europe. Power is very important in the scapegoating process, given that it involves the demonization of the relatively powerless by those in a position of relative power and influence. Crude stereotypes are often used in the demonization process as scapegoating also involves drawing simplistic (and thus readily digestible) boundaries between good and evil (Murji, 2001: 255–256). An example of extreme scapegoating occurred in Nazi Germany with its propaganda against its Jewish population. Here, **anti-Semitism** was widely used to present Jews in unfavourable ways and especially to blame them for the country's economic and social decline. This resulted in prejudice, hatred and attacks against members of the Jewish faith, and ultimately had severe and genocidal consequences (Braham and Zargani, 2003: 73). Consider also Bhattacharayya's (2008: 75) argument on how newer racialized and gendered stereotypes about South Asian (Muslim) men actually serve to 'relegitimise state racism'.

Case study: Victims and offenders in the Jyoti Singh Pandey case

One evening in 2012, a 23-year-old female medical intern, Jyoti Singh Pandey,[9] was travelling on a bus with a male friend through a South Delhi neighbourhood. Also on the bus were six other men, including the bus driver, all of whom gang raped Pandey and beat up her friend. Over two weeks later Pandey died from the injuries she had sustained during the attack. The attack attracted heightened attention by the world's media and led to a number of public protests highlighting the issue of rape in India and the failure of India's government to provide adequate security for women. The six men accused of the attack were all arrested and charged with sexual assault and murder, and (in light of India's overburdened legal system) were put on trial in a fast-track court. In March 2013, one of the accused was found hanged in his cell, and later that year the remaining five accused were all found guilty and sentenced. One (juvenile) was given the maximum sentence of three years' imprisonment in a reform facility, and the others were sentenced to death by hanging. Following the case, the issue of rape (especially of women) in India became the subject of widespread discussion.

Although anti-rape and women's rights organizations valued the heightened attention into the vulnerability of women to rape in India, critics argued that, in reality, the incidents of rape per population are no greater than figures in the USA. Critics went on to claim that the media's selective, biased and sensationalist reporting of the case actually served to damage the reputation of *all* Indian men and to present the nation as backwards and culturally deficient. This was illustrated with the wide reporting of comments made by one of the attackers in a documentary called *India's Daughter*, which was made about the case. Very much like other rapists across the world, he 'justified' his actions via the use of a victim-blaming logic: 'A decent girl won't roam around at nine o'clock at night ... a girl is

(Continued)

(Continued)

far more responsible for a rape than a boy' (Mukesh Singh, quoted in *India's Daughter*, broadcast on the BBC (UK), 4 March 2015). In discussing the cultural reasons for the rape, a *New York Times* Editorial contrasted 'India's "patriarchal village culture" with the ostensibly true cosmopolitanism of Western cities, which, in doing so relied on the problematic assumption that the latter is somehow definitionally safer for women' (Roychowdhury, 2013: 283–284). The context of rape anywhere, argued critics, is about the gender inequalities and power imbalances that exist everywhere – not just in India – and, as such, the issue of rape must be addressed as a global issue, not just as a symptom specific to Indian culture. However, Roychowdhury (2013: 282–283) goes on to note that the international media presented 'their' Pandey as 'emblematic of a decidedly modern Indian woman' who became a symbol of 'the battle between two Indias: the first, new and modern, and the second, old and backward'. The attack on Pandey was, the international press suggested, the result of a misogynistic culture's attempt to control and suppress women who dared to modernize, liberate and empower (by which we read 'Westernize') themselves.

The international media's reporting of the Delhi gang rape case marks out a number of salient issues regarding the use of race, or, more specifically, a racialized culture, which when unavoidably intertwined with (the presentation of) other social variables result in a repositioning of status. Pandey was undeniably a victim of rape. However, her enhanced status of 'victim' was possible because she was *presented*[10] as an educated and aspirational woman, who desired to be an active consumer, and thus economically and socially upwardly mobile. Pandey was also an attractive woman who (according to media reports of interviews with her father) wore Western clothes and her long hair flowing and down. She refused to be confined to the home, and instead visited malls and movie theatres (*Daily Mirror*, 2013, cited in Roychowdhury, 2013: 283). These additional social variables helped to elevate Pandey to a higher status of victimhood, which in turn evoked greater sympathy – she was, in the media's eyes, 'a true victim'. In addition, this 'victim' status was weighted even more because of its positioning against Pandey's attackers, or, more specifically, 'their' social variables, which located them firmly as traditional and backward village folk, who were considered undesirable and thus ranked lower on the scale of international social acceptance. Colonial echoes of the attackers as dangerous brown men helped to elevate them into positions of undesirability. The (white Eurocentric) international media played on the colonial legacy of exoticism, which sees 'white men saving brown women from brown men' (Spivak, 1988, cited in Roychowdhury, 2013: 284).

ACTIVITY

When the international media reports on cases such as that of Pandey in the way that it did, what impact does this have for all rape victims everywhere?

CONCLUDING THOUGHTS

This chapter has considered the significance of other social variables, such as gender, sexuality, age, class, geography and the urban environment, and how these variables intertwine with that of race in order to deliver a varied set of experiences for the human subject. This is undoubtedly a political process as well as a social one, and like all socially constructed events is not entirely fixed, but rather is open to negotiation and change. The reporting of the gang rape of Jyoti Singh Pandey in Delhi (India) has been used as a case to illustrate some of the salient issues on how a racialized culture, combined with other social variables, is used to re-present bodies and reassign victim-hood status. The chapter asks questions about how and why a racial hierarchy is influenced by other social variables, and the positioning of power within this dynamic.

MAIN POINTS

- Racism is ordinary.
- Racism, sexism and class oppression are interlinked, and in combination create a hierarchy of discrimination.
- There remains in contemporary society, a presence of the imperialist gaze.
- There is widespread use of scapegoating which serves to blame racialized groups for wider social problems.

STUDY QUESTIONS

1. In what ways is racism normalized? What are the consequences of this?

2. To what extent are the arguments around intersectionality evident in contemporary society?

3. What is the legacy of imperialism for women? Do women of different racial and ethnic backgrounds have a shared or divided experience of that legacy?

4. Is racism the same for all those who experience it?

FURTHER READING

Bhattacharayya, Gargi (2008) *Dangerous Brown Men: Exploiting Sex, Violence and Feminism in the War on Terror.* London: Zed Books.
hooks, bell (2013) *Writing Beyond Race: Living Theory and Practice.* New York: Routledge.
Rhodes, James (2011) '"It's not just them, it's whites as well": Whiteness, class and BNP support', *Sociology*, 45(1): 102–117.

REFERENCES

Ali, Suki (2005) 'Uses of the exotic: Body, narrative, mixedness', in C. Alexander and C. Knowles (eds.), *Making Race Matter: Bodies, Space and Identity*. Basingstoke: Palgrave Macmillan. pp. 153–171.

Andrisani, Paola (2011) 'A 360° view: Chronicles of ordinary racism'. *Lunaria, Rome*. English translation by Davide Di Pietro and Clara Marshall. pp. 131–140.

Anthias, Floya and Yuval-Davies, Nira (1993) *Racialized Boundaries: Race, Nation, Gender, Colour and Class and the Anti-Racist Struggle*. London: Routledge.

Braham, Peter and Zargani, Aldo (2003) 'Anti-semitism', in G. Bolaffi, R. Bracalenti, P. Braham and S. Gindro (eds.), *Dictionary of Race, Ethnicity and Culture*. London: Sage. pp. 15–17.

Cohen, Robin and Kennedy, Paul (2013) *Global Sociology*. Third Edition. Basingstoke: Palgrave Macmillan.

Cooper, Anna Julie (1892) *A Voice from the South*. Xenia, OH: Aldine Printing House.

Crenshaw, Kimberlé (1989) 'Demarginalizing the intersection of race and sex: A black feminist critique of antidiscrimination doctrine, feminist theory and antiracist politics', *University of Chicago Legal Forum*, 140: 139–167.

Crenshaw, Kimberlé (1995) 'Mapping the margins: Intersectionality, identity politics, and violence against women of colour', in K. Crenshaw, N. Gotando, G. Peller and K. Thomas (eds.), *Critical Race Theory: The Key Writings that Formed the Movement*. New York: The New Press. pp. 357–383.

Daily Express (2009) 'Stop giving benefits and this feckless underclass will stop breeding', *Daily Express Online*, 16 February 2009 (www.express.co.uk/comment/blogs/85054/Stop-giving-benefits-and-this-feckless-underclass-will-stop-breeding).

Daily Mail (2014) 'How can rewarding the underclass and punishing the hardworking be the right way to support families?' *Daily Mail Online*, 19 August 2014 (www.dailymail.co.uk/debate/article-2728446/How-rewarding-feckless-punishing-hardworking-right-way-support-families-By-Jill-Kirby.html).

Davis, Angela (1980) *Women, Race and Class*. London: The Women's Press.

Delgado, Richard and Stefancic, Jean (2001) *Critical Race Theory: An Introduction*. New York: New York University Press

Franks, Myfanwy (2000) 'Crossing the borders of whiteness? White Muslim women who wear the hijab in Britain today', *Ethnic and Racial Studies*, 23(5): 917–929.

Garner, Steve (2010) *Racisms: An Introduction*. London: Sage.

Gindro, Sandra (2003a) 'Exoticism', in G. Bolaffi, R. Bracalenti, P. Braham and S. Gindro (eds.), *Dictionary of Race, Ethnicity and Culture*. London: Sage. pp. 112–113.

Gindro, Sandra (2003b) 'Infibulation', in G. Bolaffi, R. Bracalenti, P. Braham and S. Gindro (eds.), *Dictionary of Race, Ethnicity and Culture*. London: Sage. p. 147.

Harris, Angela (2000) 'Race and essentialism in feminist legal theory', in R. Delgado and J. Stefancic (eds.), *Critical Race Theory: The Cutting Edge*. Second Edition. Philadelphia, PA: Temple University Press. pp. 261–274.

Healey, Joseph F. (2012) *Diversity and Society: Race, Ethnicity and Gender*. Newbury Park, CA: Pine Forge Press.

Hill-Collins, Patricia (2000) *Black Feminist Thought*. Second Edition. London: Routledge.

hooks, bell (1982) *Ain't I a Woman*. London: The Women's Press.

hooks, bell (1995) *Killing Rage: Ending Racism*. New York: Henry Holt and Company.

Hunter, Margaret L. (2005) *Race, Gender, and the Politics of Skin Tone*. New York: Routledge.

Law, Ian (2010) *Racism and Ethnicity: Global Debates, Dilemmas, Directions*. Harlow: Longman.

McLaughlin, Eugene (2001) 'Underclass', in E. McLaughlin and J. Muncie (eds.), *The Sage Dictionary of Criminology*. London: Sage. pp. 310–311.

Moody-Ramirez, Mia and Dates, Janette L. (2014) *The Obamas and Mass Media: Race, Gender, Religion, and Politics*. New York: Palgrave Macmillan.

Murji, Karim (2001) 'Scapegoating', in E. McLaughlin and J. Muncie (eds.), *The Sage Dictionary of Criminology*. London: Sage. pp. 255–256.

Murray, Charles (1984) *Losing Ground: American Social Policy 1950–1980*. New York: Basic Books.

Murray, Charles (1990) *The Emerging British Underclass*. London: Institute of Economic Affairs.

Okely, Judith (1983) *The Traveller-Gypsies*. Cambridge: Cambridge University Press.

Phoenix, Ann (2003) 'Underclass', in G. Bolaffi, R. Bracalenti, P. Braham and S. Gindro (eds.), *Dictionary of Race, Ethnicity and Culture*. London: Sage. pp. 324–325.

Rattansi, Ali (2003) 'Orientalism', in G. Bolaffi, R. Bracalenti, P. Braham and S. Gindro (eds.), *Dictionary of Race, Ethnicity and Culture*. London: Sage. pp. 212–214.

Roychowdhury, Poulami (2013) '"The Delhi Gang Rape": The making of international causes', *Feminist Studies*, 39(1): 282–292.

Said, Edward (1978) *Orientalism*. London: Routledge.

Spencer, Stephen (2006) *Race and Ethnicity: Culture, Identity and Representation*. London: Routledge.

Stone, Sarah Rene (2004) 'Mail Order Brides: Taking a look from a new perspective', *Popcenter Online*, 10 March 2015 (www.popcenter.org/problems/trafficked_women/PDFs/Stone_2004.pdf).

The Telegraph (2011) 'Conservative Party Conference 2011: We must tackle "feral underclass", says Ken Clarke', *The Telegraph Online*, 4 October 2011 (www.telegraph.co.uk/news/politics/conservative/8806128/Conservative-Party-Conference-2011-we-must-tackle-feral-underclass-says-Ken-Clarke.html).

Walter, Bronwen (2001) *Outsiders Inside: Whiteness, Place and Irish Women*. London: Routledge.

Williams, Fiona (1989) *Social Policy – A Critical Introduction: Issues of Race, Gender and Class*. Cambridge: Polity Press.

Wray, Matt (2006) *Not Quite White: White Trash and the Boundaries of Whiteness*. Durham, NC: Duke University Press.

NOTES

1. Murray later went on to rename 'the underclass', referring to them instead as 'the new rabble', although the key characteristics of each group remained similar (McLaughlin, 2001: 310).
2. The BNP stands for British National Party, a far-right political party in the UK.
3. Structural intersectionality refers to poverty and economic considerations, such as access to housing, employment and welfare. Political intersectionality refers to how black and minority ethnic women are situated between at least two subordinated groups whose political interests conflict, as white women and black minority and ethnic men (Crenshaw, 1995: 358–359).
4. It is important to note that not all of those who come under the category of physically appearing to be white, or at least much closer to it than other black minority ethnic women, actually escape negative gendered and racialized stereotyping. Consider, for instance, the case of Irish

women (see Walter, 2001) who have struggled with their own specific anti-Irish and anti-female hostility, resulting in a very specific type of human declassification and victimization experience.

5. However, Okely (1983: 201) notes in her study of several Traveller-gypsy communities living in south-east England how the 'Gypsy woman' has also been subjected to similar sexually promiscuous images: she is 'presented as sensual, sexually provocative and enticing'.

6. The Philippines exports the highest number of brides per year in comparison to any other country (Stone, 2004).

7. This is a legacy of the US military presence in Asia during the Second World War and, in particular, its 'Rest and Recreation' (R&R) programme. For instance, recall Thailand's provision of 'R&R' services to US troops following a contract signed by the Thai government and the World Bank President Robert McNamara in 1967 (Bishop and Robinson, 1998, in Garner, 2010: 45–46). The programme created a triangle of exploitation, where (young, poor) Asian women became sex workers, economically exploited by Asian men, who also economically exploited the US troops, who then sexually exploited the Asian women (Garner, 2010: 46). Within this exploitation triangle, the Asian women are always placed at the bottom, facing exploitation from both the Asian and US men.

8. Bhattacharayya (2008: 91) goes on to illustrate her argument further with reference to the highly sexualized torture used in 'war on terror' detention camps.

9. India does not allow the press to publicize a rape victim's name, and so initially Singh had become widely known as 'Nirbhaya', which translates as 'fearless'.

10. The use of italics for the word 'presented' refers to how an examination of the facts into the backgrounds of Pandey and her attackers reveal that they had come from quite similar backgrounds, for example, in terms of caste and socioeconomic status. Yet, the international media had chosen to overlook these similarities selectively, focusing instead on exaggerated differences (Roychowdhury, 2013: 284). The use of italics is not intended to question or deny that Pandey was not as she was presented, rather that there were key similarities between her and her attackers that were ignored in media reports.

7

MASKING RACISM IN SOCIETY

INTRODUCTION

This chapter invites the reader to consider some of the more damaging consequences of racial categorizations in society. It does this by discussing how a new language of race has been popularized within a context that denies the existence of racism or claims that if there are racially discriminatory practices, then they are somehow justified, say in the name of national identity/pride and in the wider security of the country. The concepts covered in the chapter include ethnicity; hierarchy of whiteness; Islamaphobia; neo-colonialism; political correctness; and xenophobia. The case study included in this chapter discusses the experiences and perceptions of whites who choose to convert to Islam. The key question raised is: To what extent is the new language of race a reworking of older racist ideas?

KEY TERMS

- Critical whiteness studies

- Ethnicity

- Hierarchy of whiteness

- Islamaphobia

- Neo-colonialism

- New racism

- Political correctness

- Roma

- White backlash

- Xenophobia

- Xeno-racism

A LANGUAGE OF DENIAL

The failure to significantly improve the disadvantages that threaten the lives of black and minority ethnic groups, or to meaningfully remove racism from the structures of society, is rooted in the reluctance to accept racism and racial disadvantage as an issue in itself. Indeed, in many instances, racial discrimination is viewed as a thing of the past, and many white groups do not feel themselves accountable for what they consider to be the racism of the past, such as slavery (Gallagher, 2003). Thus, racial disadvantage persists not only because, as preceding chapters have illustrated, there is an invested belief in a natural hierarchy of race, but also partly because there is a denial of racism. Sometimes this denial is a false presentation covering a true, yet private acknowledgement of racism, but at other times the denial is based on a genuine belief that racism no longer exists (in a way that limits life chances). It has been argued elsewhere that the denial of racism is almost as common as the problem of racial discrimination and, moreover, the practice of denying racism can actually 'cause' and perpetuate racism (Bhavnani, Mirza and Meetoo, 2005: 51). This is linked to the notion of 'white victimhood', as mentioned in Chapter 4. White identities, which by default include their privileged status and future potential, become perceived as vulnerable and victimized in particular contexts, such as multicultural-ism or pursuit of racial equality. Research here has found that white groups: (1) perceive their white identities as being unfairly accused of racism – as black and minority ethnic groups are *just* over-sensitive and have easy access to the 'race card' as well as the agenda of 'political correctness' having gone too far; (2) have no spe-cial niche devoted for them within popular culture – unlike black and minority ethnic groups who (are allowed to) have special groups, magazines/newspapers and holidays; and (3) are forced to accept other cultures – with the view that diversity, in particular, does not add anything positive to the white life and environment. These perceptions not only provide a basis for notions of white victimhood, but also gener-ate envy and resentment among white populations (McKinney, 2003: 39–52). Despite the relative non-threatened position of white advantage, there is within the victimhood rationale a genuine belief that the white identity is at risk of becoming a minority, and with this comes the panic that whiteness may not always bring with it its automatic and unchallenged benefits (McKinney, 2003: 41). This fear is sustained by the array of news stories and political debates which over-focus on the danger of whites becoming a minority:

> White Britons 'will be minority' by 2066, says professor (*The Telegraph*, 2 May 2013)

> Census: White children to become minority by 2020 (UPI, 5 March 2015)

> In 19 states, Whites have become the minority (*Madame Noire*, 20 April 2015)

In a state of 'racial hyperprivilege', that is, the way in which white males hold a disproportionate amount of power above and over women and black and minority ethnic people, thus giving them the power to both recreate and challenge racial paradigms (Carbrera, 2014: 31), it is important to examine the interplay between racialized control and challenges to racism in those very spaces where whiteness normalization is most powerful, for example with the fraternity/sorority system within the higher education campus environment (Cabrera, 2014: 31–32).[1] Sociological examination into the normalization and power of whiteness is referred to as **critical whiteness studies**. This is a body of scholarship which seeks to 'reveal the frequently invisible social structures that continually recreate white supremacy and privilege' (Cabrera, 2014: 34). The concerns of critical whiteness studies can be separated into two categories: (1) that which examines the formation of whiteness – in particular, how it was that 'Europeans *became* white' (emphasis added); and (2) that which considers the use of public statements, such as 'I'm not racist but...', for permitting continued practices of racial discrimination and reinforcing white supremacy (Cabrera, 2014: 34).

Policies and practices that address social concerns, which themselves emerge from the perceived threat of racialized populations, are often justified within a context that uses narratives of economic instability, social inequality and vulnerable national security.

This narrative moves away from using racial terms, or indeed the suggestion of racial significance. However, the narrative uses a number of other mechanisms in order to support racial ideology. For instance, euphemisms are used to mask racist ideology. The use of euphemism in race talk can be clearly witnessed in the media, political and public discourse on 'illegal immigration' (Bhavnani et al., 2005: 51). Here, recent coverage of 'illegal immigration' in Europe has over-focused our attention on the supposed threatening and over-burdening presence of migrants (and asylum seekers), and not on the array of related issues and human rights infringements commonly experienced by these groups, such as prolonged detention in holding centres, sexual exploitation, domestic slavery, separation from family, and post-traumatic stress disorder (often following war and state violence). Euphemism allows the self-deluded perception of support for equality, while actually contributing to structures of racism. This is because euphemism allows speakers to officially deny (and even criticize) racist policies and practices. So, for instance, the social concern and action on addressing 'illegal immigration' doesn't factor in the mis-labelling of all black and minority ethnic people as migrants, and 'illegal migrants' at that, but is claimed to be a mere reflection of a citizen's normal economic and social concerns.

Similarly, a new language of race is used to sanitize racialized references. This is one of the claims made about use of the term '**ethnicity**'. In an attempt to differentiate the two terms 'race' and 'ethnicity', G. Vacher de las Pouge in 1896 used the latter to describe the cultural, psychological and social characteristics of collectives, as opposed to the physical characteristics of the first (Gindro, 2003: 94). Today, the term ethnicity (or ethnic group) refers to a collective that shares common cultural characteristics, such as religion, language, nationality and political beliefs. Some of the characteristics marking out an ethnic group may be biologically based (in terms of racially based attributes), but sociological thinking generally agrees that the concept of ethnicity transcends racial boundaries. Because of its largely socially constructed nature, ethnic identity formation is complex and fluid. However, it has been suggested that use of the term in contemporary society is often as a euphemism for race, allowing for a delivery of racist ideas under the illusion of celebrating diversity and supporting multiculturalism (Moore, 2003: 96).

In addition, if race is overtly talked about or alluded to, bias occurs through the use of selective language and imagery which presents whiteness as good, law-abiding and sincere, and blackness as evil, criminal-prone and dangerous. In drawing on the work of van Dijk, it is argued that processes of denial which utilize such constructions of black deviance and white victimhood also serve the positive self-presentation of white superiority (van Dijk, 1993, cited in Bhavnani et al., 2005: 52). Reference to (biological and genetic) racial difference can remain absent from the conversation, but notions of racial difference can still dominate the conversation by operating through assertions about cultural features (dress, religious performance, etc.) which in themselves draw on racialized ideas about difference and hierarchy (Dunn, Klocker and Salabay, 2007: 565). This narrative is most clearly illustrated in the discussions about Muslim identities in Western (white, Christian majority) countries such as Britain and Australia. Contemporary stereotypes about the dangerous Muslim Other, coupled with the historically dominant Orientalist ideas about Islam as oppressive and culturally inferior, serve to permit anti-Muslim hostility. The use of racist ideology when discussing Muslim populations within a period that claims that Muslims are not racial groups, and as such cannot be victims of racism, has led to the term **Islamaphobia** being used. This refers to anti-Muslim sentiment, including prejudice against and hatred towards people of the Muslim faith, and a fear of the religion of Islam itself. In recent times, the term is often used to describe an unfounded dread or dislike of Muslims, which then results in discriminatory and exclusionary practices (Runnymede Trust, 1997). It is argued that following world events such as 9/11 in America, Islamaphobia has not only risen dramatically, but has become more explicit and relatively acceptable – national security concerns are often held up as a justification for anti-Muslim hostility in lay society, and for the state's selective surveillance, increased control and ultimate detention/removal of Muslims. This discrimination is not helped by various mass media outlets which have been accused of stoking anti-Muslim hostility by presenting Islam as oppressive, anti-Western, barbaric and extreme in its use of violence (namely non-discriminatory terrorism). As discussed in previous chapters, the media, in particular press outlets, can be accused of contributing massively to the new racism and reproducing racial inequality, not least because they have a powerful influence over the shaping of the knowledge and attitudes held by its readers, who are made up of both lay members of society and people working within elite organizations (van Dijk, 2000: 36).

Defensive rationales are also often used in processes of denial. This is illustrated in the white victimization and minority privilege logic, a 'sincere fiction' whereby multi-culturalism is considered to be a form of 'reverse racism' which favours black and minority ethnic groups at the expense of whites. What is interesting about this logic is that it conveniently ignores the fact that black and minority ethnic groups actually lack the power to practise racial oppression against white groups (Carbrera, 2014: 45–49). Such sentiments of victimhood contribute to the production of a '**white backlash**'. This refers to a growing movement in which white people lay claim to being racially oppressed and, as such, seek redress against policies, practices and legislation which in their view discriminate against them (Hughey, 2014: 721). The white backlash rests on two beliefs: (1) the black and minority ethnic person who unfairly receives resources and opportunities that they are undeserving of and unable to use correctly; and (2) the victimization of the white person, including the withholding of said resources and opportunities from them, which is considered to be especially unjust given that they view themselves to have the intelligence and moral ability to use them correctly (Hughey, 2014: 722–724). A white backlash can also occur following demographic changes, usually as a result of migration, where there is a change in the proximity between black and minority ethnic and white communities.

The white backlash serves to reproduce racial inequality. Within a post-racial era, in which America has seen the election of a Black African-American (and what some consider to be a 'non-authentic') president, the creation of movements such as the Tea Party and the Birthers indicates a revival of the white backlash sentiment. Quite literally, the movements consider President Obama to have taken control of the nation and see a need for this to be reclaimed, as indicated by the Tea Party's slogan 'Take It Back, Take Our Country Back' (Hughey, 2014: 723). Despite the mass of data that shows increasing levels of black and minority ethnic victimization and racial disadvantage in comparison to their white counterparts, who continue to inhabit a powerful status and all the privileges which that position brings, whiteness in a post-racial era continues to be constructed as victimized and vulnerable. This has also allowed for 'struggles of whiteness' (in terms of identity and space) to be viewed with sympathy, and for its ensuing discriminatory practices to be re-presented as honourable and valuable (Hughey, 2014: 727). This is even the case when such activities are clearly problematic, such as the occurrence of violent racist hate crimes. For instance, a study by Ray, Smith and Wastel (2004) into perpetrators of racist violence found that offending behaviour is linked to a sense of disadvantage and shame, resulting in 'rage' against South Asians who are perceived as illegitimately successful. Racist violence is therefore used as an expression of that 'rage' and to counter perceived notions of white victimhood. The relative permitting of racist violence remains unchallenged because of its occurrence within a cultural context that permits racism and violent behaviour (Ray et al., 2004: 350).

Social concerns and the ensuing policy and practice regarding race, racism and ethnicity in society continue to be pre-loaded with racialized ideas about white supremacy and black and minority ethnic inferiority. This is coupled with a denial of racism, which then allows the problem of racism not only to survive, but to thrive in what is often referred to as a post-racial era. As Bhavnani et al. (2005: 52) note:

> ...the label 'racism' refuses to stick to the everyday manifestations of racist discourse. Thus the vitriolic media discourse on asylum seekers, multi-culturalism and Britishness, or the reporting of localized working-class discontent, all of which are deeply imbued with racialized meaning, appear 'unraced', neutral, and unattached to their source of origin – that is, the politically powerful and influential. They are therefore 'legitimately denied'.

POPULARIZING NEW RACISM

The term 'new racism' refers to a form of racially based discrimination whereby one's rights are confined because they are viewed as having deviant cultural characteristics (Dunn et al., 2007: 567). It is suggested that this new type of racism is more difficult to detect in comparison to the older racism of a post-Fascist/Nazi era, which was considered to be more overt. New racism gathered marked popularity in the 1980s within the context of a new wave of anti-immigrant sentiment. For instance, it is argued that the then British Prime Minister, Margaret Thatcher, moved away from the racism of the past, which had often been associated with Fascism and Nazism, and in its place utilized cultural racism to depict immigrants as a cultural, social and economic threat to the British national identity and its global standing (Sniderman et al., 1991: 424). This can be most clearly illustrated with a speech given by Thatcher in February 1978, in which she used culture (*or* race) to object to immigration:

...it means that people are really rather afraid that this country might be swamped by people of a different culture. The British character has done so much for democracy, for law, and done so much throughout the world that if there is any fear that it might be swamped, then people are going to be rather hostile to those coming in. (Cited in Solomos, 1989: 129)

Such racialized constructions are in abundance in today's reporting of refugee and migrant movements. For instance, in August 2015, significant numbers within the European press, political arena and lay public presented their 'concern' about what was reported to be the high volumes of refugees and migrants who were attempting to enter parts of Europe. For instance, Britain's Foreign Secretary, Philip Hammond, stated: 'The gap in standards of living between Europe and Africa means there will always be millions of Africans with the economic motivation to try to get to Europe. ... So long as there are large numbers of pretty desperate migrants marauding around the area, there always will be a threat to the [Channel] tunnel security' (Philip Hammond, quoted in The *Guardian*, 10 August 2015a). The use of the term 'marauding' not only scaremongers, but also dehumanizes, and suggests that migrants are a threat to European civilization and social order (The *Guardian*, 10 August 2015b). Similar terms, such as 'swarms' and 'floods', have also been commonly used in the reporting of the 'crisis'. It is suggested here that the use of the word 'crisis' in media coverage and political debates is not referring to the humanitarian crisis[2] faced by refugees and migrants,[3] but is instead being used to refer to the supposed civilization crisis of white Europeans who consider themselves at risk of being 'swamped' by masses of people with supposed alien, incompatible and deviant cultures. Even in those instances when Britain sought to present itself as sympathetic and humanitarian, it could still not escape the use of negative association. For instance, consider Britain's Labour Party leadership candidate, Andy Burnham, who in September 2015 stated that Britain should do more to share the 'burden' of housing Syrian refugees: 'What we have got is no one taking ownership of the problem. ... It is wrong to let Greece and Italy shoulder an enormous burden' (Andy Burnham, quoted in *The Telegraph*, 29 August 2015).

By moving away from biologically based racist ideology, new racism instead satisfied the racist agenda by conflating the relationship between cultural identity and citizenship rights. As awareness grew about the socially undesirable expression of racial prejudice, new racism emerged as a disguised, indirect and continued way to express it (Sniderman et al., 1991: 424). In his article on news organizations' reproduction of new racism, van Dijk (2000: 41) argues that racialized opposition presents itself in the underlying attitudes of news stories about the 'ingroup' and the 'outgroup' via a series of 'disclaimers' that are woven into sentences which ultimately realize strategies of 'positive self-presentation' and 'negative other-presentation':

- Apparent denial – 'We have nothing against foreigners, but...'

- Apparent concession – 'There are also nice foreigners, but on the whole...'

- Apparent empathy – 'Of course it is sad for refugees that... but...'

- Transfer – 'I have nothing against foreigners, but my clients...' (van Dijk, 2000: 41).

As Dunn et al. (2007: 567) note, '"new racism" presumes a meaningful departure from "old" *biological* racism' (emphasis added), and this is problematic and misleading as new racism(s) continue to utilize old biological racism logic. New racism then 'wants to be democratic and respectable, and hence first off denies that it is racism' (van Dijk, 2000: 34). In this sense, new racism gains its power from the very notion that it is *not* racism, but is rather a genuine concern about cultural differences. Dunn et al. (2007) go on to illustrate this point with the wave of anti-Muslim hostility in Australia, and more specifically with a discussion of the Baulkham Hill case, where, in objecting to the building of a mosque, locals raised concerns about the safety of girls and women, whom they feared would be at risk from the Muslim men. Muslim men here are presented as animalistic and sexually aggressive, themes that are echoed in Bhattacharyya's discussion on 'browning' (2008: 75) – see Chapter 4. The new racism of Baulkham Hill clearly echoed the biologically based assumptions of 'old racism', not least through its discourse of 'Otherness': a process that marks out the identity of individuals and groups as different (specifically, problematically alien) from the mainstream. However, the Islamaphobic sentiments were presented as mere concerns about incompatible cultural difference.

The use of new racism to sanitize spaces of black and minority ethnic presence has risen dramatically within the context of the global war on terror, where debates about citizenship, identity and national security have intertwined with one another to present 'brown bodies' as especially dangerous (Patel, 2013). This is illustrated by the hostility shown towards Muslim women who use the veil and who are seen as a particular type of threat to Western culture – not only for choosing to make a visible statement of separation and difference. Western perception and (mis)understanding of the veil has shifted from viewing it as a source of eroticism to seeing it as a sign of victimhood of a backward, patriarchal religion, to now viewing it as an undesirable object that is primarily used to indicate a rejection of Western (which is read as 'progressive') cultures in countries such as America, Australia, Britain, Canada and France (Khiabany and Williamson, 2008: 70).

ACTIVITY

Khiabany and Williamson (2008: 73) note that 'Muslims make up only 2.8 per cent of the British population and women who wear the full face veil are a tiny minority of that figure'. In light of this comment, consider if there is a valid reason for concern about the veil.

Islamaphobia is one type of new racism. Another is what Fekete (2001: 2) refers to as xeno-racism (see Chapter 9). This term is derived from **xenophobia**. In its strict sense, xenophobia means an uncontrollable fear of strangers. In recent times, though, and especially following the events of 9/11, xenophobia has become a popular term in sociological thought and is often discussed within the context of racism and the ensuing disproportionate reactions towards an imagined threat. Fekete (2001) draws on the term to discuss the emergence of a new type of (post-racial) racism: **xeno-racism**. Fekete (2010) argues that in Britain, xeno-racism became popular in the late 1990s with the use of 'deterrence' as a guiding principle in asylum policy. This later grew into a position of strictly 'managed migration', which was more popular across Europe. This allowed for 'structures of discrimination' and 'culturally acceptable racism' against asylum seekers – including all those perceived and imagined to be asylum seekers (Fekete, 2001: 24). The term xeno-racism not only highlights the racialized hatred of (perceived strangers or) 'Others', but also draws our attention to the increasing use of defensive measures in immigration and asylum policy as a way of securing the white majority privileged position.

The preference for use of the terms 'culture' and 'cultural' also contributes to a move towards new racism, and significantly fails to consider the role of racialized power in constructions of the cultural Other. In examining child welfare policies in Canada, Pon (2009: 59) argues that the politics of 'cultural competency' popularizes 'an obsolete view of culture' by failing to acknowledge Canada's history of colonialism and racism. Culture in this context is viewed as neutral and fails to consider the role of power in the oppressive and essentialized construction of the Other cultural group (Sakamoto, 2007, cited in Pon, 2009: 60). For instance, the cultural constructions used in Canada – and other similar countries – fail to factor in the(ir) own use of power and control in colonial times. Cultural definitions are therefore informed by a history of racism and power. However, culture is not only presented as neutral, it is being used to replace and/or mask older, openly expressed biologically based racialized language. Although the language has changed, the old (racist) narrative and its meanings nevertheless remain the same – as does its discriminatory impact on the racialized Other and its contribution to ensuring the maintenance of power structures in wider society. The use of culture to mark out the Other ensures that accusations of racism are eluded (Pon, 2009: 61). This is because discourses about social cohesion, cultural preservation and national identity are now used to label, categorize and exclude, but without use of a biologically based racial ideology left over from Hitlerism (Baker, 1981, cited in Pon, 2009: 61).

One response to growing accusations of new forms of racism (and, as mentioned above, to notions of 'white victimhood') is to argue that an equality of opportunity agenda has now been achieved, and is now being abused by black and minority ethnic groups in order to obtain unfair advantage in identity politics as well as areas such as employment, health care and housing. The term **'political correctness'** (or 'PC') is used to refer to an attempt to transform common language so that it includes people of all backgrounds and avoids certain terms, action or policies that may be perceived as offending, excluding or marginalizing particular members/groups of society who are vulnerable to discrimination and disadvantage (as in matters of race, ethnicity, gender and sexuality). In recent years, though, the term has come to be promoted in the tabloid press as a way of drawing attention to its supposed excessive use – such as in the (later revealed to be fiction) reporting of how a school in Britain had altered the nursery rhyme 'Baa baa black sheep' to 'Baa baa rainbow sheep' (*The Times*, 7 March 2006). Hence the term is no longer used in isolation, but within sentences such as 'political correctness gone mad!' It is argued that these media-generated aspects of popular culture, and its (fictional) stories of political correctness, only serve to detract from inequality issues and ensure the continued use of race and racism to privilege some at the expense of others.

SAME OLD, SAME OLD?

The distinct features of new racism, especially within what is claimed to be a post-racial era, clearly differ from the older racism of the past. This chapter has so far outlined the ways in which this is the case. Older racism appeared more 'basic' and overt. In comparison, new racism is more complex and masks itself under notions of cultural differences and incompatibilities. Indeed, new racism attempts to present itself as anything but racist. However, this is problematic, not least because, as Gines (2014: 75) notes, 'there is something old and familiar about an ideal that is imagined to be new – the postracial ideal'. Claims of being in a post-racial state rely on a number of assumptions, including the view that racial oppression only operated on a black–white racial binary, and that the appointment of key figures (such as President Obama in the USA) is now sufficient to erase a history of racial oppression (Gines, 2014: 77). Not only does this challenge the notion of the post-racial, but it also disputes the very claim that we are currently living in post-racial times.

Indeed, a by-product of its over-focus on cultural difference means that new racism has actually expanded the categories of the undesirable (racial) Other. This means that groups which had previously escaped Otherization labels have now become viewed as undesirable. This is interesting given that many of these groups 'appear' biologically and phenotypically 'white'. Thus, a **hierarchy of whiteness** has been redeveloped to create more levels and sub-levels. What informs positioning on this hierarchy are not only racialized factors but, as discussed in Chapter 6, gender, age and class variables, as well as the wider socio-political context in which the hierarchy exists. Thus, there is a growing category of those who are white but 'not white enough'. They appear (biologically and/or phenotypically) white, but are ultimately considered insufficient in their 'cultural whiteness'. For instance, in her study of Bosnian refugees in Australia, Colic-Peisker (2005: 615–618) argues that Bosnians were considered to be Australia's 'preferred humanitarian immigrants during the 1990s', and that this was largely due to their 'whiteness'/'Europeanness' and 'assimilability' potential. The perceived 'invisibility' of Bosnian refugees was considered by Australian politicians as enabling a smoother resettlement and transition period for the Bosnians and limited disruption to the Australian way of life – in terms of its culture and identity. However, the actual settlement proved difficult for Bosnians, not least because of language barriers which contributed to cultural, economic and social exclusion. Indeed, Colic-Peisker (2005: 632) makes the point that:

> The argument of cultural proximity of Europeans to 'white Australia' should ... be viewed with extreme caution. Within the current immigration intake, highly qualified and English-speaking urban Sri-Lankan, Indian or Taiwanese migrants, for example – as bearers of a dominant culture which can nowadays be described as global, middle-class, English-speaking, computerized and 'cyberspaced' – are culturally closer to urban Australians than Bosnian villagers.

Although occupying a low level in the racialized hierarchy, some whites may actually boost their ranking and thus reposition themselves on a higher level. They do this by undertaking positive self-presentation and negative other-presentation. This was undertaken by some of the Bosnian refugees in Colic-Peisker's study, who chose to use their 'white European' identity to liken themselves to the (white) Australian identity and thus claim inclusion. However, this 'socio-psychological mechanism of advantageous self-identification' meant that the Bosnian refugees had to distance themselves from other refugee groups in Australia, and in many instances even embark on the stigmatization of other refugee groups (Colic-Peisker, 2005: 624). The Irish are also a good example of how status repositioning on a racial hierarchy has been achieved. As mentioned in Chapter 4, it was Noel Ignatiev (1995) who looked at how Irish Catholic immigrants in America eventually shifted from an underclass position with relative non-citizenship status (for example, they were barred from voting and Catholic orphans were brought up within the Protestant religion) to then occupying an improved position in which they were considered to be more 'valuable' than their black African counterparts. The Irish achieved this by using notions of racial difference and superiority to distance themselves from black Africans, so much so that they themselves were considered to be particularly aggressive racists (Ignatiev, 1995). As Fox (2013: 1874) notes: 'Putatively shared whiteness does not guarantee that migrants will not be victims of racism. ... But it does help' – not least because the very ability to claim (some degree of) whiteness 'affords a privileged vantage point from which they can effectively assign other minorities a less white (and lower) status'.

However, it can also be argued that there are greater commonalities between older and newer forms of racism in that there have always been particular groups who 'appeared' biologically and phenotypically 'white', but have always failed to escape racial discrimination. For instance, this category would include Roma and members of the Travelling community, who have both over a very long time experienced stigmatization, inequality, racial discrimination and victimization – an experience that continues today. The **Roma** people are often considered to have their own distinct ethnic identity, which includes a nomadic lifestyle and the Romani language.[4] Over the years, Roma people have been widely discriminated against, with many considering them to be the most persecuted people in Europe. This persecution continues with a range of practices which deny them basic social and citizenship rights (Eksner and Muecke, 2003: 294). With the recent emphasis on claims about self-segregation acting as a barrier for societal harmony among different racial/ethnic groups, the Roma people are often viewed as being to blame for their victimization – a view not helped by problematic misrepresentations of them in the media. This combination makes them the one group in Europe who are most vulnerable to racist discrimination (Law, 2010: 182). Similarly, members of the Travelling community comprise an ethnic group (according to British law) who are of Irish heritage. Many of them live in Ireland, although there are also sizeable numbers in Britain and the USA. Travellers not only experience prejudice from other members of society – indeed, they are the most discriminated-against group in Ireland (Danaher et al., 2009: 119) – but they also face structural isolation and exclusion from services provided by mainstream institutions, such as education and healthcare.

The thread of commonality that runs from old racism to new racism can in recent historical terms be linked to Empire-building and colonial rule. In his discussion of the construction of Britishness, Gilroy (2005) suggests that the British identity is not only largely informed by its history of Empire and colonial rule, but is shaped by an excessively optimistic and romanticized view of this period, which conveniently forgets the abuses it perpetrated against its colonial subjects. Thus, Britain's uneasy understanding of its own Empire and postcolonial history creates 'the neurotic development of postcolonial or post-imperial melancholia' which has a tendency to view Britishness through an 'airbrushed, nuanced and nostalgic filter' (Gilroy, 2005: 434–437). The legacy of colonial rule therefore still thrives today and, it has been suggested, has ultimately fed into contemporary thinking about race, nationhood and power. Indeed, the term **neo-colonialism** is often used to refer to the view that political decolonization has not in practice disrupted the West's monopolistic control over the power and economy of former colony countries.

Coupled with this, it has been suggested that old racisms continue to have distinct avenues which allow their continued expression. Cisneros and Nakayama (2015) illustrate this point with their discussion of racism in new social media outlets, such as *Twitter*. The nature of instant messaging and relative anonymity afforded by *Twitter* permit latent discriminatory views that draw on older logics of racism to be very easily expressed and popularized. The ease of accessibility means that anyone can self-publish material online, whether that material is factually correct or not. Cisneros and Nakayama (2015) argue that *Twitter*, and other social media like it, specifically allow for crude racist stereotypes and rhetoric about 'white supremacy, biological/ cultural essentialism and ethnic exclusion' to work through a phenomenon called 'context collapse', which is where the 'social, geographic/spatial, and temporal contexts that are key to understanding and interpreting specific messages' become collapsed so that the audience is 'invisible and acontextual' (Cisneros and Nakayama, 2015: 117). There is therefore no one exclusive audience or identity involved in receiving the 'Tweet' or specific message. The racist rhetoric therefore spreads fast and wide.

ACTIVITY

In challenging the notion of 'new racism', Colin Wayne Leach (2005: 434) argues that there is nothing 'new' about it, in that 'formal expressions of cultural difference or the denial of societal discrimination' have long featured in Western societies. What does Leach mean by this comment and is there any weight to his claims?

Case study: White converts to Islam

It is argued that within contemporary society white bodies inhabit a privileged and powerful position. This means that when they embark on deviant or criminal behaviour they are more able to evade stigmatization. For instance, consider the behaviour of right-wing extremist groups, such as the English Defence League (EDL),[5] which are able to mask their racist, Islamaphobic ideology by claiming (rights to) a positive cultural and national identity. Framing their arguments within this context allows them to pursue a white social order without using pro-white terminology. However, the exclusivity of whiteness does not fall on all those appearing to be phenotypically white. There are Other white populations who are placed upon the lower rungs of a racial hierarchy, for example, those referred to as 'white trash'. They are considered undesirable and are met with similar (although never greater) levels of distaste to those of their black and minority ethnic counterparts. These 'abject whites' are 'seen to embody an unsettling mix of whiteness, "working classness", and poverty' (Haylett, 2001, cited in Rhodes, 2011: 107). They are considered prone to laziness and criminal behaviour, and their very presence threatens (white) social order (Patel, 2013: 43). This white hierarchy tells us that whiteness is also flexible and, moreover, that it and the privileges which accompany it are negotiated on an 'intra-racial' basis (Hartigan, 2005, cited in Rhodes, 2011: 107). One illustration of this process is the case of white people who convert to Islam.

In contemporary Western society, white converts are often viewed by the white majority with confusion and sympathy. As I have stated elsewhere (Patel, 2013: 43), white converts are considered by other whites as oppressed and confused – especially female converts. They are viewed with pity, for having fallen under the spell of the brown body, and for ultimately having denied themselves *their* own right to superiority (Franks, 2000). In this sense, the white convert is considered to be the victim. For some, though, white converts are viewed with distaste, a fact illustrated by the abusive label often thrown at them: 'white Paki' (Franks, 2000). In an honest account of her own experience of abuse following conversion, Bristol (England) resident Kelly Ziane recalled how she had been spat at by a man, who also tried to pull off her hijab, was called a 'Paki' and a 'raghead', and how a man verbally attacked her after he had driven his car directly towards her and her three children as they crossed a road (*The Bristol Post*, 27 March 2014). There are numerous such accounts that are increasingly being reported by some quarters of the press and victim organizations, as well as in the academic literature. Converts are considered to be traitors to the white race (Franks, 2000). This is especially true for those converts who choose to mark out their faith, for instance by wearing ethnic clothing typically taken to be Islamic attire (Patel, 2013).

Although white converts experience discrimination and disadvantage, they are ultimately able to mask their Muslim identity – or 'tell white lies' (Jensen, 2008: 400). This can be done by choosing the ways in which they wish to express their

(Continued)

(Continued)

faith and, ultimately, who they make aware of their conversion. For instance, not all female converts may wish to wear the hijab, jilbab or niqab, and not all male converts may wish to grow a beard or wear *sunnah* clothes. In addition, not all may wish to openly state if and when they pray. It is possible for white converts to be 'invisible Muslims' if they choose. In comparison, brown-bodied Muslims are 'limited' by their very skin colour and the perceptions that accompany the brown body in an era marked out by the 'war on terror' and other events which have given rise to anti-Muslim sentiment (Patel, 2013). A brown body will more often be perceived as Muslim, whether there is any visible suggestion of this or not – and regardless of whether they are actually of the Muslim faith or not. In comparison, a white body that visibly demonstrates their Muslim faith will get often get a double take, a second glance, because of the very inconceivable incompatibility of whiteness and Islam.

Indeed, in looking at Islamaphobia and some of its more subtle practices, Moosavi (2014: 41) argues that white converts 'are well placed to expose this "subtle Islamophobia" because their intimate and regular contact with non-Muslims makes them particularly susceptible to frank remarks about their Muslim identity'. What must be considered, though, is the ability of white converts to 'mask race', as well as the continued and persistent power of whiteness in this pursuit of 'exposing subtle Islamophobia', namely the way in which it is precisely *their* whiteness that remains constant – despite conversion to Islam – and how this constant whiteness affords them the power to 'expose' (or not) the discrimination. White converts then inhabit a relatively powerful position, which can vary depending on the degree to which they choose to 'show' their Muslim-ness.

ACTIVITY

Do white converts to Islam really experience anti-Muslim racism in the same ways that their 'brown' Muslims do?

CONCLUDING THOUGHTS

In examining the various ways in which racism is masked in society, this chapter has focused on the continued use of whiteness to assert power and control, despite claims we are now living in a post-racial society. There has been a discussion on the ways in which whiteness reaffirms its position of privilege and the impact of this on black and minority ethnic groups and outsider white groups. One of the key points made is that there is common use of a new and popular language of race which continues to have a racially discriminatory impact yet claims to work within the boundaries of a post-racial society. The case of white converts to Islam was considered particularly as an illustration of the ability for converts to forever draw on their whiteness to cover their Muslim identity, and thus escape discrimination and disadvantage. The key question in this chapter invites a consideration of the extent to which the new language of race is actually a reworking of older racist ideas.

MAIN POINTS

- There is a language of race which denies the existence of racism yet uses a number of narrative techniques to support racial ideology.

- Forms of 'new racism' over-focus on deviant cultural characteristics, which ultimately permit continued practices of racially based discrimination.

- An over-focus on cultural difference has expanded the categories of the undesirable (racial) Other to include outsider white categories.

STUDY QUESTIONS

1. How does the 'new racism' satisfy the racist agenda within the post-racial era?

2. Is there a context within which the 'white backlash' is justified?

3. Islamaphobia is one type of new racism. What other types are there?

FURTHER READING

Cabrera, Nolan León (2014) 'Exposing whiteness in higher education: White male college students minimizing racism, claiming victimization, and recreating white supremacy', *Race, Ethnicity and Education*, 17(1): 30–55.
Hughey, Matthew W. (2014) 'White backlash in the "post-racial" United States', *Ethnic and Racial Studies*, 37(5): 721–730.
McKinney, Karyn D. (2003) '"I feel 'whiteness' when I hear people blaming whites"': Whiteness as cultural victimization', *Race and Society*, 6: 39–55.

REFERENCES

Bhattacharyya, Gargi (2008) *Dangerous Brown Men: Exploiting Sex, Violence and Feminism in the War on Terror*. London: Zed Books.
Bhavnani, Reen, Mirza, Heidi Safia and Meetoo, Veen (2005) *Tackling the Roots of Racism*. Bristol: Polity Press.

Cisneros, David J. and Nakayama, Thomas K. (2015) 'New media, old racisms: Twitter, Miss America, and cultural logics of race', *Journal of International and Intercultural Communication*, 8(2): 108–127.

Colic-Peisker, Val (2005) '"At least you're the right colour": Identity and social inclusion of Bosnian refugees in Australia', *Journal of Ethnic and Migration Studies*, 31(4): 615–638.

Danaher, Patrick Alan, Kenny, Máirín and Leder, Judith Remy (2009) *Traveller, Nomadic and Migrant Education*. Abingdon: Routledge.

Dunn, Kevin M., Klocker, Natascha and Salabay, Tanya (2007) 'Contemporary racism and Islamaphobia in Australia: Racializing religion', *Ethnicities*, 7(4): 564–589.

Eksner, Julia and Muecke, Tim (2003) 'Roma', in G. Bolaffi, R. Bracalenti, P. Braham and S. Gindro (eds.), *Dictionary of Race, Ethnicity and Culture*. London: Sage. pp. 291–295.

Fekete, Liz (2001) 'The emergence of xeno-racism', *Race and Class*, 43(2): 23–40.

Fox, Jon E. (2013) 'The uses of racism: Whitewashing new Europeans in the UK', *Ethnic and Racial Studies*, 36(11): 1871–1889.

Franks, Myfanwy (2000) 'Crossing the borders of whiteness? White Muslim women who wear the hijab in Britain today', *Ethnic and Racial Studies*, 23(5): 917–929.

Gallagher, Charles A. (2003) 'Playing the White ethnic card: Using ethnic identity to deny contemporary racism', in A.W. Doane and E. Bonilla-Silva (eds.), *White Out: The Continuing Significance of Racism*. New York: Routledge. pp. 145–158.

Gilroy, Paul (2005) 'Multiculture, double consciousness and the "War on Terror"', *Patterns of Prejudice*, 39(4): 431–443.

Gindro, Sandra (2003) 'Ethnicity', in G. Bolaffi, R. Bracalenti, P. Braham and S. Gindro (eds.), *Dictionary of Race, Ethnicity and Culture*. London: Sage. pp. 94–96.

Gines, Kathryn T. (2014) 'A critique of postracialism: Conserving race and complicating blackness beyond the Black-white binary', *Du Bois Review*, 11(1): 75–86.

Ignatiev, Noel (1995) *How the Irish Became White*. Abingdon: Routledge.

Jensen, Tina G. (2008) 'To be "Danish", becoming "Muslim": Contestations of national identity?', *Journal of Ethnic and Migration Studies*, 34(3): 389–409.

Khiabany, Gholam and Williamson, Milly (2008) 'Veiled bodies, naked racism: Culture, politics and race in *The Sun*', *Race and Class*, 50(2): 69–88.

Law, Ian (2010) *Racism and Ethnicity: Global Debates, Dilemmas, Directions*. Harlow: Longman Pearson.

Leach, Colin Wayne (2005) 'Against the notion of a "New Racism"', *Journal of Community and Applied Social Psychology*, 15: 432–445.

Madame Noire (2015) 'In 19 states, whites have become the minority', *Madame Noire Online*, 20 April 2015. Reported by: Ann Brown (http://madamenoire.com/527005/in-19-states-whites-have-become-the-minority/).

Moore, Robert (2003) 'Ethnicity', in G. Bolaffi, R. Bracalenti, P. Braham and S. Gindro (eds.), *Dictionary of Race, Ethnicity and Culture*. London: Sage. pp. 96–99.

Moosavi, Leon (2014) 'The racialization of Muslim converts in Britain and their experiences of Islamophobia', *Critical Sociology*, 41(1): 41–56.

Patel, Tina G. (2013) 'Ethnic deviant labels within the "war on terror" context: Excusing white deviance', *Ethnicity and Race in a Changing World*, 4(1): 34–50.

Pon, Gordon (2009) 'Cultural competency as new racism: An ontology of forgetting', *Journal of Progressive Human Services*, 20(1): 59–71.

Ray, Larry, Smith, David and Wastel, Liz (2004) 'Shame, rage and racist violence', *British Journal of Criminology*, 44(3): 350–368.

Rhodes, James (2011) '"It's not just them, it's Whites as well": Whiteness, class and BNP support', *Sociology*, 45(1): 102–117.

Runnymede Trust (1997) *Islamaphobia: A Challenge for Us All*. London: Runnymede Trust.

Sniderman, Paul M., Piazza, Thomas, Tetlock, Philip E. and Kendrick, Ann (1991) 'The new racism', *American Journal of Political Science*, 35(2): 423–447.

Solomos, John (1989) *Race and Racism in Contemporary Britain*. London: Macmillan Educational.

The Bristol Post (2014) '"My hell as a white Muslim living in Bristol": Woman says she is racially abused every day'. *The Bristol Post*, 27 March 2014 (www.bristolpost.co.uk/TOUGH-LIFE-WHITE-MUSLIM-LIVING-CITY/story-20851359-detail/story.html#ixzz3lhslzKTM).

The *Guardian* (2015a) '"Marauding" migrants threaten standard of living, says foreign secretary', The *Guardian*, 10 August 2015. Reported by: Frances Perraudin (www.theguardian.com/uk-news/2015/aug/09/african-migrants-threaten-eu-standard-living-philip-hammond).

The *Guardian* (2015b) '10 truths about Europe's migrant crisis', The *Guardian*, 10 August 2015. Reported by: Patrick Kingsley (www.theguardian.com/commentisfree/2015/aug/10/migration-debate-metaphors-swarms-floods-marauders-migrants).

The Telegraph (2013) 'White Britons "will be minority" by 2066, says professor', *The Telegraph Online*, 2 May 2013. Reported by: Rosa Silverman (www.telegraph.co.uk/news/uknews/immigration/10032296/White-Britons-will-be-minority-by-2066-says-professor.html).

The Telegraph (2015) 'Andy Burnham tells David Cameron to accept quotas of Calais migrants to help with his EU renegotiation', *The Telegraph*, 29 August 2015. Reported by: Christopher Hope (www.telegraph.co.uk/news/politics/andy-burnham/11832643/Andy-Burnham-tells-David-Cameron-to-accept-quotas-of-Calais-migrants-to-help-with-his-EU-renegotiation.html).

The Times (2006) 'Why black sheep are barred and Humpty can't be cracked', *The Times*, 7 March 2006. Reported by: Alexandra Blair.

UPI (2015) 'Census: White children to become minority by 2020', *UPI Online*, 5 March 2015. Reported by: Doug G. Ware (www.upi.com/Top_News/US/2015/03/05/Census-White-children-to-become-minority-by-2020/9751425612082/).

van Dijk, Teun A. (2000) '(New)s racism: A discourse analytical approach', in S. Cottle (ed.), *Ethnic Minorities and the Media*. Milton Keynes: Open University Press. pp. 33–49.

NOTES

1. Cabrera (2014: 32) argues that fraternity/sorority sub-environments unofficially permit racial segregation – white enclaves where the collectives' identity and actions create social comfort, which serves to perpetuate feelings of white victimization.

2. Such as escape from war, dictatorial oppression, and religious extremism, which are, for instance, faced by refugees from Syria, Eritrea and Afghanistan (The *Guardian*, 10 August 2015b).

3. In the reporting of these events, the terms 'refugee' and 'migrant' have been used interchangeably to present all within the movement as merely seeking to improve social life chances, as opposed to being forced to leave their own countries of origin for humanitarian reasons.

4.   The term 'Roma' refers to those people who describe themselves as Romany, Gypsies, Manouches, Kalderdash, Machavaya, Loari, Churari, Romanichal, Gitanoes, Kalo, Sinti, Rudari, Boyash, Ungaritza, Luri, Bashaldé, Romungro, Yenish, Xoraxai. The term differs from 'Traveller', which specifically refers to members of the Irish Traveller community native to Ireland (Law, 2010: 165).
5.   The English Defence League is a far-right movement that formally emerged in England in 2009. It is known for using street protest as a way of demonstrating opposition to what it considers to be a spread of Islamism, Sharia Law and Islamic extremism in England.

8

RACE IN SOCIAL INSTITUTIONS AND ORGANIZATIONS

INTRODUCTION

This chapter considers the significance of race in key social institutions and organizations that have significant power and influence in contemporary society over how we construct views about race, label bodies and think about ourselves in relation to others. The theory and concepts covered include: black criminality; institutional racism; positive discrimination; and tokenism. The case study in the chapter is about racism in football. The key question raised in the chapter is: Are there particular spaces where problematic ideas about race and society are especially powerful and, if so, what is the impact of this for progressing thinking about race and society more widely?

KEY TERMS

- Black criminality

- Criminalization

- Cultural deficit theory

- Institutional racism

- Positive discrimination and affirmative action

- Tokenism

RACIALIZED RELATIONS AND DAMAGING REPRESENTATIONS

There are a number of key social institutions where stereotypical and damaging views about members of black and minority ethnic communities are in abundance. These tend to pathologize people as having limited intelligence and deviant tendencies. For instance, within the education system biologically based ideas about race and IQ dominated educators' views on black and minority ethnic potential and achievement. These views were popularized in Britain by the work of Hans Eysenck (1971), and around the same time in the USA by Arthur Jenson (1969). These authors argued that in comparison to their white counterparts, black and minority ethnic children had limited natural abilities to allow them to develop educationally. Although later research soundly challenged the dubious claims about limited IQ levels, they later re-emerged in the form of socio-biological explanations – illustrated in the work of Richard Herrnstein and Charles Murray (1994). This later gave rise to various elements of 'cultural deficit theory', especially in relation to those of black African-Caribbean or South Asian background (Ratcliffe, 2004: 73–75). The **cultural deficit theory** holds that people of black and minority ethnic groups (some more than others, such as black African-American populations) have limited educational abilities and attainment aspirations in comparison to their white counterparts. It maintains that the reason that these groups fail to thrive educationally is because they are 'culturally deprived' of values coherent with the education system – in other words, their family and cultural setting does not instil in them the value of education, especially in relation to self-determination, success and for becoming active members of society. The theory has been widely critiqued for failing to consider structural inequalities within the education system. Unsurprisingly, such patterns of discrimination and inequality are also mirrored in the employment and labour market experiences of black and minority ethnic populations, who are much more likely to be unemployed in comparison to their white counterparts (Ratcliffe, 2004: 92).

There are also higher rates of black and minority ethnic patients in the mental health system, with research finding that black African-Caribbean men especially have higher rates of admittance to mental health institutions such as psychiatric hospitals (Nacro, 2007). Practitioners have argued that this is a direct result of the tendency for this population group to have more mental health issues. For instance, research shows that there are higher rates of schizophrenia among members of the black African-Caribbean and black African-American population groups. However, the accuracy of data available on race and mental health has been heavily questioned and deemed unreliable (Williams and Earl, 2007).

Yet, the crudest demonstration of black and minority ethnic negative pathologization and vulnerability is within the criminal justice system, especially in terms of interactions with the police. Statistics on offending seem to suggest that members of the black and minority ethnic population commit more crimes. However, a plethora of research over the last 40 years has found that discriminatory practices across all aspects of the criminal justice system have led to racialized disproportionality – that is, a selective focus and increased levels of punishment of members of the black and minority ethnic population. It has been found that extensive police (ab)use of stop and search[1] on members of the black and minority ethnic population, especially black African-Caribbean men, has led to more members of this group having encounters with the criminal justice system, and in particular experiencing a range of harassment and violence by the police (Rowe, 2012: 115–116). This not only effectively ignored white suspects, but also led to a vicious cycle. Here, 'police lore'[2] and its victimization of members of the black and minority ethnic population led to tense relations in which some members of these population groups developed a lack of trust, and suspicion of the police and the wider criminal justice system. This in turn created strained interactions, which the police then used to justify their notion of a problematic, criminal and hostile black culture. In more recent years following 9/11,[3] there has been a focus on increasing national security through the use of an array of anti-terror[4] measures. Thus, attention has shifted on to members of the South Asian community (who are taken to be Muslims). In England and Wales, sections 44 and 45 of the 2000 Terrorism Act[5] give the police increased stop and search powers, above and beyond its predecessor, the Police and Criminal Evidence Act (1984).[6] These powers are allowed to occur because they have the support, if not the demand, of majority (white) society. Thus, as Patel (2013a: 39) notes, 'racist sentiments are being re-presented, distorted and used in ways to gain support for ever more intrusive and controlling measures' against various members of the black and minority ethnic population.

Similar patterns of discrimination and over-representation have also been found in the court system, especially regarding sentencing patterns. However, the actual degree to which race matters in this part of the criminal justice system is less easy to determine. This is linked to methodological implications, which makes it difficult to determine the degree to which race, as opposed to other factors, influences court processes and sentencing (Hood, 1992). Of the little research that does exist, there is evidence to support the view that not only is racial bias present, but that this bias also impacts on court decisions and sentencing outcomes (Abrams et al., 2008; Austin and Allen, 2000;

Baldus et al., 1998; Hood, 1992; Mauer and King, 2007; Mitchell et al., 2005; Steffensmeier and Demuth, 2000). Data from the USA has found that the stereotypical physical features of a black African-American defendant influences outcome, especially when the case involves a white victim (Blair, Judd and Chapleau, 2004; Eberhardt et al., 2006; Forsterlee et al., 2006). For instance, in a study of death-eligible cases in the USA, Eberhardt et al. (2006: 383) found that the stereotypical physical traits associated with black African-American people, namely broad nose, thick lips and dark skin, functioned 'as a significant determinant of deathworthiness'. Similarly, Steffensmeier, Ulmer and Kramer (1998) found that the defendant's age and gender, in addition to their racial background, were also significant factors in courtroom experiences. For instance, young black African-American males are more harshly sentenced. Agozino (1997, 2008) argues that black women of African heritage are especially prone within the criminal justice system to being seen as 'foreign' others, and this additional layer of 'deviance' makes them particularly susceptible to being more harshly punished.

One impact of such racism on members of the black and minority ethnic community is their susceptibility to (over-)criminalization. **Criminalization** refers to the ways in which certain behaviour is met with widespread disapproval and condemnation. Criminalization is considered to be a social activity, meaning that it is a technical process in which the social reaction itself is an important point of analysis, for instance, the ways in which the behaviour is outlawed and becomes a 'crime'; how it is regulated through law enforcement; and how it comes to be punished by the courts. Not all crimes are harmful, and not all acts of harm come to be seen as a crime. This means that criminalization is a political, economic and ideological process which involves selective policing and punishment (Chadwick and Scraton, 2001: 68). When members of the black and minority ethnic population are racially criminalized in this way, the notion of '**black criminality**' becomes popularized and used to justify their selective surveillance and punishment. Often crime concerns become racialized, in that they are blamed on supposed 'cultural dysfunctions' of a black and minority ethnic population group. For instance, consider the presentation of the problem of gang affiliation and gun crime in Britain. Not only does this narrative echo the earlier racial panics, such as those of street crime and muggings in the 1970s, but it has explicitly been linked to issues within the black African-Caribbean population. The racialized language in the gun crime narrative, however, is not as overt as it was in the 1970s, which is unsurprising given that we are now in a post-Macpherson era. Nevertheless, the narrative still uses 'signifiers of race' and draws on notions of cultural difference – especially the idea of a problematic black culture – to frame the context. For example, terms which carry the image and legacy of previous (pre-Macpherson) racialized crime panics continue to be used to make reference to race, without naming it as such, for instance, terms such as 'urban', 'gangstas', 'feckless families' and 'absent fathers' (Rowe, 2012: 67–68). Another example is the increased attention given to members of the Muslim community, who in recent years have all come to be construed as potential terrorists – an image reinforced in narratives across popular culture, the mass media, crime prevention and politics about national identity, immigration and security. The result is the introduction of specialist nationality integration and crime-(terrorism) avoidance programmes, which actually serve to reinforce the 'mythical image' (Gilroy, 2008: 114)[7] of the 'militant Muslim' willing to carry out indiscriminate terrorist activity. For example, consider Britain's *Prevent Strategy* (Home Office, 2011),[8] criticized not least because:

> The term 'Prevent' lends itself to the idea that there lies a dormant terrorist within Muslims; that somewhere, entwined in their instincts and licensed by their religious beliefs, there is the possibility that some, albeit very rarely, will turn to terrorism against the state. And so we must do everything to 'prevent' that from happening. (Islamic Society of Britain, 2010, quoted in Rowe, 2012: 165)

Another impact of such racism is that there is a tendency to ignore black and minority ethnic victimization, especially the crimes which are perpetrated on them, which can also lead to them being treated as if they were themselves the problem. For instance, consider the police's (mis)treatment of Duwayne Brooks in the Stephen Lawrence case.[9] Indeed, black and minority ethnic people have often reported feeling as if the police and other criminal justice bodies fail to protect them when they have been victims of crime, especially from violent racism. For example, studies indicate the failure of the police to deal sufficiently with reports of racial violence; racist stereotyping by police officers themselves when dealing with members of black and minority ethnic community; the tendency of officers to deny or even play down the racial motive; and problems in accurate police recording of racially motivated crimes (Bjorgo and Witte, 1993; Bowling, 1999; Bowling and Phillips, 2002; Gordon, 1990; Holdaway, 1983, 1996; Maynard and Read, 1997; Reiner, 2000; Skogan, 1994). This not only impacts on the satisfaction and confidence levels that black and minority ethnic people have in the police (Barrett, Fletcher and Patel, 2013), but also on how they view themselves (Apena, 2007) and the developmental opportunities that are available to them, for instance in education and employment.

INSTITUTIONAL RACISM

It is argued that what remains insufficiently dislodged are the racially discriminatory ideas that exist about black and minority ethnic potential and victimization, and the ways in which this is powerfully influenced by an institutionally racist system. The term '**institutional racism**' was first introduced by Stokely Carmichael (later Kwame Touré) and Charles Hamilton in 1967:

> ... when in ... Birmingham, Alabama – 500 black babies die each year because of the lack of proper food, clothing, shelter and proper medical facilities, and thousands more are destroyed or maimed physically, emotionally and intellectually because of conditions of poverty and discrimination in the black community, that is a function of institutional racism. (Carmichael and Hamilton, 1967: 6)

Carmichael and Hamilton used the term to highlight the pervasive and systematic racism in the USA, which they argued was a long-standing and structural feature which influenced all aspects of society for black minority ethnic people, especially African Americans (Murji, 2003: 147). Institutional racism is seen as the less overt set of racist assumptions, customs and routine practices which are the institutionalized norms of key structures and organizations in society. It is attributed to white power and privilege. In using the phrase 'web of institutional racism' to refer to nine types of interconnected institutional racism,[10] Miller and Garran (2007: 60) note that institutional racism 'is nearly invisible to many white people who pass through it unimpeded. White people maintain the illusion that many societal institutions, policies, living and working arrangements, programs and organizations are race neutral ... [but] that is not possible in a racialized society.' Carmichael and Hamilton argued that institutional racism was a form of 'internal colonialism' in the USA, given that in theory it gave citizenship status to its American minority ethnic groups, but in practice it placed them as colonial subjects within white society (Murji, 2003: 148). This is supported by Sivanandan (2005), who states 'the racism that needs to be contested is not personal prejudice, which has no authority behind it, but institutionalized racism, woven over centuries of colonialism and slavery into the structures of society and government'.

In the UK, the concept of institutional racism gained widespread public recognition following an inquiry into the Metropolitan Police Force's investigation of the murder of Stephen Lawrence in London (Macpherson, 1999). The Macpherson Report (1999) attempted to acknowledge, define and investigate institutional racism, noting that it existed within the culture of policing as well as in the views and practices of individual racist officers (Ratcliffe, 2004: 119). As Macpherson (1999: para 6.34) notes:

> The collective failure of an organisation to provide an appropriate and professional service to people because of their colour, culture or ethnic origin. It can be seen and detected in processes, attitudes, and behaviour which amount to discrimination through unwitting prejudice, ignorance, thoughtlessness, and racist stereotyping which disadvantage minority ethnic people.

There were a number of key elements introduced with the Macpherson definition: first, the failure to act properly, and, secondly, the idea of unintentional actions (Garner, 2010: 102). Another key aspect was the idea of 'perception', and in particular the perception of the victim or any third party that the incident was racist.

However, criticism offered by Floya Anthias (1999) of the Macpherson Report and its conceptualization of 'institutional racism' noted that the definition fails to adequately differentiate between the racism of the institution and its policies and the racism of the individuals within institutions. Others argue that it poses the danger of interjecting 'race' into an incident where it actually has no place, because the over-focus on race overshadows the consideration of other forms of discrimination and exclusion, such as those around gender and social class (Miles and Brown, 2003). The concept can also detract from the ideal fulfilment of true justice for all

(Ignatieff, 2000, cited in Garner, 2010: 107). Some go further and argue that the concept and its encouraged use actually perpetuate racism by constructing a system of racial preference which gives advantages to ethnic minority groups (Green, 2000, in Garner, 2010: 107). Unsurprisingly, the Report's findings were strongly criticized by many individual officers in the police force, who felt that it had accused them of being individually racist in the undertaking of their policing duties. Indeed, some officers found the concept confusing. For instance, Souhami's (2007: 80) study into officers' reactions following Macpherson found that officers were especially confused about the concept of 'institutional racism' itself – in particular, the relationship between the institution and the individuals who comprise it. Souhami (2007: 81–82) notes that police culture is an important source of mediation when it comes to police service delivery, yet officers were unable to recognize how the institution and its culture shape how officers understand their social reality, and thus their behaviour as discretionary decision makers (and vice versa).[11]

Institutional racism has also been found in other influential social institutions, such as the education system (Gilborn, 2008; Gill, Mayor and Blair, 1992; Troyna and Williams, 2012). In the past, such racism was more overt, as illustrated by the use of the race and IQ theory to justify offering lower-quality teaching to black and minority ethnic students. In recent years, though, institutionally racist practices have been found in those settings that consider themselves to work according to race equality measures. Yet, unconsciously (due to dominating white normative structures) they continue to racially discriminate against its black and minority ethnic students and their families. Carlile (2011: 191–192) argues that racism in educational settings appears to be approached as undesirable, and indeed the subject of various initiatives that claim to 'celebrate diversity', but in reality established practices at administrative levels can constitute institutional racism, one example being a lack of adequate translation facilities for parents of excluded children which, in effect, undermines their participation in exclusion/inclusion processes. Thus, institutionally racist practices can emerge from those measures that appear to be race-neutral or even appear to satisfy race equality agendas (Taylor and Clark, 2009: 115). Pilkington (2012: 242) interestingly argues that particular educational settings, namely higher education institutions, are unlikely to take meaningful measures to promote race equality because of a common belief that universities are liberal institutions which, by their very nature, are committed to equality of opportunity. Like others, Pilkington (2012) notes that as institutions whose whiteness remains the normative and centralized power, the actual privilege of whiteness goes unnoticed and overlooked.

The world of sport is another social institution that has faced continual accusations of institutionalized racism. It has been argued that the institution of sport is dominated by policies, processes and practices which favour white hegemonic privilege (Bradbury, 2013: 305). Take, for instance, the case of recruitment, selection and promotion practices of amateur and elite football in European countries (Bradbury, 2013; Burdsey, 2004, 2007; Council of Europe: European Commission against Racial Intolerance, 2008; Halm, 2005). Although there are a number of players from black

African-Caribbean background, there remain very few players of other black and minority ethnic backgrounds, such as those of South Asian background, for instance, despite their numbers in the general population. In an article examining this issue, Northcroft (2008) noted how the number of professional footballers of South Asian background was five. Of greater concern is the racist stereotyping about supposed inherent cultural differences that are used to justify their relative absence – such as the idea that South Asians are physically weak: '…physically frail, lacking in stamina and likely to underachieve in physical education' (Carrington and McDonald, 2001, cited in Saeed and Kilvington, 2011: 606). Such views mean that little attention is paid to the discriminatory, closed practices of football organization and the invisible, normal and central structures of whiteness that allow racially biased practices to maintain 'the status quo of racialized power relations' (Bradbury, 2013: 305).

Racism in football raises some interesting issues about institutional racism in general. In terms of the 'performance of racism', King (2004) usefully draws our attention to the dichotomy of 'onside racism' – the visible and conscious – and 'offside racism' – the invisible and unconscious – to understand how whiteness, namely white masculine identities, perform and function within football institutions. In drawing on the work of Erving Goffman (1959) and Franz Fanon (1967), King argues that racialized performance in football sees black and minority ethnic players 'adjusting' to racial stereotypes about the black body in order to survive in football. They do this by 'adopting the white man's standards of behaviour through the use of the "white mask"' in their public, or front-stage, performance so that they move beyond being perceived simply as black or Asian bodies to be controlled by white men (King, 2004: 3–4). Football also illustrates the unsettled relationship between racist behaviour and a racist person. Here, alleged racism in football has in the last few years been more commonly reported. For instance, recall the case of Chelsea defender (and England captain) John Terry, who in October 2011 faced accusations of racially abusing the mixed-race Queens Park Rangers player Anton Ferdinand (Song, 2014: 108–109).[12] In drawing on the work of Ali Rattansi (2007, cited in Song, 2014: 116), Miri Song notes that what is especially interesting about the Terry/Ferdinand case is that although there is agreement that Terry behaved in a racist way towards Ferdinand, there is a wider debate about whether or not Terry is actually a racist person. This is because there is a question mark over whether Terry consistently behaves in this way towards other black and minority ethnic people. This analysis raises further questions about the content of racism or being a racist person – for instance, should a single incident of racist behaviour be met with the label 'racist'? If so, surely we are all racists, given that it is almost impossible not to have behaved in a (consciously or unconsciously) racist way at one point in our lives? Similarly, is the expression of a racist view against a white person by a black and minority ethnic person – what is commonly referred to a 'reverse racism' – equally damaging in its consequences, given that, yes, it is a form of racial essentializing, but is not considered to entail the same detrimental impact as white against black and minority ethnic racism, due to differences in motivation, history and social experience (Song, 2014: 120–121). Or, would it be more useful to view racism as existing on a continuum, ranging from soft to hard racism? (Rattansi, 2007, cited in Song, 2014: 120).

--- **ACTIVITY** ---

Are we all racists? Explain your answer. What does this say about the future of anti-racist measures?

Attempts to deal with problems of institutional racism include seeking to improve representation (in terms of the number of black and minority ethnic staff) within institutions. This has included the use of specialist recruitment initiatives, which many argue amounts to a form of **positive discrimination** (also known as '**affirmative action**' in the USA). Positive discrimination is a way to support socially discriminated against and disadvantaged groups. The initiative allows for these groups to receive preferential treatment as a way of reversing and overcoming inequalities – in particular, those which have some historical basis. Although a popular initiative that is still is use in the USA, affirmative action has been widely criticized, not least for the way in which it may suggest that black minority ethnic groups, such as African Americans, who are subject to preferential treatment, may have this treatment justified on the basis of an implied inferiority (Valeri, 2003: 4–5). Thus, the core component of racist views remains unchallenged. These 'advantageous' practices have also been criticized for the way in which they bring the danger of placing obstacles in the way of black and minority ethnic staff, especially their acceptance as credible members of staff who have the ability to undertake duties. Such initiatives have also been criticized for the way in which they may meet recruitment targets, but actually fail to make any serious impact on the retention and progression of black and minority ethnic staff, and ultimately the removal of racism and achievement of equality in practice. This has led to the charge of superficial 'window dressing' or 'tokenistic' appointments being made. The concept of **tokenism** was popularized in America in the late 1950s and refers to a policy or practice which moves towards the inclusion of members of a minority group. However, the effort is seen as superficial and is used to create the appearance of equality and inclusiveness, as well as to deflect accusations of discrimination. Token appointments are often seen as representatives of their minority group – whether this is their choice or not. Another critique is the discourse of 'reverse racism' (Feagin and O'Brien, 2003, cited in Cabrera, 2012: 45). Linked to notions of 'white victimhood', 'reverse racism' is the belief that multiculturalism and anti-racist measures actually serve to victimize white populations, with equality and positive action measures in particular marginalizing whites. Within this perspective, whites perceive themselves as victims of racism (Bonilla-Silva, 2002, cited in Cabrera, 2012: 45).

ALL ABOUT RACE?

There are many demonstrations of the tendency to racialize social events, especially by those who use it to reinforce views about the supposed problematic presence of black and minority ethnic groups. For instance, one case is the designation of social conflict (also commonly known as 'riots', 'urban unrest' and 'street violence'), as caused by racial difference. This was illustrated with the comments made by historian David Starkey following the August 2011 disturbances in England and Wales. Commonly referred to as 'riots', the disturbances started on 4 August 2011 in Tottenham, a northern suburb of London, following the suspicious police shooting of a young man of African-Caribbean heritage, Mark Duggan. The riots lasted a week and spread to 66 different areas across England and Wales (Lowe, 2013: 279). David Starkey referred to 'a profound cultural change' and after disclosing that he had re-read Enoch Powell's 'rivers of blood' speech,[13] Starkey stated that '[Powell's] prophecy was absolutely right in one sense. The Tiber did not foam with blood but flames lambent, they wrapped around Tottenham and wrapped around Clapham.' In tapping into racial panics about black and minority ethnic people of immigrant heritage, Starkey was assigning some of the blame for the disturbances on 'whites who have become black' and who had adopted a 'violent, destructive, nihilistic gangster culture', and he went on to say that 'this language, which is wholly false, which is this Jamaican patois that has been intruded in England and that is why so many of us have this sense literally of a foreign country' (*Newsnight*, 12 August 2011). Although Starkey's comments were met with criticism and correction, his views were nevertheless supported in some quarters.

The common reference to such social conflict as 'race riots', or the suggestion of them being raced events, is inaccurate and problematic, not least because they are (also, if not more) about broader social disadvantages and injustices, such as those in education, employment and housing. Yes, they may include race and/or ethnicity (unsurprisingly, given that black and minority ethnic groups are most likely to be seriously disadvantaged here), but they also often cut across racial borders. This was evident in the 1981 Toxteth (Liverpool, UK) disturbances, which emerged from long-standing tensions between the Merseyside Police Force and the residents in Toxteth, many of whom were of black and minority ethnic background. Although police and community relations were poor, following perceptions of police racism in stop and search under the 'sus laws',[14] the disturbances were set off following what was considered to be police heavy-handedness and the excessive use of force in the arrest of Leroy Alphonse Cooper (who was of black African-Caribbean heritage) on 3 July 1981. However, that period saw an economic recession in the UK, with one of the highest rates of unemployment being in Toxteth. Although race – or, in particular, accusations of racist policing – played a role in the accumulation of anger and hostility leading up to the disturbance, the events in Toxteth were not solely or primarily even about race, despite the attempt of the media and politicians to label them as 'race riots'. Indeed, following the riots, Mr Kenneth Oxford, the then Chief Constable of Merseyside, stated that in his opinion the Toxteth disturbances were not 'race riots', a point which is consistent with the narratives of residents in the area, who indicated that a significant number of the 'rioters' were actually of a white working-class background (Vulliamy, 2011). Similarly, initial perceptions of the August 2011 events were that they were due to criminal gangs, feral youth and young thugs (Lowe, 2013: 280). This was clearly illustrated by the then Prime Minister David Cameron, who blamed people from 'sick and broken pockets of society' who 'feel the world owes them something' (UK Riots, 2011, cited in Lowe, 2013: 281). Many discussions then started to blame supposed problematic black cultures – namely irrational and angry black African-Caribbean people with a readiness to use physical violence and to participate in criminal behaviour (vandalism and looting) – as was clearly illustrated by David Starkey's comments. However, as Lowe (2013) highlights, the causes of the 2011 events were much more complex and no one group or reason was to blame. This was supported by the conclusions of the Riots Communities and Victims Panel (2012). Thus, Lowe (2013) argues, what was ignored in the media and political commentary was how the 'rioters' were unconsciously communicating their heightened position of inequality and disempowerment in a particular socioeconomic and political context (see Lowe, 2013: 286–287).

We therefore need to consider the social injustice element as a cause of social events described as 'riots' or 'urban unrest'. Benyon and Solomos (1987: 181) argue that we must view disorders in terms of broader social injustice issues related to the political, social, cultural and economic contexts in which they occur – as opposed to the idea of 'human wickedness' or a 'greed for looting' or 'black criminality' being the causes for social unrest. This is because such unrest only arises under certain conditions, for example, in times of high unemployment, widespread deprivation, manifestations of racial (or other types of) discrimination and disadvantage, political exclusion and powerlessness, and a common mistrust of, and hostility to, criminal justice institutions, such as the police. Indeed, it has also been suggested that such social events, especially where 'looting' and 'theft' are involved, can also be viewed as rational responses to the consumer pressures and desires that exist in contemporary society (Hayward, 2007; Patel, 2013b; Young, 2007).

In addition to socioeconomic disadvantage, there are other factors that help to explain the outbreak of disorder or unrest as a violent reaction to social situations. Here, there is a stimulus to set the violent reaction in motion. Thus, there is tinder which is created by the underlying conditions, but it is ignited by a particular event which provides the spark (Benyon and Solomos, 1987: 181–182). This can be events which are interpreted as personifications or brutal illustrations of social injustice, such as the death of a suspect in police custody, as we saw, for example, in the cases of Michael Brown[15] (Missouri, USA) and Mark Duggan (Tottenham, England). The latter, for instance, was considered to spark the 2011 disturbances in England and Wales.

--- **ACTIVITY** ---

Following the August 2011 riots in cities across England and Wales, the historian David Starkey partly blamed the events on 'whites who have become black' and who have adopted a black 'gangster' culture (*Newsnight*, 12 August 2011). Why was Starkey able to make such a comment and in some quarters gain support for it, despite the fact that race was not a significant factor in these events?

Case study: Racism in football

In February 2015, footage emerged in the UK showing Chelsea football supporters singing a racist chant, 'We're racist, we're racist and that's the way we like it', and preventing a man of black African-Caribbean heritage from boarding a Métro train in Paris. After trying to board the Métro at the Richelieu-Drouot station, the footage appeared to show the man being pushed out of the door and back onto the platform. The incident occurred just before the Champions League game between the English football team Chelsea and France's Paris Saint-Germain (The *Guardian*, 18 February 2015). Following an investigation of the incident, five men were arrested and sought to fight against the imposition of a football banning order (under the Football (Disorder) Act, 2000). This failed and they were each given a banning order of between three and five years. Such banning orders require recipients to surrender their passports during specified periods, such as around international games, and to report to a police station at the start (kick-off time) of specified football matches.

Following the incident, Chelsea Football Club were quick to speak out against the fans' behaviour, stating:

> Such behaviour is abhorrent and has no place in football or society. We will support any criminal action against those involved and should evidence point to involvement of Chelsea season-ticket holders or members, the club will take the strongest possible action against them, including banning orders. ... The point has to be made there were 2,000 Chelsea fans there. The vast majority are not racist. We are a multi-racial club, you only have to look at our team. (The *Guardian*, 18 February 2015)

Although the Paris incident itself is upsetting and shocking, what is interesting is the club's reference to its (black and minority ethnic) team members for validation that it is a 'multi-racial' club – and thus, in their logic, a claim to being non-racist. This is 'tokenism' at its fullest.

As discussed earlier in this chapter, racism is considered to have a strong foothold in football, given the dynamics of identity, heritage and sense of place. For instance, in talking about the English football team, Back, Crabbe and Solomos (1999: 222) argue that 'following England has become something that lies beyond football results; it is framed by a discourse characterized by notions of pride, passion, loyalty and a set of normative codes and assumptions that go with "being English"'. Indeed, by virtue of its imperialist phase, racism in English football remains closely linked to notions of Imperialist patriotism, illustrated not least by a well-known racist chant: 'Stand by the Union Jack, send those niggers back; if you're white, you're alright, if you're black, send 'em back ... there ain't no black in the Union Jack, send the bastards back.' Such ingrained perceptions help to explain the behaviour of the Chelsea fans in the Paris case. Racism in football is relatively unsurprising given the cultural, political and historical background of football, and football fandom in particular, which one can argue is strongly rooted in nationalism – and thus whiteness – and the idea of excluding all those who fall outside this identity. For example, consider the high volume of race hate found among fans, which in recent times has been especially evident and voluminous on social networking sites. Recall, for instance, the racist tweets and trolling of Anton Ferdinand in 2011 (*London Evening Standard*, 1 November 2011). Indeed, some have suggested that in contemporary society it is still not yet possible to be both black and English within institutions of English sport (Gilroy, 1987, cited in King, 2004: 14). This is symbolically illustrated by the absence of black in the Union Jack, and the insistence of supporters that black-ness does not belong in the Union Jack, as the well-known neo-fascist chant (which commonly echoed around football grounds in the 1970s) goes: 'Ain't no black in the Union Jack, send the bastards back!' (Back et al., 1999: 420).

ACTIVITY

Is the performance of national identity in football inevitably racist? Explain your answer.

CONCLUDING THOUGHTS

This chapter has looked at the ways in which ideas about race continue to reside in various social institutions and organizations. Not only do these ideas draw on his-torical biases and crude stereotypes, but they have also been re-presented in palatable ways so that they are considered as normative facts. The power of influence of these ideas is reflected in the views and actions of lay society, despite attempts to discredit them and ensure equality of opportunity. To illustrate some of these points, the case of racism in football has been discussed, in particular the 'Chelsea supporters in Paris' incident in February 2015. In examining these issues, the key question raised is why do particular spaces especially allow for racist views not only to continue, but to thrive?

MAIN POINTS

- The negative pathologization of black and minority ethnic groups has contrib-uted to their vulnerability within institutions and organizations.

- The persistence of institutional racism, especially within the criminal justice system, has led to over-criminalization and a denial of victimhood status.

- There is a tendency to label urban unrest in areas dominated by black and minority ethnic populations as 'race riots'.

STUDY QUESTIONS

1. Explain the readiness to believe that crime can be racially determined?

2. Why is institutional racism still present?

3. What are the social and political motivations of urban unrest?

FURTHER READING

Abrams, David S., Bertrand, Marianne and Mullainathan, Sendhil (2008) 'Do judges vary in their treatment of race?', *American Law and Economics Association Annual Meetings*, 93: 1–44.

Bourne, Jenny (2001) 'The life and times of institutional racism', *Race and Class*, 43(2): 7–22.

Bradbury, Steven (2013) 'Institutional racism, Whiteness and the under-representation of minorities in leadership positions in football in Europe', *Soccer and Society*, 14(3): 296–314.

Gilroy, Paul (1982) 'The myth of black criminality', *The Socialist Register*, 19 (http://socialist register.com/index.php/srv/issue/view/417#.Uzp9IFfBn3A).

REFERENCES

Agozino, Biko (1997) *Black Women and the Criminal Justice System*. Aldershot: Ashgate.

Agozino, Biko (2008) 'Foreign women in prison', *African Journal of Criminology and Justice Studies*, 23(2): 1–33.

Anthias, Floya (1999) 'Institutional racism, power and account', *Sociological Research Online*, 31 March 1999 (www.socresonline.org.uk/4/lawrence/anthias.html).

Apena, Feyishola (2007) 'Being black and in trouble: The role of self-perception in the offending behaviour of black youth', *The National Association for Youth Justice*, 7(3): 211–228.

Austin, Roy L. and Allen, Mark D. (2000) 'Racial disparities in arrest rates as an explanation of racial disparity in commitment to Pennsylvania's prisons', *Journal of Research in Crime and Delinquency*, 37: 200–220.

Back, Les, Crabbe, Tim and Solomos, John (1999) 'Beyond the racism/hooligan couplet: Race, social theory and football culture', *British Journal of Sociology*, 50(3): 419–442.

Baldus, David C., Woodworth, George, Zuckerman, David, Weiner, Neil A. and Broffitt, Barbara (1998) 'Racial discrimination and the death penalty in the post-*FURMAN* era: An empirical and legal overview, with recent findings from Philadelphia', *Cornell Law Review*, 83: 1638–1770.

Barrett, Giles, Fletcher, Samantha M. and Patel, Tina G. (2013) 'Black minority ethnic communities and levels of satisfaction with policing: Findings from a study in the North of England', *Criminology and Criminal Justice*, 14(2): 196–215.

Benyon, John and Solomos, John (eds.) (1987) *The Roots of Urban Unrest*. New York: Pergamon.

Bjorgo, Tore and Witte, Rob (eds.) (1993) *Racist Violence in Europe*. London: St Martin's Press.

Blair, Irene V., Judd, Charles M. and Chapleau, Kristine M. (2004) 'The influence of Afrocentric facial features in criminal sentencing', *Psychological Science*, 15: 674–679.

Bowling, Benjamin (1999) *Violent Racism: Victimisation, Policing and Social Context*. Oxford: Oxford University Press.

Bowling, Benjamin and Phillips, Coretta (2002) *Racism, Crime and Justice*. Harlow: Longman.

Burdsey, Daniel (2004) 'Outside race? Race, racism and the recruitment of Asian professional footballers', *Patterns of Prejudice*, 38(3): 279–299.

Burdsey, Daniel (2007) *British Asians and Football: Culture, Identity and Exclusion*. London: Routledge.

Cabrera, Nolan León (2012) 'Exposing whiteness in higher education: White male college students minimizing racism, claiming victimization, and recreating white supremacy', *Race, Ethnicity and Education*, 17(1): 30–55.

Carlile, Anna (2011) 'An ethnography of permanent exclusion from school: Revealing and untangling the threads of institutionalised racism', *Race, Ethnicity and Education*, 15(2): 175–194.

Carmichael, Stokely and Hamilton, Charles V. (1967) 'Black power: The politics of liberation in America', in E. Cashmore and J. Jennings (eds.), *Racism: Essential Readings*. London: Sage. pp. 111–121.

Carrington, Ben and McDonald, Ian (2001) *'Race', Sport and British Society*. Abingdon: Routledge.

Chadwick, Kathryn and Scraton, Phil (2001) 'Criminalization', in E. McLaughlin and J. Muncie (eds.), *The Sage Dictionary of Criminology*. London: Sage. pp. 68–69.

Council of Europe: European Commission against Racial Intolerance (2008) *ECRI General Policy Recommendation No. 12 on Combating Racism and Racial Discrimination in the Field of Sport*. Brussels: Council of Europe.

Eberhardt, Jennifer L., Davies, Paul G., Purdie-Vaughns, Valerie J. and Lynn Johnson, S. (2006) *Looking Deathworthy: Perceived Stereotypicality of Black Defendants Predicts Capital-Sentencing Outcomes*. Research Report 06-012. New York: Cornell Law School.

Eysenck, Hans (1971) *Race, Intelligence and Education*. London: Temple Smith.

Fanon, Franz (1967) *Black Skin, White Mask*. London: Pluto Press.

ForsterLee, Robert, ForsterLee, Lynne, Horowitz, Irwin A., and King, Ella (2006) 'The effects of defendant race, victim race, and juror gender on evidence processing in a murder trial', *Behavioral Sciences and the Law*, 24(2): 179–198.

Garner, Steve (2010) *Racisms: An Introduction*. London: Sage.

Gilborn, David (2008) *Racism and Education: Coincidence or Conspiracy?* Abingdon: Routledge.

Gill, Dawn, Mayor, Barbara and Blair, Maud (eds.) (1992) *Racism and Education: Structures and Strategies*. London: Sage.

Gilroy, Paul (2008) 'The myth of black criminality (a revised essay)', in B. Spalek (ed.), *Ethnicity and Crime: A Reader*. Maidenhead: Open University Press. pp. 113–127.

Goffman, Erving (1959) *The Presentation of Self in Everyday Life*. New York: Doubleday.

Gordon, Paul (1990) *Racial Violence and Harassment*. London: Runnymede Trust.

Halm, Dirk (2005) 'Turkish immigrants in German amateur football', in A. Tomlinson and C. Young (eds.), *German Football: History, Culture and Society*. London: Routledge. pp. 73–92.

Hayward, Keith J. (2007) 'Consumer culture and crime in late modernity', in C. Sumner (ed.), *The Blackwell Companion to Criminology*. Oxford: Blackwell. pp. 143–161.

Herrnstein, Richard J. and Murray, Charles (1994) *The Bell Curve: Intelligence and Class Structure in American Life*. New York: The Free Press.

Holdaway, Simon (1983) *Inside the British Police Force: A Force at Work*. Oxford: Basil Blackwell.

Holdaway, Simon (1996) *The Racialisation of British Policing*. Basingstoke: Palgrave Macmillan.

Home Office (1824) *Vagrancy Act 1824*. London: The Stationery Office.

Home Office (2000) *Terrorism Act 2000*. London: The Stationery Office,

Home Office (2000) *Football (Disorder) Act 2000*. London: The Stationery Office.

Home Office (2011) *Prevent Strategy*. London: Home Office.

Hood, Roger (1992) *Race and Sentencing: A Study in the Crown Court*. Oxford: Clarendon Press.

Jenson, Arthur (1969) 'How much can we boost IQ and scholastic achievement?', *Harvard Educational Review*, 39(1): 1–123.

Kalra, Virinder (2003) 'Police lore and community disorder: Diversity in the criminal justice system', in D. Mason (ed.), *Explaining Ethnic Differences: Changing Patterns of Disadvantage in Britain*. Bristol: Policy Press. pp. 139–152.

King, Colin (2004) *Offside Racism: Playing the White Man*. Oxford: Berg.

London Evening Standard (2011) 'Anton Ferdinand is the victim of racist abuse on Twitter', *London Evening Standard*, 1 November 2011. Reported by: Tom Collomosse.

Lowe, Frank (2013) 'The August 2011 riots: Them and us', *Psychodynamic Practice: Individuals, Groups and Organisations*, 19(3): 279–295.

Macpherson, William (1999) *The Stephen Lawrence Inquiry*. Cm. 4262-1. London: Home Office (www.archive.official-documents.co.uk/document/cm42/4262/4262.htm).

Martin, Gus (2010) *Understanding Terrorism: Challenges, Perspectives and Issues*. London: Sage.

Mauer, Marc and King, Ryan S. (2007) *Uneven Justice: State Rates of Incarceration by Race and Ethnicity*. Washington, DC: The Sentencing Project.

Maynard, Warwick and Read, Tim (1997) *Policing Racially Motivated Incidents*. Crime Detection and Prevention Series – Paper 84. London: Home Office/Police Research Group.

Miles, Robert and Brown, Malcolm (2003) *Racism*. Second Edition. London: Routledge.

Miller, Joshua and Garran, Ann Marie (2007) 'The web of institutional racism', *Smith College Studies in Social Work*, 77(1): 33–67.

Mitchell, Tara, Haw, Ryann M., Pfeifer, Jeffrey, E. and Meissner, Christian A. (2005) 'Racial bias in mock juror decision-making: A meta-analytic review of defendant treatment', *Law and Human Behaviour*, 29(6): 621–637.

Murji, Karim (2003) 'Institutional racism', in G. Bolaffi, R. Bracalenti, P. Braham and S. Gindro (eds.), *Dictionary of Race, Ethnicity and Culture*. London: Sage. pp. 147–151.

Nacro (2007) *Black Communities, Mental Health and the Criminal Justice System*. London: Nacro [Mental Health Unit].

Newsnight (2011) *Newsnight*. Broadcast on BBC 2, 12 August 2011. BBC England.

Northcroft, Jonathan (2008) 'Why are there no Asian football stars?', *The Sunday Times*, 10 February 2008 (www.thesundaytimes.co.uk/sto/sport/football/article80380.ece).

Patel, Tina G. (2013a) 'Ethnic deviant labels within the "war on terror" context: Excusing White deviance', *Ethnicity and Race in a Changing World*, 4(1): 34–50 (www.man chesteruniversitypress.co.uk/data/ip/ip021/docs/Vol_4_Iss_1.pdf).

Patel, Tina G. (2013b) '"We'll go grafting, yeah?" Crime as a response to urban neglect', *Criminology and Criminal Justice*, 14(2): 179–195.

Pilkington, Andrew (2012) 'The interacting dynamics of institutionalised racism in higher education', *Race, Ethnicity and Education*, 16(2): 225–245.

Police and Criminal Evidence Act (1984).

Ratcliffe, Peter (2004) *'Race', Ethnicity and Difference: Imagining the Inclusive Society*. Maidenhead: Open University Press.

Reiner, Rob (2000) *The Politics of the Police*. Oxford: Oxford University Press.

Riots Communities and Victims Panel (2012) *After the Riots: The Final Report of the Riots Communities and Victims Panel*. London: Riots Communities and Victims Panel.

Rowe, Michael (2012) *Race and Crime*. London: Sage.

Saeed, Amir and Kilvington, Daniel (2011) 'British-Asians and racism within contemporary English football', *Soccer and Society*, 12(5): 601–612.

Sivanandan, Ambavalener (2005) 'Why Muslims reject British values', The *Guardian (Observer)*, 16 October 2005.

Skogan, Wesley G. (1994) *Contacts between Police and Public: Findings from the 1992 British Crime Survey*. Home Office Research Study 132. London: Home Office.

Song, Miri (2014) 'Challenging a culture of racial equivalence', *The British Journal of Sociology*, 65(1): 107–129.

Souhami, Anna (2007) 'Understanding institutional racism: The Stephen Lawrence Inquiry and the police service reaction', in M. Rowe (ed.), *Policing Beyond Macpherson: Issues in Policing, Race and Society*. Cullompton, Devon: Willan. pp. 66–87.

Steffensmeier, Darrell and Demuth, Stephen (2000) 'Ethnicity and sentencing outcomes in U.S. federal courts: Who is punished more harshly?', *American Sociological Review*, 65: 705–729.

Steffensmeier, Darrell, Ulmer, Jeffrey and Kramer, John (1998) 'The interaction of race, gender, and age in criminal sentencing: The punishment cost of being young, black, and male', *Criminology*, 36(4): 763–798.

Taylor, Dianne L. and Clark, Menthia, P. (2009) '"Set up to fail": Institutional racism and the sabotage of school improvement', *Equality and Excellence in Education*, 42(2): 114–129.

The *Guardian* (2015) 'Paris police launch inquiry after Chelsea fans seen abusing black man on film', The *Guardian Online*, 18 February 2015 (www.theguardian.com/foot ball/2015/feb/18/met-police-join-search-chelsea-fans-caught-abusing-black-man-film-paris-metro).

Troyna, Barry and Williams, Jenny (2012) *Racism, Education and the State*. Abingdon: Routledge.

Valeri, Mauro (2003) 'Affirmative action', in G. Bolaffi, R. Bracalenti, P. Braham and S. Gindro (eds.), *Dictionary of Race, Ethnicity and Culture*. London: Sage. pp. 4–6.

Vulliamy, Ed (2011) 'Toxteth revisited, 30 years after the riots', The *Guardian Online*, 3 July 2011 (www.theguardian.com/uk/2011/jul/03/toxteth-liverpool-riot-30-years).

Williams, David R. and Earl, Tara R. (2007) 'Commentary: Race and mental health – more questions than answers', *International Journal of Epidemiology*, 36(4): 758–760.
Young, Jock (2007) *The Vertigo of Late Modernity*. London: Sage.

NOTES

1. Stop and search gives a police officer permission to stop and search someone, their clothes and anything they may be carrying. The officer must explain that they are stopping and searching you and that they are doing so for items that could be used in connection with a crime (drugs, weapons or stolen property) or for items that could be used to commit a crime or to cause criminal damage.

2. Kalra (2003: 139) defines 'police lore' as the routines and customs that the police apply when dealing with particular people, meaning that black and minority ethnic people are marked for special (negative) treatment.

3. This refers to the terrorist attacks in the USA on 11 September 2001 – commonly known as '9/11' – and other later related terrorist activity, for example, the attacks in Bali, London and Madrid.

4. 'Anti-terror' refers to defensive enhanced security and surveillance measures designed to deter or prevent terrorist attacks (Martin, 2010: 463). It differs from 'counter-terror', which refers to proactive policies designed to eliminate terrorist environments and groups (Martin, 2010: 463).

5. Sections 44 and 45 of the Terrorism Act (2000) enabled the police and the Home Secretary to define any area in the country and a time period wherein they could stop and search any vehicle or person, with section 45 allowing this power to be exercised 'for the purpose of searching for articles of a kind which could be used in connection with terrorism, and … may be exercised whether or not the constable has grounds for suspecting the presence of articles of that kind' (Terrorism Act 2000, section 44, 1-a/b). In January 2010 these stop and search powers were ruled illegal by the European Court of Human Rights, and at the time of writing this book the British Government were reviewing its use and powers.

6. In England and Wales, the Police and Criminal Evidence Act (1984) states that it is unlawful for a police officer to discriminate on the grounds of race or ethnicity. However, an update of the Act following the Terrorism Act (2000) does allow officers to take into account the individual's ethnicity in their selection of persons to search: '…There may be circumstances, however, where it is appropriate for officers to take account of a person's ethnic origin in selecting persons to be stopped in response to a specific terrorist threat, for example, some international terrorist groups are associated with particular ethnic identities' (Police and Criminal Evidence Act 1984, code A, para. 2.25).

7. Gilroy (1982, 2008) argues that racialized 'imagery of alien violence and criminality personified in the "mugger" and the "illegal immigrant"' has been an important political tool in racial and national politics (Gilroy, 2008: 114). Gilroy does not deny that some members of the black and minority ethnic population commit crimes, but rather he notes how the images and representations of black criminality have achieved a powerful and mythic status, and ignore the relationship between race and crime – specifically how black and minority ethnic populations in countries such as Britain and the USA are still over-concentrated in poor and deprived areas, and thus consideration of their law-breaking should not solely be racialized but also considered within the context of their poverty and relative deprivation (2008: 124).

8. 'Prevent' has been introduced to stop the radicalization of people vulnerable to recruitment to terrorist ideology and activities (Rowe, 2012: 164).

9. Duwayne Brooks was with Stephen Lawrence when he was murdered on 22 April 1993. In referring to inadequacies in the investigation of the murder and, more specifically, to a series of failures by the Metropolitan Police Force, the Macpherson Report (1999: section 5.12) stated that Duwayne Brooks was dismissed as a victim: 'We are driven to the conclusion that

Mr Brooks was stereotyped as a young black man exhibiting unpleasant hostility and agitation, who could not be expected to help, and whose condition and status simply did not need further examination or understanding. We believe that Mr Brooks' colour and such stereotyping played their part in the collective failure of those involved to treat him properly and according to his needs.'

10. These are residential, educational, employment, accumulation of wealth and upward mobility, environmental and health, mental health, criminal justice, political and media (Miller and Garran, 2007: 35).

11. For more on this, see work on the police 'canteen culture' (Reiner, 2000).

12. Although not convicted in the Magistrate's courts, Terry was later found guilty of racial abuse by the Football Association's Independent Commission, which gave him a four-match ban and a £220,000 fine (Song, 2014: 108–109).

13. In April 1968, Conservative Member of Parliament Enoch Powell criticized proposed Commonwealth immigration and anti-discrimination legislation in the UK. The speech became known as the 'rivers of blood' speech, given its allusion to a line from *The Aeneid*.

14. This term (from 'suspected person') was the informal name given to laws on stop and search. It allowed police officers to stop, search and arrest people for being in breach of the Vagrancy Act 1824, whom they suspected were intending to commit an offence.

15. In 2014, Michael Brown, an unarmed 18-year-old black African-American man, was shot several times by Darren Wilson, a police officer of white ethnic background. In November that same year, a grand jury decided not to indict Wilson, and in 2015, the US Department of Justice cleared Wilson of civil rights violations stating that the evidence showed that Wilson shot Brown in self-defence.

9

HUMAN RIGHTS, EQUALITY AND LEGISLATION

INTRODUCTION

This chapter considers race and ethnicity matters in terms of their relationship to human rights and the law on equality and anti-discrimination. The chapter documents some of the existing legislation in this area, offering some historical context to its development. The discussion then focuses on the limitations of this legislation for addressing newer and unresolved issues around race and society. The legislation covered in this chapter includes: the Immigration Acts 1971 and 1978; the Race Relations (Amendment) Act 2000; and the Racial and Religious Hatred Act 2006; and their equivalents in Europe, the USA and Australia, such as the Civil Rights Acts

1964 and 1991 in the USA and the Commonwealth Racial Discrimination Act 1975 in Australia. The concepts covered include: citizenship; ghettos; hate crime; positive action; and public policy. The case study in the chapter concerns the discriminatory use of CCTV surveillance in Birmingham (UK). The key question raised in this chapter is: How sufficient is existing legislation for protecting the rights of those who suffer disproportionately from race discrimination and inequality?

KEY TERMS

- Compulsory dispersal

- Citizenship

- Equality

- European Convention of Human Rights

- Fortress Europe

- Freedom of expression

- Ghettos

- Hate crime

- Hate speech

- Public policy

LEGISLATIVE MEASURES

The protection of rights is outlined in **public policy**. Public policy is made up of various formal and informal actions on the part of government bodies in order to protect social principles, interests or relationships – making it a highly political process that is underpinned by special interest and the exercise of power. In terms of race and ethnicity, public policy has focused on inequalities by specifically seeking to prohibit prejudicial behaviour, rectify systematic oppression or reverse existing policy (McIlwain and Caliendo, 2011: 38). However, in Western countries such as the UK, USA, Australia and Canada, it has been argued that public policy on race and ethnicity is rooted in an Imperial past (including slavery), which has resulted in a Eurocentric tendency to support a white privileged hierarchical racial order. Therefore, although it must be noted that public policy has made a number of key steps towards protecting rights and avoiding discriminatory abuse, it must also be recognized that public policy has also negatively impacted on the movement, rights and freedoms of some black and minority ethnic people.

Included under the category of formal public policy is legislation. In terms of race and ethnicity in society, there has been a mass of legislative measures which can broadly be divided into two categories: first, legislation that has sought to restrict the presence of particular racial/ethnic groups; and, secondly, legislation that has sought to address the inequalities and discriminations faced by particular racial/ethnic groups. Legislation under the first category includes:

- British Nationality Act (1948) – Britain

- Commonwealth Immigrants Acts (1962) (1968) – Britain

- Immigration Acts (1971) (1978) – Britain

- Immigration Act (1976) – Canada

- Immigration and Refugee Protection Act (2002) – Canada

- Nationality Act (1981) – Britain

The British Nationality Act 1948 extended residency rights to all colonial subjects and allowed citizens of the new Commonwealth countries the right to freely enter Britain in order to work. They were also permitted to settle with their families. Records on immigration were poorly kept with the introduction of the 1948 Act, but it is estimated that new Commonwealth immigration was at 5,400 by 1951 (Hennessy, 2006: 442). In the years following the passing of the Act, there was, in particular, an increased number of Commonwealth migrants arriving from the Caribbean, India, Pakistan, Africa and the Far East, which is unsurprising given that these areas were actively targeted for specialist recruitment drives as a way of dealing with the post-war labour shortage in Britain. By the mid-1950s, however, there emerged panic and hostility among the white British population, who viewed these migrants as 'job-takers', and they eventually became demonized as alien, deviant and a threat to white British society. British anti-immigration campaigns grew, and eventually played a key role in the introduction of immigration control legislation, namely the Commonwealth Immigrants Acts of 1962 and 1968, the 1971 and 1978 Immigration Acts and the 1981 British Nationality Act (see Mason, 1995, for a concise description of their content). In essence, these Acts sought to restrict the entry into Britain of what was then known as 'coloured migrants', by leaving the rights of entry of 'old' Commonwealth citizens (namely Australia and Canada) and removing rights of 'new' Commonwealth citizens (namely India and Pakistan) (Mason, 1995: 27–29). It is unsurprising, then, that this suite of legislation has come to be known as racialized immigration policy, which seriously curbed the rights of British citizens who were not white. Most recently, following Britain's membership of the European Union and the permitting of free movement of labour between EU member states, terms such as **fortress Europe** became popularized as a way of making reference to policies which lowered internal European borders, but made external borders more secure (McGhee, 2005: 54).

The Canadian 1976 Immigration Act, which was later replaced by the Immigration and Refugee Protection Act 2002, firmly established three classes of immigrant – family, independent and humanitarian. The Act focused on who could gain entry into Canada rather than on who should be kept out, and in this sense alone it differed significantly from legislation in other countries. However, the Canadian law's criteria for entry were considered by some as tough. For instance, under its points-entry system, those under the class of 'independent' immigrant had to demonstrate skills and value for Canada. Despite this critique, its points-entry system has been credited for having led to the existence of communities of recent immigrant heritage/status who are more settled, better educated and earning higher salaries in comparison to other countries with broader immigration policies, such as the USA.

ACTIVITY

Consider the advantages and disadvantages of (1) a points-entry system and (2) an unrestricted approach to immigration. What is the potential for racial bias to enter each of these?

Debates surrounding these legislative measures have often utilized the notion of **citizenship** to determine who has the right to belong (and not belong) to a given country. Citizenship refers to the legal status of an individual who belongs to a political unit (namely, a state), which then gives them a series of civil, political and social rights (Melotti, 2003: 36), as well as setting out a series of duties to be fulfilled that are based around adhering to the rules of that given state. However, social scientific discussion of citizenship notes how it has come to acquire a complex set of meanings, which within racialized spaces are often unevenly assigned, most notably with non-white populations being marked out as 'outsiders' and 'foreign others' unworthy of citizenship status – even in cases where formal citizenship has been awarded (Mason, 1995: 109).

The discrimination experienced by black and minority ethnic populations has also been addressed in legislation. Here, legislative measures have made attempts to address the inequalities and discriminations faced by particular racial/ethnic groups. They include:

- Anti-Racism Law (1981) – Belgium
- Civil Rights Acts (1871) (1964) (1991) – USA
- Commonwealth Racial Discrimination Act (1975) – Australia
- Crime and Disorder Act (1998) – Britain
- Employment Equity Act (1995) – Canada
- Hate Crimes Prevention Act (1999) – USA

- Human Rights Act (1977) – Canada

- Human Rights Act (1993) – New Zealand

- Promotion of Equality and Prevention of Unfair Discrimination Act (2000) – South Africa

- Race Relations Acts (1965) (1968) (1976) – Britain

- Race Relations Act (1971) – New Zealand

- Race Relations (Amendment) Act (2000) – Britain

- Racial and Religious Hatred Act (2006) – Britain

This suite of legislation (which is by no means exhaustive) in various ways and to varying degrees addresses the concept of 'hate', especially within the context of criminal behaviour. In official terms, a **hate crime** is defined as being an act which 'constitutes a criminal offence, perceived by the victim or any other person as being motivated by prejudice or hate' (Association of Chief Police Officers, 2005: 9). It is argued that hate crimes are different from and more serious than other crimes, given that the victims of hate crimes may suffer more psychological and physical trauma (Gerstenfeld, 2011: 18–22). **Hate speech** is often used interchangeably with hate crime, although there are important distinctions. For example, although it is often harmful and dangerous (as it can create an atmosphere that encourages criminal behaviour), hate speech is often considered to be outside the law. Indeed, in the USA, it is argued that any prohibition on speech (whether it be motivated by hate or otherwise) violates the First Amendment (of the 1791 United States Constitution) on freedom of speech (Gerstenfeld, 2011: 35).

In the USA, hate crime legislation developed following the period of the Civil War, when, in an era that saw the emergence of the Ku Klux Klan, discrimination, and violence against black African-American Southerners, hate crime became a serious problem. For example, between 1882 and 1930, at least 2,300 African Americans in the South were lynched (Tolnay and Neck, 1995, cited in Gerstenfeld, 2011: 11). More recently, there is the US Hate Crimes Prevention Act 1999, which prohibits certain acts of violence because of actual or perceived racial, religious or national origin. In Britain, the Crime and Disorder Act 1998 and the Racial and Religious Hatred Act 2006 are just two of many Acts that contain provisions relating to racially aggravating offences and incitement to religious hatred. However, social scientific and indeed legal debate has struggled with the evidencing of hate in such events, given that the motivation of hate is not always clearly expressed. Hate crime is relative – it is 'dynamic and in a state of constant movement and change, rather than static and fixed' (Bowling, 1993: 238). It is argued that we should consider the wider social, cultural, structural and political context of hate, and in doing so highlight the everyday and normalized occurrence of racially, ethnically and religiously based hate crimes.

In terms of equality and anti-discrimination, US legislation also includes the Civil Rights Acts of 1871, 1964 and 1991, which, in combination, criminalize behaviour that interferes with the enjoyment of activities and benefits if that interference is due to 'race, colour, religion, or national origin' (Gerstenfeld, 2011: 13). Similarly, the Australian Commonwealth Racial Discrimination Act 1975 makes racial discrimination unlawful. As do New Zealand's Race Relations Act 1971 and Human Rights Act 1993; the Belgian Anti-Racism Law 1981; and South Africa's Promotion of Equality and Prevention of Unfair Discrimination Act 2000. In Britain, the Race Relations Acts of 1965, 1968, 1976, and the later Amendment of 2000, prohibited incitement to racial hatred and made racial discrimination in certain places illegal, while actively seeking to promote equality of opportunity. Significantly, the Human Rights Act 1998 allowed individuals to enforce the **European Convention of Human Rights** in UK courts, further supporting rights to be free of discrimination, and protection of liberty and security, freedom of conscience, thought and religion, and the right to a fair trial (Bhavnani, Mirza and Meetoo, 2005: 72).

The right to **freedom of expression** is considered to be a basic human right and is covered accordingly under the Universal Declaration of Human Rights and the International Covenant on Civil and Political Rights:

> ...everyone shall have the right to hold opinions without interference ... [and] ...shall have the right to freedom of expression; this right shall include freedom to seek, receive and impart information and ideas of all kinds, regardless of frontiers, either orally, in writing or in print, in the form of art, or through any other media of his choice. (United Nations General Assembly, 1976: Article 19(2))

Additionally, the Covenant recognizes that such rights to freedom of expression also bring with them a 'special duty and responsibility' with regards to 'respecting the rights and reputations of others' or for 'the protection of national security or of public order (*ordre public*), or of public health or morals' (International Covenant on Civil and Political Rights, 1976: Article 19(3b)). Thus, one's freedom of expression may be the subject of restrictions under certain conditions. Despite the Covenant's clear guidance, in practice, dispute and tension have arisen over freedom of expression, especially when the content of that expression is at odds with the views of (an)other. For example, consider the controversy surrounding the publication of cartoons depicting the Prophet Muhammed by the Danish newspaper *Jyllands-Posten* in September 2005.

WHOSE PROTECTION?

Postcolonial constructions of black and minority ethnic people as subhuman has led to their presence in countries such as Britain, Australia, France and the United States of America being seen as a social problem – as an ill of society which in the short term needs to be remedied and in the long term needs to be prevented. This is never more evident than in the areas of immigration and asylum policy, social housing, education and employment, where it is argued that, despite claims to equality of opportunity and access, there nevertheless remains an approach which believes that support and protection needs to be offered to members of the 'host' society (here taken as white majority), who are presented as being at risk of an 'unmanageable' level of black and minority ethnic presence. This view dominates despite evidence which suggests favourable treatment of white populations, often at the expense of black and minority ethnic ones.

Immigration, economic migration and asylum have regularly been presented as a social problem. A quick scan of the national and international press illustrates this well. For many politicians and lay members of society, immigration controls (including a reduction in the number of refugee and asylum application acceptances, and active use of deportation measures) are considered to be a necessity in society – especially in terms of crime reduction,[1] resource allocation[2] and 'community cohesion'. Panics about immigration and the presence of black and minority ethnic 'others' have become a disproportionate preoccupation, largely assisted by the use of unreliable statistics and problematic data, as well as the utilization of highly emotive language and imagery (Skellington, 1996: 64–68). This has contributed to the development of **compulsory dispersal** programmes for asylum seekers. These claim to prevent the over-concentration of asylum seekers in areas such as London by moving people out to other parts of the country. Such dispersal was introduced in Britain under the Immigration and Asylum Act 1999, despite hostility and criticism. This notion of 'burden sharing' is seen in similar programmes used across Europe, for instance, in Sweden (since 1985) and Germany (since 1974) (Hynes and Sales, 2010: 39–42). In this sense, as Sivanandan (2001: 2) notes, immigration and asylum policy draws on 'xeno-racism' – a fear and hatred of strangers that is motivated by racial/ethnic ideas – along with the use of defensive measures at an increased rate as a way of attempting to preserve the 'host' peoples' position (for instance, identity, way of life and standard of living). This presents the pursuit of anti-immigration and anti-asylum measures as socially acceptable (Fekete, 2001).

ACTIVITY

Collect news reports (narratives and images) on immigration and asylum. List the ways in which the characteristics of immigrants and asylum seekers are presented. What social scientific data are there to support these character presentations?

The panic about immigration and asylum is also used as a rationale to justify measures which make it even more difficult to obtain citizenship status. Recent citizenship processes have adopted the view that citizenship is a 'rite of passage' – where orientations are given, followed by the practical tools to contribute to that society (McGhee, 2005: 73). Based on the idea of citizenship rooted in integration, this approach is a response to the view that there is a community cohesion crisis because migrant groups have self-segregated and remained culturally different. This was an argument used following the 2001 urban unrest in the English towns of Bradford and Oldham – see Alexander (2004) and Amin (2003). The notion of citizenship rooted in integration echoes the integrationist policy used by France in the mid-1980s – a policy that perceived French citizenship as rejecting, in the public sphere at least, any distinctions that are based on race and ethnicity. France's integrationist policy differed from the then British integrationist approach of multiculturalism, and instead encouraged immigrants to France to retain their own distinctive cultures but asked that they also integrate themselves into French culture, traditions and values. However, the value of such a policy was questioned following the urban unrest (in areas with populations of recent immigrant heritage) that occurred in Paris and other French cities during October and November 2005.

The negative re-presentation of black and minority ethnic populations, especially those of recent immigrant heritage, fails to consider the widespread and inter-connected nature of inequalities faced by (and indeed targeted at) these groups. For instance, it is argued that social housing policy has been used as a tool for satisfying an agenda of spatial segregation and exclusionary practice. Pockets of the city, often termed **ghettos**, contain members of an ethnic minority group who are subjected to social, legal or economic pressures. Its residents often feel excluded as they are restricted to these spaces and segregated from mainstream society. The existence of ghettos, or what Marcuse (1996, cited in Ratcliffe, 2004: 61) calls 'outcast ghettos', is a global phenomenon, witnessed in a range of countries from the USA to South Africa to India. These neighbourhoods often come to be seen as unsafe spaces, con-taining dangerous (black and minority ethnic) people, leading to the place and its people becoming further stigmatized and the subject of heightened policing. For example, consider the case of Detroit (USA) following the 1967 riot, and similarly Toxteth (Liverpool, UK) following the 1981 unrest. These neighbourhoods conse-quently became the target of urban regeneration and gentrification projects, which, some argue, further exclude existing disempowered residents.

Another area which racially labels and excludes members of the black and minor-ity ethnic population, despite the existence of equality policy, is within the education system. It can be argued that racism within the education system damaged the edu-cational experience of black and minority ethnic populations (Codjoe, 2010; Gillborn, 2007; Solórzano, 2000). A number of measures have been introduced, ranging from diversity education (such as educating students about different heritages) to supplementary educational resources (for instance, specialist schools which offer additional education to black and minority ethnic populations outside mainstream education[3]). However, these approaches, too, have been heavily criticized, the first for essentializing racial and ethnic differences, and the second for creating insular and self-segregating communities.[4]

Unsurprisingly, issues of discrimination and inequality also extend to areas of employment. This is despite a number of policy and practice initiatives to ensure anti-discrimination and equality of opportunity. For example, in the UK, there is the Equality Act 2010 and the Protection from Harassment Act 1997; in Canada, the Employment Equity Act 1986, later amended in 1995; and in the USA there is 'positive discrimination' (or 'affirmative action'), known as 'reservation' in India and 'positive action' in the UK. However, equality of access and fair treatment once in the workplace are still problematic for people of black and minority ethnic back-ground, in the form, for instance, of bullying, harassment and rejection for promotion (Deitch et al., 2003; Fox and Stallworth, 2005; Mistry and Latoo, 2009). There are various sociological explanations on why this is the case (see Ratcliffe, 2004: 97–98). While equality initiatives have led to increased access for some black and minority ethnic people, and at the very least have heightened awareness and created the image of an atmosphere of inclusion, it is argued that in reality people of black and minor-ity ethnic background continue to face discrimination, harassment and exclusion in regards to employment opportunities (Bhavnani et al., 2005: 82).

LIMITATIONS FOR EQUALITY

The term **equality** encompasses the ethical, moral and legal principles which guide the ideal status and relations between human beings. It implies the need to consider how all human beings can have their needs, interests and desires delivered, given that they are all important in a democratic society developed on a majority rule system (Peltzel, 2003: 88). Equality between citizens is an assumed principle of society, although it has been necessary to enshrine it in policy, for example the Unanimous Declaration of the Thirteen United States of America (1776), known most commonly as the Declaration of Independence: 'We holds these truths to be self-evident, that all men are created equal … with certain unalienable Rights, that among these are Life, Liberty and the Pursuit of Happiness' (quoted in Peltzel, 2003: 88). Some groups, such as those of particular racial or ethnic background, have considered themselves to be in a less equal position, especially when compared to their white counterparts. Thus, they often refer to a history or position of inequality followed by a struggle for equality, either ethically, morally or legally. It is important to recognize that here the perceptions of equality often differ between groups, depending on their collective desires as a racial or ethnic category. For example, in their study on the perception gaps between white Americans and Americans of black and ethnic minority back-ground, Eibach and Ehrlinger (2006) found that white Americans tended to use comparisons with the past to assess progress on equality – thus deciding that there was greater equality between groups – while minorities used the measure of ideal standards – thus deciding that there was less equality.

_____ **ACTIVITY** _____

Is equality an outdated concept?

Differing perceptions of equality often mean that a true state of universal equality can never be achieved. This is illustrated in a South African study by Dixon, Durrheim and Tredoux (2007: 867) which suggested that among the white popula-tion, 'there remains a stubborn core of resistance to policies designed to rectify the injustices of apartheid'. Despite resistance, progress has been made, and policy initiatives have been developed that have sought to make black and minority ethnic populations equal citizens. For instance, in 2005, the UK's Commission for Racial Equality (which has now become part of the Equality and Human Rights Commission),produced a guide called *Promoting Good Race Relations*. The guide identified five key principles considered necessary for achieving equality for all and, ultimately, good race relations. These are:

1. Equality in the rights and opportunities for everyone in all areas of activity.

2. Respect in the acceptance of the individual right to identify with, maintain and develop one's particular cultural heritage, as well as explore other cultures.

3. Security to a safe environment for all, which is free from racism.

4. Unity in terms of the acceptance of belonging to a wider community, and of shared values and responsibilities, which are rooted in a sense of common citizenship and humanity.

5. Cooperation between individuals and groups and in the achievement of common goals, and in order to resolve conflict and create community cohesion. (Commission for Racial Equality, 2005, cited in Johnson and Tatam, 2008: 4)

Indeed, a key example is the American civil rights movement, which helped to end a two-tier system of race relations, replacing it instead with a universal system of formal legal racial equality. Yet in practice, racial inequality remains prominent in American society (Sears et al., 1997: 16).

However, in those instances where equality may be produced in policy, there is the reality that it may not be delivered or achieved in practice. This is partly due to how the racism of the past – often the racism covered by equality policy – has now changed and morphed into newer presentations of discrimination, which have not only allowed racist practices to continue, but to do so in a way that makes racism palatable and acceptable. For example, in his discussion of racism within the context of the 'war on terror', Sivanandan (2006: 1–3) notes that newer and popular forms of racism now include:

1. Civilizational racism – the notion of a superior (white) civilization, a 'super-nation' containing 'super-people, a chosen people on a mission to liberate the world'. Most notably this is the view taken by the US government in their approach to Iraq and what they view to be the threat of an Islamic regime.

2. Nativism – racism that is used to justify ideas about preserving and defending the culture and status of the 'host' population – 'our people'.

3. Islamaphobia – a racism that is directed at Muslims on the basis of their religion.

4. Xenophobia – the racial discrimination directed at asylum seekers and migrants, which is presented as some sort of 'natural' and thus rational fear.

ACTIVITY

What are the similarities and differences between 'new' and 'old' forms of racism?

In addition, those areas in which racial inequality is likely to exist have now become the target of anti-discrimination and pro-equality measures. However, the problem with this is that 'a new politics of documentation' – that is, the documentation which expresses commitment to race equality promotion – is used in itself as a good indicator of race equality. The actual delivery and impact of such documented commitment therefore become irrelevant. Indeed, it has been argued that such documents also work to conceal racism (Ahmed, 2007: 590). Although some pro-equality measures may see limited overt discrimination and greater equality, it also means that discrimination and inequality against black and minority ethnic groups may exist in more subtle ways which are rationalized as non-prejudicial (Brigham, 1993: 1935). For instance, Fekete (2001: 24) argues that xenophobia has now become fully incorporated into the UK's policy on asylum seeking, namely by making 'deterrence' a priority, rather than the protection of human rights. Kundnani (2001: 44–45) notes that in addition to this 'logic of deterrence', there also exists a 'logic of suspicion' towards asylum seekers. This allows for a social acceptance of racism towards asylum seekers, both by the state and by lay society as a whole. Xenophobia, the racism directed at asylum seekers, argues Fekete (2001: 23–24), has thus become culturally acceptable within a wider framework that seeks to use racism as a means to socially sort bodies in the name of economic prosperity and national identity, and it can be additionally argued in the name of security.

It may be suggested that racism and inequality still persist in society as a whole, and especially within areas such as immigration, social housing, education and employment, because of the power and persistence of institutional racism (see Chapter 8). Despite the findings and recommendations of the Macpherson Report (Macpherson, 1999) and other anti-discrimination and equality legislation, institutionalized racism continues to be practised, albeit in more covert than overt ways. Sivanandan (2006: 3) argues that this is unavoidable given that institutionalized racism has been 'woven, over centuries of colonialism and slavery, into the structures of society and into the instruments and institutions of government, local and central'. So powerful are the racialized ideas that dominated during Imperialism, that constructions of the 'post-colonial enemy within' have resurfaced at intermittent times in the years since (McGhee, 2005: 65). In seeking to understand the persistence of such racism, Gilroy (2006: 433–434) usefully talks about the existence of a 'post-colonial melancholia' in Britain, which includes an anxiety about identity and a reluctance to accept the loss of empire (and its accompanying greatness). This melancholic state in turn feeds the resentment and hate that is directed at those whose heritage lies in ex-colonies, and those who are seen as posing a threat to the (already diminishing) British identity. This, though, leads us to ask questions about notions of Britishness and what constitutes a British identity (as discussed in Chapter 5).

Case study: Challenging discriminatory CCTV surveillance in Birmingham (UK)

The over-zealous readiness to equate 'Muslim' populations with 'terrorism' is widespread in security measures that seek to prevent crime. The problem here not only lies with the Islamaphobic and focused targeting of all Muslim populations, but also with the way in which officials falsify or withhold information in order to undertake monitoring of Muslims (and all those they perceive to be Muslim). However, the response of targeted populations serves to act as a challenge to human rights abuses. One case is that of the CCTV surveillance in the Washwood Heath and Sparkbrook areas of Birmingham (UK). Known to be areas predominantly populated by Muslims, residents were told that more than 200 CCTV cameras were going to be erected as part of a general crime-reduction strategy, in particular to protect residents against vehicle crime, drugs offences and anti-social behaviour.

However, it was discovered that the surveillance system included 40 cameras that were classified as 'covert', many of which were believed to have been hidden in trees and walls (The *Guardian*, 17 June 2010). It was also later discovered that the cameras had been paid for by a government grant from the Terrorism and Allied Matters Fund, which provides grants for projects that seek to deter or prevent terrorist activity or help to prosecute those responsible for terrorism. These were important pieces of information that had not been disclosed to the residents of Washwood Heath and Sparkbrook. Residents raised concerns about the cameras' negative impact on their human rights, as well as their broader Islamaphobic underpinnings and the claim that they were populations who needed to be monitored because they were considered to be 'at risk' of extremism (The *Guardian*, 17 June 2010). The misjudgement of officials, namely the Association of Chief Police Officers which administered the project (named Project Champion), was noted by the then West Midland Police Chief Constable Chris Sims, who stated that he was 'deeply sorry' that his force had, in this instance, misjudged 'so wrong[ly]' the balance between counter-terrorism initiatives and the excessive intrusion into people's lives (cited in *The Telegraph*, 30 September 2010). The last of the cameras was finally dismantled in June 2011.

The Birmingham case illustrates two key 'facts' for Muslims today. First, there is the perception that all Muslims are terrorists or, at the very least, potential terrorists. For instance, as one person said about her experiences following the Birmingham case:

Whether we like it or not, we are the 7/7 bombers. We are the ones who bought down the twin towers. We are Al Qaeda and Osama Bin Laden. That's how people see us. We're the new Jews and we're the new blacks. (Young Muslim female interviewed in the aftermath of Project Champion, cited in Isakjee and Allen, 2013: 752)

(Continued)

(Continued)

Secondly, the case also illustrates the extremes to which officials will go to in order to dismiss the human rights and civil liberties of Muslims. For instance, Project Champion was criticized for having been delivered in relative secrecy and via a narrative of misrepresentation (Isakjee and Allen, 2013: 758). This aggressive attack on citizenship rights is presented by officials, politicians, the media and within lay society as non-problematic because, as the terror-panic *logic* goes, there is a very real threat of terrorist behaviour from within the Muslim community, even, as in the Birmingham case, from those such as the second- and third-generation children of immigrants, who very much identify themselves as 'British'. Thus, as Brown (2010) notes, a dichotomy is established between Islamic radicalism and British values (cited in Kalra and Mehmood, 2013: 164) which presents British Muslims as essentially hostile to and incompatible with British values, and so of suspect citizenship status. They are therefore considered as being in need of increased surveillance, albeit at the expense of their human rights and civil liberties. However, the Birmingham case also demonstrates how community-level challenges in response to Islamaphobic over-surveillance measures can heighten evidence of victimization as well as hold officials accountable for their discriminatory behaviour.

ACTIVITY

Assess the view that in insecure times it is completely justifiable to use ethnic profiling in surveillance measures.

CONCLUDING THOUGHTS

This chapter has outlined a handful of legislative measures in various countries that are designed to deliver equality in matters relating to racial discrimination and human rights. The discussion has noted that although these laws are important, they are nevertheless limited in their ability to actually uphold the rights and freedoms of those populations and groups who are especially susceptible to racial discrimination and disadvantage. This is not least because of the history of racism, which is rooted in notions about a racial hierarchy and the structures of (white) power that continue to dominate contemporary society. Ultimately, then, there is equality in policy but not in practice. There has also been a consideration of how racially based infringements on human rights are commonplace and, more worryingly, how they are now seen as acceptable given wider concerns about population control and national security. The case of the CCTV surveillance in Birmingham (UK) has been used to illustrate the everyday and routinized strategies of surveillance on those black and minority ethnic population groups who are considered 'undesirable', and how these measures are not passively accepted, but are challenged and resisted. The chapter asks questions about the sufficiency of existing legislation to protect from racial discrimination and inequality, and encourages a further consideration of balancing human rights with the right to freedom of expression.

MAIN POINTS

- Legislative measures have sought to reduce the number of black and minority ethnic migrants as well as address the inequalities and discrimination that they face.

- There are various human rights granted to all people, including the social and political right to freedom of expression (with special conditions and responsibilities).

- There are still moral panics about immigration and asylum, with contemporary panics echoing earlier ones about black and minority ethnic deviance.

STUDY QUESTIONS

1. Is citizenship an obtainable status for all?

2. Is freedom of expression universal?

3. In what ways are debates about immigration and asylum blurred?

FURTHER READING

Ahmed, Sara (2007) 'You end up doing the document rather than doing the doing': Diversity, race equality and the politics of documentation', *Ethnic and Racial Studies*, 30(4): 590–609.

Eibach, Richard P. and Ehrlinger, Joyce (2006) '"Keep your eyes on the prize": Reference points and racial differences in assessing progress toward equality', *Personality and Social Psychology Bulletin*, 32(1): 66–77.

Sears, David O., van Laar, Colette, Carillo, Mary and Kosterman, Rick (1997) 'Is it really racism? The origins of white Americans' opposition to race-targeted policies', *The Public Opinion Quarterly*, 61(1): 16–53.

REFERENCES

Alexander, Claire (2004) 'Imagining the Asian gang: Ethnicity, masculinity and youth after "the riots"', *Critical Social Policy*, 24(4): 526–549.

Amin, Ash (2003) 'Unruly strangers? The 2001 urban riots in Britain', *International Journal of Urban and Regional Research*, 27(2): 460–463.

Association of Chief Police Officers (2005) *Hate Crime: Delivering a Quality Service – Good Practice and Tactical Guidance*. London: Home Office Police Standards Unit.

Bhavnani, Reena, Mirza, Heidi Safia and Meetoo, Veena (2005) *Tackling the Roots of Racism: Lessons for Success*. Bristol: Policy Press.

Bowling, Benjamin (1993) 'Racial harassment and the process of victimization', *British Journal of Criminology*, 33(2): 231–250.

Brigham, John C. (1993) 'College students' racial attitudes', *Journal of Applied Social Psychology*, 23(23): 1933–1967.

Codjoe, Henry M. (2010) 'Fighting a "public enemy" of black academic achievement: The persistence of racism and the schooling experiences of black students in Canada', *Race, Ethnicity and Education*, 4(4): 343–375.

Commission for Racial Equality (2005) *Promoting Good Race Relations: A Guide for Public Authorities*. London: CRE.

Deitch, Elizabeth A., Barsty, Adam, Butz, Rebecca M., Chan, Suzanne, Brief, Arthur P. and Bradley, Jill C. (2003) 'Subtle yet significant: The existence and impact of everyday racial discrimination in the workplace', *Human Relations*, 56(11): 1299–1324.

Department of Justice and Constitutional Development (2000) *Promotion of Equality and Prevention of Unfair Discrimination Act 2000*. Cape Town: Parliament of South Africa.

Dixon, John, Durrheim, Kevin and Tredoux, Colin (2007) 'Intergroup contact and attitudes toward the principle and practice of racial equality', *Psychological Science*, 18(10): 867–872.

Federal Parliament (1981) *Anti-Racism Law 1981*. Belgium: Moniteur Belge.

Fekete, Liz (2001) 'The emergence of xeno-racism', *Race and Class*, 43(2): 23–40.

Fox, Suzy and Stallworth, Lamont E. (2005) 'Racial/ethnic bullying: Exploring links between bullying and racism in the US workplace', *Journal of Vocational Behaviour*, 66(3): 438–456.

Gerstenfeld, Phyllis B. (2011) *Hate Crimes: Causes, Controls and Controversies*. London: Sage.

Gillborn, David (2007) 'Education policy as an act of white supremacy: Whiteness, critical race theory and education reform', *Journal of Education Policy*, 20(4): 485–505.

Gilroy, Paul (2006) 'Multiculture, double consciousness and the "war on terror"', *Patterns of Prejudice*, 39(4): 431–443.

Hennessy, Peter (2006) *Never Again: Britain 1945–1951*. Second Edition. London: Penguin Books.

Home Office (1948) *British Nationality Act 1948*. London: The Stationery Office.

Home Office (1962) *Commonwealth Immigrants Act 1962*. London: The Stationery Office.

Home Office (1965) *Race Relations Act 1965*. London: The Stationery Office.

Home Office (1968a) *Race Relations Act 1968*. London: The Stationery Office.

Home Office (1968b) *Commonwealth Immigrants Act 1968* London: The Stationery Office.

Home Office (1971) *Immigration Act 1971*. London: The Stationery Office.

Home Office (1976) *Race Relations Act 1976*. London: The Stationery Office.

Home Office (1978) *Immigration Act 1978*. London: The Stationery Office.

Home Office (1981) *The British Nationality Act 1981*. London: The Stationery Office.

Home Office (1997) *Protection from Harassment Act 1997*. London: The Stationery Office.

Home Office (1998a) *Crime and Disorder Act 1998*. London: The Stationery Office.

Home Office (1998b) *Human Rights Act 1998*. London: The Stationery Office.

Home Office (1999) *Immigration and Asylum Act 1999*. London: The Stationery Office.

Home Office (2000) *Race Relations (Amendment) Act 2000*. London: The Stationery Office.

Home Office (2006) *Racial and Religious Hatred Act 2006*. London: The Stationery Office.

Home Office (2010) *Equality Act 2010*. London: The Stationery Office.

House of Commons (1976) *Immigration Act 1976*. Ottawa: The Government of Canada.

House of Commons (1977) *Human Rights Act 1977*. Ottawa: The Government of Canada.

House of Commons (1986) *Employment Equity Act 1986*. Ottawa: The Government of Canada

House of Commons (1995) *Employment Equity Act 1995*. Ottawa: The Government of Canada

House of Commons (2002) *Immigration and Refugee Protection Act 2002*. Ottawa: The Government of Canada.

House of Representatives (1975) *Commonwealth Racial Discrimination Act 1975*. Canberra: The Office of Parliamentary Counsel.

House of Representatives (1999) *Hate Crimes Prevention Act 1999*. Washington, DC: The Government Printing Office.

Hynes, Patricia and Sales, Rosemary (2010) 'New communities: Asylum seekers and dispersal', in A. Bloch and J. Solomos (eds.), *Race and Ethnicity in the 21st Century*. Basingstoke: Palgrave Macmillan. pp. 39–61.

Isakjee, Arshad and Allen, Chris (2013) '"A catastrophic lack of inquisitiveness": A critical study of the impact and narrative of the Project Champion surveillance project in Birmingham', *Ethnicities*, 13(6): 751–770.

Johnson, Nick and Tatam, John (2008) *Good Relations: A Conceptual Analysis*. Manchester: Equality and Human Rights Commission.

Kalra, Virinder S. and Mehmood, Tariq (2013) 'Resisting technologies of surveillance and suspicion', in N. Kapoor, V.S. Kalra and J. Rhodes (eds.), *The State of Race*. Basingstoke: Palgrave Macmillan. pp. 163–180.

Kundnani, Arun (2001) 'In a foreign land: The new popular racism', *Race and Class*, 43(2): 41–60.

Macpherson, William (1999) *The Stephen Lawrence Inquiry*. Cm. 4262-1. London: Home Office (www.archive.official-documents.co.uk/document/cm42/4262/4262.htm).

Mason, David (1995) *Race and Ethnicity in Modern Britain*. Oxford: Oxford University Press.

McGhee, Derek (2005) *Intolerant Britain? Hate, Citizenship and Difference*. Maidenhead: Open University Press.

McIlwain, Charlton D. and Caliendo, M. (2011) 'Race, politics and public policy', in S.M. Caliendo and C.D. McIlwain (eds.), *The Routledge Companion to Race and Ethnicity*. London: Routledge. pp. 38–46.

Melotti, Umberto (2003) 'Citizenship', in G. Bolaffi, R. Bracalenti, P. Braham and S. Gindro (eds.), *Dictionary of Race, Ethnicity and Culture*. London: Sage. pp. 36–38.

Ministry of Justice (1971) *Race Relations Act 1971*. Wellington: Parliamentary Counsel Office.

Ministry of Justice (1993) *Human Rights Act 1993*. Wellington: Parliamentary Counsel Office.

Mistry, Minal and Latoo, Javed (2009) 'Uncovering the face of racism in the workplace', *British Journal of Medical Practitioners*, 2(2): 20–24.

Peltzel, Susanna (2003) 'Equality', in G. Bolaffi, R. Bracalenti, P. Braham and S. Gindro (eds.), *Dictionary of Race, Ethnicity and Culture*. London: Sage. pp. 88–90.

Ratcliffe, Peter (2004) *'Race', Ethnicity and Difference: Imagining the Inclusive Society*. Maidenhead: Open University Press.

Sivanandan, Ambalavaner (2001) 'Poverty is the new black', *Race and Class*, 43(2): 1–6.

Sivanandan, Ambalavaner (2006) 'Race, terror and civil society', *Race and Class*, 47(1): 1–8.

Skellington, Richard (1996) *'Race' in Britain Today*. Third Edition. London: Sage.

Solórzano, Daniel (2000) 'Critical race theory, racial microagressions, and campus racial climate: The experiences of African American College students', *The Journal of Negro Education*, 69(1/2): 60–73.

The *Guardian* (2010) 'Birmingham Stops Muslim CCTV Surveillance Scheme', The *Guardian Online*, 17 June 2010 (www.theguardian.com/uk/2010/jun/17/birmingham-stops-muslim-surveillance-scheme).

The Telegraph (2010) 'Police apologise for putting 200 CCTV cameras in Muslim area', *The Telegraph Online*, 30 September 2010 (www.telegraph.co.uk/news/uknews/law-and-order/8034999/Police-apologise-for-putting-200-CCTV-cameras-in-Muslim-area.html).

United Nations General Assembly (1976) *International Covenant on Civil and Political Rights 1976*. New York: United Nations.

United States Congress (1776) *Unanimous Declaration of the Thirteen United States of America 1776*. Washington, DC: The Government Printing Office

United States Congress (1791) *United States Constitution 1791*. Washington, DC: The Government Printing Office.

United States Congress (1871) *Civil Rights Acts 1871*. Washington, DC: The Government Printing Office.

United States Congress (1964) *Civil Rights Acts 1964*. Washington, DC: The Government Printing Office.

United States Congress (1991) *Civil Rights Acts 1991*. Washington, DC: The Government Printing Office.

NOTES

1. In particular, this has come to refer to terrorism.
2. In the areas of housing, healthcare, education and employment, for instance.
3. The supplementary school movement was pioneered by African-Caribbean and South Asian communities in 1960s Britain, who were responding to what they perceived was a discriminatory and insufficient mainstream schooling system.
4. More recently, the UK has also seen an increase in the number of allegations about abusive behaviour by some supplementary schools teachers.

10

RESEARCHING RACE AND SOCIETY

INTRODUCTION

This chapter describes traditional research practices into the subject of race and society, and highlights the limitations of these for contemporary race and society issues, instead offering direction on how research can be undertaken. The approach suggested would offer a more qualitative and in-depth understanding of the key issues, built on trust and support for the research subjects. More importantly, the suggested approach would access data from those directly involved in the matters. An outline, justification and some suggested avenues for undertaking such an approach is presented. The theory and concepts covered in the chapter include: critical research; feminist epistemology; over-researched; post-positivism; and racial minority perspectives. The case study in the chapter concerns the victimization and abuse of research subjects as well as the unethical methods used in the Tuskegee Syphilis study. The key question that is raised is: Do some racial groups have valid reasons for being suspicious of researchers?

KEY TERMS

- Bias

- Critical research

- Feminist epistemology

- Gatekeeper

- Over-researched

- Positivism

- Post-positivism

- Qualitative research

- Quantitative research

- Race-based epistemologies

- Research

- Research design

- Social constructionism

- Victimology

- Victim surveys

THE TRADITION OF RESEARCHING RACE AND SOCIETY

In the social sciences, **research** refers to a project that seeks to produce outcomes which develop knowledge. Crow and Semmens (2008: 7–8) note that good research will usually be original, to a degree; theoretically informed; systematic and follow scientific method; have conclusions that are generalizable; and adhere to ethical principles. Research should ultimately seek to discover 'truth' and in doing so create new knowledge and enhance understanding, with a view to improving life chances. In the social sciences, particular types of research methodology, usually distinguished as **quantitative research** and **qualitative research**, will often be used to understand particular topics and experiences.

Quantitative research has been linked to **positivism** – the view that objective knowledge, namely facts, can be collected from observation by the researcher who is value-free and independent. Following critique of this element of the positivist approach, **post-positivism** emerged which, although sharing many of its predecessor's views about objectivity, differed in its acknowledgement of the possibility of researcher limitations and influence. Quantitative research methods remain concerned with the systematic collection and analysis of observable phenomena using numerical data – asking the *what*, *where* and *when* about action. As such, it often produces information or 'facts' in the form of percentages and statements, which are usually favoured by lay society given their tendency to be readily digestible. Methods commonly favoured by the quantitative approach include questionnaire surveys and statistical tests. Yates (2004: 8) usefully lists the core parts of conducting a quantitative research study.[1] These are:

1. Theory
2. Hypothesis
3. Operationalization of concepts
4. Selection of respondents or causes
5. Research design
6. Collection of data
7. Analysis of data
8. Findings

In comparison, qualitative research is concerned with words. It seeks to discover an in-depth meaning behind human behaviour and social interaction – asking *why* and *how* about an action. Although the philosophical underpinnings of the qualitative approach vary, it is most commonly associated with **social constructionism**. This is the view that 'social properties are constructed through interactions between people' (Yates, 2004: 24). Therefore, meanings are interpreted and negotiated by social actors (human beings) depending on socio-political factors. Qualitative research methods include document/content analysis; semi-structured or unstructured in-depth interviews; participant/non-participant observation; and focus group discussions.

Each research approach offers its own advantages to the study of race and society. Similarly, they are not without their limitations.[2] It has therefore been increasingly common to see the adoption of a multi-strategy research approach – also known as mixed method research – which uses both qualitative and quantitative research methods to collect data in a subject area (Robson, 2011: 161). The approach can be quite effective. For instance, in her study of rural racism, Charlotte Williams (2007: 748 and 759) used both quantitative methods (in the form of 'desk-based analysis of data provided by the 2001 Census') and qualitative methods (in the form of 'semi-structured interviews with key stakeholders'), emerging with an interesting insight into the 'shifting territories' of rural racism and British multiculturalism.

The design of a research study is very important, especially when researching marginalized and excluded populations. **Research design** is the strategic plan for undertaking research, including: the aims and objectives of the research, and whether it is policy- or theory-orientated; information on methods to be used for the collection of data; and the methodological analysis to be deployed (Scott and Marshall, 2005: 564). Based on the view that society is consensual and ordered, social research emphasizes being open about the nature of the study, cooperating with informants, establishing trust and rapport, and empathy between the researcher and researched (Bulmer, 2001: 48). However, the reality is that society is conflictual in terms of members' goals, values and interests (Douglas, 1976, cited in Bulmer, 2001: 48). This means that social researchers, who, some argue, can never truly be neutral and value-free, need to ensure that they are aware of ethical issues and can adopt strategies to reduce harm to research subjects. Poorly designed research which fails to consider these issues not only risks the danger of producing invalid data and harming the well-being of research participants, but it also runs the risk of impacting negatively on any future willingness of subjects to actively engage in research. Research projects usually have to adhere to an established and professional ethical code set down by their own academic institutions, subject disciplines and often by the organization from which their sample population is drawn. For instance, in the UK, social science research is guided by the British Sociological Association (BSA) and the Social Research Association (SRA). Their ethical guidelines (which are accessible online) offer advice on how to conduct good practice in social research, as well as provide the social researcher with awareness of ethical dilemmas that can arise during research.

At its most foundational level, research must ensure that it is not exploitative or harmful. The pursuit of knowledge development and respect for individual/group rights and privacy must be carefully balanced (Barnes, 1979, cited in Bulmer, 2001: 49). There is a long history of these standards not having been met in research, especially in social, psychological and medical studies involving black and minority ethnic populations, for example, the now famous case of the Tuskegee Syphilis study (discussed in more detail in the case study in this chapter). In an attempt to counteract research suspicion and hostility, the principle of informed consent is identified as being a core ethical consideration of social research. Informed consent is the research participant's voluntary consent to taking part in the research and it has to be based on knowledge of what the research is about; why it is being undertaken; who is carrying it out; who is funding the research; how the research will be used; and what is required from research participants, including their right to withdraw from participation at any time and for any reason, which they may or may not wish to disclose. Consenting to research under these conditions is vital given that it is 'needed to protect the important ethical principle of autonomy – the right to exercise self-determination' (Kent, 2000: 81). Anonymity and confidentiality are also core ethical principles. These principles refer to the data collection process as well as to how the data is stored and disseminated. They assure the research participant that their identity and participation in the research will not be known by anyone other than themselves and the researcher. This principle is also subject to external policy measures, such as the Data Protection Act (1998) in the UK. These principles are particularly important in research where there is the threat of violence or harm, such as in research on racist hate crimes.

However, once in the field and/or at dissemination, the (intended or unintended) potential for misuse of samples or data is constantly present, and can occur for a variety of reasons. Research relating to race and society has tended to disproportionately suffer from bias, which is unsurprising given the Eurocentric roots of the social science discipline. **Bias** in social research refers to the politics of research, namely how the social scientific research is influenced by the political context in which it occurs. Bias is a threat in qualitative research, especially given that qualitative analysis 'is always from someone's point of view' (Becker, 1967, cited in Hammersley and Gomm, 1997, paras. 1–5). This 'point of view' is frequently never declared or acknowledged, despite it overshadowing the entire data collection, analysis and dissemination process. Some go further and argue that epistemologies themselves[3] are racially biased. This is what is referred to as 'epistemological racism' (Scheurich and Young, 1997: 4).

Research data on black and minority ethnic groups has traditionally been quantitative in nature, and used to monitor their numbers and geographical presence. Consider, for instance, the Census data collected in the UK, which since 1991 has asked questions about ethnicity. Although the Census is considered by many as sound, critics argue that its simplistic reporting of data fails to capture a more meaningful understanding of black and minority ethnic presence. This (type of) data set also has the potential to generate fear and concern, especially when reported on by other outlets. For example, in December 2011, The *Guardian* newspaper (in the UK) ran with an article which, in presenting Census data, stated that:

> Christians down 13 percentage points to 59% ... Muslim population up from 3% to 5% ... White ethnic group down five points to 86% ... 13% in England and Wales born outside UK ... India, Poland and Pakistan are top three countries foreign-born people in England and Wales come from. (The *Guardian*, 11 December 2011)

What this overly simplistic presentation of data does is present black and minority ethnic presence (especially selective black and minority ethnic presence) as something that is massively and speedily growing to an extent that the white Christian ('indigenous') population are at a real risk of being shifted from majority to minority status. Clearly, the mapping nature of such data is not a neutral and value-free exercise, but a political and ideological one (Skellington, 1996: 28). Skellington notes that such data – what he calls 'racialized data' – are not merely a reflection of objective reality. Rather, it is data that have been *racialized*: 'that is, "race" has been introduced into the definition or data-collection exercise as a factor of some importance and the subjects have been defined, at least partly, in racial terms' (Skellington, 1996: 23). This can often lead to the creation of 'false pathologies' (Phillips and Bowling, 2003: 271). This is the use of data – usually quantitative data – to present images of black and minority ethnic people as problematic, namely as inherently criminal or socially deviant. Quantitative mapping of race data also fails to allow for changing categorizations of race (and ethnicity) across space, time and context, as well as how people do not have one fixed view of their racial selves (Skellington, 1996: 24).

Some research into the identity and experiences of black and minority ethnic populations have used more qualitative methods, although this has not been without its criticisms. For instance, John Howard Griffin (1961) wanted to gain an insight into the experiences of black African Americans living in the South. To do so, Griffin used a form of covert participant observation over a six-week period: he 'blackened' his face and other parts of the body that were visible, and behaved in a way that he deemed typical of the black African-American character. Griffin felt he was treated as someone of black African-American background (and disadvantaged) in a period of racial segregation. Griffin's work drew widespread criticism, not least because of questions surrounding the ability to truly experience 'blackness' within the context of racial segregation without having many years of personal experience, which his brief experiment could never allow (Bryman, 2012: 44). Erikson (1967, cited in Bulmer, 2001: 47) notes that such covert research is also problematic given that social interaction is complex and it is impossible to 'conceal' one's own identity from others by 'playing' a role that you have, at best, only partially viewed from the outside. Data collected in such ways are highly susceptible to bias, distortion and error (Bulmer, 2001: 47). Such a methodological approach also fails to consider the intersectional dynamics of racialized identities. For instance, as discussed earlier in this book, the Black feminist critique would place equal emphasis on gender and ethnicity (or, race) as sites of inequality, with others later adding class oppression as an equal co-factor. Thus, Griffin may have presented himself (and been perceived by some) as 'black', but he also needed to factor in how his experiences were influenced by (perceptions of) gender and class, alongside that of race.

Research into black and minority ethnic populations has also been used to generate fear, and to provide an avenue for increased surveillance and the use of control strategies. For example, in the context of events such as the 9/11 and 7/7 terror attacks and the 2001 urban disturbances in towns such as Bradford (UK), there has more recently been a mass of research into Muslim communities, especially in the areas of: conversion to Islam; identity and community relations; and crime and deviance[4] (for example, see Alexander, 2005; Brown and Saeed, 2014; Franks, 2000; Midden and Ponzanesi, 2013; Moosavi, 2014; Silvestri, 2011; Sirin et al., 2008; and Soutar, 2010, to name a few). This heightened research attention has made Muslim populations more visible (Khoury, 2009). Research has increased attention to Muslim populations, and this heightened attention has (albeit inadvertently) contributed to the climate of fear, panic and suspicion that exists about Muslim populations as a whole (Sanghera and Thapar-Björkert, 2008: 546). This has in turn contributed to the development of initiatives which claim to 'secure borders', prevent crime (terrorism), 'integrate communities' and reduce the risk of radicalization. For instance, consider the UK's *Contest* (Home Office, 2011a) and *Prevent* (Home Office, 2011b) strategies. Critics have argued that in reality such initiatives actually seek to curb immigration and control ethnic 'Others', and that the research process is abused, and the data misused, in order to support measures that would otherwise be disallowed.

HOSTILITY, SUSPICION AND ACCESS

Criminology has recently attempted to correct the previous body of problematic work into black and minority ethnic presence in the criminal justice system. In considering the experience of justice, this updated critical consideration has highlighted how black and minority ethnic populations actually suffer disproportionately in comparison to their white counterparts – largely because of the persistent stereotype of 'black criminality' and institutionally racist nature of the criminal justice system. One attempt to provide a more accurate consideration has been to focus on the victimization of black and minority ethnic people. For example, in their study into rural racism in England Jon Garland and Neil Chakraborti (2004: 387) used in-depth, semi-structured interviews with victims of racial harassment living in rural areas in order to gain 'a deeper appreciation of the various facets of racist prejudice from the individuals and families who had direct experience of the problem'. Historically located in the discipline of criminology, **victimology**, the study of victimization in terms of crime and human rights violations, has been marked out as an important way of providing insight into the lived experiences of racial groups, especially those of black and minority ethnic background. Use of **victim surveys**, namely questionnaires, interviews, focus groups, and so on, have especially been useful in highlighting the increasing numbers of black and minority ethnic people who experience race hate attacks. They therefore offer more accurate information into the levels of and experiences of victimization, as well as reasons for the under-reporting of crime, the treatment of victims in the criminal justice system and the fear of crime (Jupp, 2001: 312).

It is claimed that black and minority ethnic populations have experienced being **over-researched** – for some examples of this see Sukarieh and Tannock (2012: 496). As Clark (2008: 953) notes: 'claims of over-researching are likely to be reported in contexts where repeated engagements do not lead to any experience of change or where the engagement comes into conflict with the primary aims and interests of the research group'. Black and minority ethnic groups have especially experienced being over-researched in the areas of intelligence and educational achievement, parenting and social deviance, and criminal behaviour. Being over-researched leads to research fatigue, or what Sanghera and Thapar-Björkert (2008: 552) refer to as 'research weariness', which can be illustrated by comments made by respondents into their study of Pakistani populations in England: 'Oh no, not another researcher' and '[it's] a bit like being an animal in a zoo' (study respondents quoted in Sanghera and Thapar-Björkert, 2008: 552). This also gives rise to the accusation of 'studying down' (Harding, 1987, Troyna, 1998, cited in Crozier, 2003: 81) – a 'white gaze' that portrays black and minority ethnic people as different, or with negative stereotypical connotations (Lawrence, 1982, cited in Crozier, 2003: 81).

In recent years, black and minority ethnic populations are a group that has suffered especially from research fatigue (Afshar et al., 2002; Butt and O'Neil, 2004; Sanghera and Thapar-Björkert, 2008). For example, in their study, Afshar, Franks, Maynard and Wray (2002: 9) found that 'a group of black women complained that they were asked the same questions over and over again but never saw any outcomes or feedback'. It was not so much that these participants didn't want to engage with the research *per se*, or did not consider its aims to be of any value, but rather that they had developed research fatigue and, eventually, 'research weariness' (Sanghera and Thapar-Björkert, 2008: 552), and demonstrated a reluctance to participate in further research because of previous research experiences and what they considered to be the limited changes it had led to. Similarly, we should not assume that all those who do participate in research do so for reasons of empowerment, as Sanghera and Thapar-Björkert (2008) highlight when they note that some groups may use research interest into their experiences for their own personal and financial gains. This was illustrated when some of the respondents in their study asked: 'How much you gonna pay me?' (study respondents quoted in Sanghera and Thapar-Björkert, 2008: 551). This raises ethical questions about 'buying research' as well as wider questions about power and access in research.

Sanghera and Thapar-Björkert argue that 'research weariness' may also be linked to the climate of fear and suspicion that exists within black and minority ethnic populations – what they call 'research wariness' (2008: 552). This refers to the idea that researchers enter the 'field', often on the promise of providing an avenue for change. They then obtain the data that they require and leave the field, having failed to deliver their promises. There is also often resentment at researchers who are seen as further abusing black and minority ethnic populations for their own interests, for instance in pursuit of career development. Indeed, some argue that the research in itself may constitute part of a wider system of surveillance and control (Sukarieh and Tannock, 2012: 497). This then further disadvantages already disempowered black and minority ethnic populations, as Smith (1999, cited in Sukarieh and Tannock, 2012: 497) notes: 'research is … inextricably linked to European imperialism and colonialism'. Thus, of the research that does exist, there has been a tendency to view black and minority ethnic populations as a problem – as culturally deficient and psychologically flawed. See, for example, the work of Herrnstein and Murray (1994).

It is not surprising, then, that there is hostility and problems of access when seeking to undertake research within black and minority ethnic populations. One key way to access research sites/samples is through the use of gatekeepers. **Gatekeepers** are individuals in a given social setting or formal organization who hold a crucial position in the flow of information and access to resources. They have the power to grant or prevent access to samples, and for this reason alone are significant figures in the research process. Often in research involving black and minority ethnic populations, some community leaders have been key gatekeepers. However, in referring to the work of Rowe (2004), Garland, Spalek and Chakraborti (2006: 426) note a word of caution when they discuss how research with minority ethnic groups must be especially careful in its selection of research participants, avoiding in particular a reliance on the views of individual community 'leaders' (original use of inverted commas), whose views may actually be biased and non-representative. In recent years and for a range of reasons, traditionally established community leaders within Pakistani Muslim populations have especially been accused of being self-appointed, self-serving individuals who are motivated by personal patronage, as opposed to being significant people who truly represent the community (Sanghera and Thapar-Björkert, 2008: 551).

Indeed, Webster goes further and comments on how some community leaders encourage a mythical and separatist ethnic identity in order to enhance their own personal prestige and power (Webster, 2003: 80).

ACTIVITY

Design a piece of research into experiences of racism. Include aims and objectives; methodology and data collection; data analysis; and dissemination of key findings and recommendations. What difficulties do you expect to encounter in the research and how can these be overcome?

The use of racial minority perspectives has been advocated as one way of overcoming the problems of exploitative and racially pathologizing research. With its roots in **feminist epistemology** – an approach that is concerned with how gender influences what is, or *should* be, considered as acceptable knowledge – racial minority perspectives adopt an approach which argues that race influences what is considered to be acceptable knowledge and the elicitation of that knowledge. In line with this, Hill Collins (2002) refers to a **race-based epistemology**, or what she specifically calls an 'Afrocentric feminist epistemology' (2002: 206). This suggests that 'black' researchers are inherently better equipped to elicit data from/about the 'black experience'. This is because of an assumption of a shared commonality and set of experiences, especially in terms of racism, which is considered by the perspective to be at the core of the black identity and sense of self. The perspective maintains that because of this shared experience, black researchers bring with them a greater degree of legitimacy and a higher likelihood of being able to elicit more detailed data. With its singular categorization of 'blackness' and the assumption of a universal shared experience, this approach has been criticized for being inherently essentialist and failing to acknowledge the shifting status and experience of race and ethnicity. In presenting a critique of this essentialist methodological view, Patel and Tyrer (2011: 138) suggest that all social researchers, regardless of race and ethnicity, should seek to contribute to the development of an anti-(racially)pathologizing perspective, and that it should not be expected to fall on the agenda of black and minority ethnic researchers only.

RESEARCHING AND SUPPORTING THE VOICES OF MINORITY RACIAL GROUPS

Attempts have been made to correct analysis into black and minority ethnic experiences by consulting subjects directly and using life history methods that allow their own narratives to be presented in a way of their (relative) choosing, for instance, through oral interviews, storytelling or visual representation. This has been viewed as an advance of knowledge because a closer version of truth is being obtained directly from the source itself. The methods also enhance visibility and enable empowerment, which in turn widens research participants' control over their own lives. This is especially important for those groups and subject areas, such as the racism experienced by black and minority ethnic communities, which have historically been ignored and under-examined.[5] This correction has largely emerged following recognition of the problematic methodologies as well as their biased motivations, which have been used to collect data on racial groups and their experiences.

It is argued that, given black and minority ethnic groups' previous experience of victimization at the hands of social scientific research, any future research with and into their experiences should take great care to be honest and transparent about its purpose and outcomes, especially if it will go on to inform social policy and intervention programmes. This research should also have a critical focus. In this sense, **critical research** refers to a research re-focus as it considers dominant 'knowledge' to be neither value-free nor neutral, but something that remains derived and reproduced via oppressive and unequal structural relations – which then go on to serve the interests of the dominant power (Scraton and Chadwick, 2001: 72). Critical research therefore seeks to unearth unequal relations and to give voice to those who suffer from its oppressive existence. This means that in terms of structural inequalities, critical research has political and economic ideological concerns, as well as socially investigative ones. In terms of race and ethnicity, we can learn from Edward Said (1994: 72–73), who argued that, as researchers, we should speak up about 'deliberate programs of discrimination, repression, and collective cruelty'.

Said also reminds us of the need to consider, in all our intellectual work (including research), the question of 'how does one speak the truth? What truth? For whom and where?' (Said, 1994: 65). In seeking to give a voice to black and ethnic minority research subjects, researchers should also carefully consider what this means and how this can be achieved, especially in white-dominated societies where the relationship between the researcher and researched can be construed as another instance of the oppressor exploiting the oppressed (Ladner, 1978, cited in Crozier, 2003: 82). Crozier (2003: 82) asks us to consider what it is we actually mean by 'giving a voice'. At the very least, researchers should ensure that their own stereotypes do not interfere with data collection. For instance, Crozier talks about how in an attempt to try to 'give a voice' to her sample of black parents, she may, on reflection, have appeared 'condescending', which risked reinforcing a racialized hierarchical position (2003: 82).

Garland, Spalek and Chakraborti (2006: 426) note that the assumption of whiteness and the white experience to be the norm or the 'commonsense' view should be challenged, especially when it is discussed in terms of 'othering' and the experiences of minority ethnic groups (2006: 424). They argue that there first needs to be a move away from the common practice of employing broad umbrella ethnic categories, such as 'Black' or 'Asian', when undertaking research into the experiences of what are commonly referred to as black and minority ethnic or minority ethnic groups (Garland et al., 2006: 423). In reporting on his study into the experiences of 'black'[6] staff in further education, Maylor (2009) provides an interesting account of the dangers of using collective terminology and assuming shared meanings. Rather, categories should consider not only ethnic and religious differences, but others such as geographical, national, class and gendered differences too. For example, research into the experiences of Muslim populations must recognize that belonging is also often defined by ethnic and national ties. Avoiding the use of umbrella categories would help avoid sweeping statements about minority ethnic groups and any consequential, misdirected, generalized research outcomes or recommendations. Garland, Spalek and Chakraborti (2006: 424) go on to argue that to move away from such limited terms would also bring the benefit of addressing the specific concerns of minority ethnic groups who are especially 'hidden' and 'forgotten'.

In their discussion of the discipline of Criminology, Phillips and Bowling (2003: 270) call for a more 'multidimensional approach' to be used when researching ethnic minorities' experiences of criminal justice. Doing so would help to challenge the creation of 'false pathologies' that has for so long dominated Criminology (2003: 271). Part of such an approach involves examining more closely the discipline of Criminology itself, mainly in terms of its predominantly white, male and middle-class standards, and its Eurocentric structures. Phillips and Bowling also call for the use of a 'distinctive minority perspective' (2003: 270), similar to Kathryn Russell's 'black criminology'[7] (1992). This 'minority perspective' moves beyond single, crude and essentialized racial and ethnic labels, namely 'black', and thus a black–white dualism, in order to embrace ethnic difference and cultural hybridity (Phillips and Bowling, 2003: 271). This approach would see a vast improvement in how data about minority groups is collected, analysed, interpreted and disseminated, ensuring that minority groups have a key role in knowledge production about their lives and experiences (Phillips and Bowling, 2003: 270). The perspective also holds value in non-exploitative research, ensuring that its research subjects are supported in their pursuit of equality and justice, as opposed to being used to facilitate the formulation of discriminatory policy or the advancement of researchers' careers.

Reference to the methodological approach of critical race theory has been presented as useful because it seeks to 'honor research participants' who have suffered from the 'white lie' (Vaught, 2008: 566). This refers to how marginalized and disempowered groups, such as those of a black and minority ethnic background, 'mask' their true selves/identity in order to manoeuvre through structural inequalities and racist institutions, in order to survive in a white-privileged society (Rodriguez, 2006: 1068). Rodriguez and other critical race theorists argue that black and minority ethnic groups need to develop a critical consciousness of residence in a racist and white supremacist society (Anzaldua, 1998; hooks, 2003; Rodriguez, 2006). To do this, Rodriguez argues that research with black and minority ethnic populations would especially benefit from methods that provide for narratives and life-story work. For Rodriguez (2006: 1069): 'Narratives can serve as a powerful means of creating a site of resistance. For the marginalized, [they] can serve as a powerful means of survival and liberation.' See, for instance, Chris Weedon's discussion of research into Aboriginal women's life-writing work (2004). Such storytelling is also a form of what Richard Delgado refers to as 'counterstorytelling' (1989), given that it serves to unmask, challenge and correct dominant racist narratives (Solórzano and Yosso, 2002), as well as bring unity and 'psychic self-preservation' for the individual concerned (Delgado, 1989, cited in Rodriguez, 2006: 1070).

Similarly, intersectionality as a methodological approach is also useful. Although its development as a research tool is still in relative infancy, considering intersectionality in research into race and society draws our attention to how there is a variety of multi-level factors and power structures in place, which ultimately impact on our life experiences. Therefore, suitable research methods must be adopted to factor in this reality. This would include recognizing that although summaries of a sampled population of, say, black and minority ethnic women and their experiences of poverty in rural England may share some similarities, there will nevertheless be a unique and individual narrative to each and every one of the sampled population. A research method that will permit and nourish the release of this individual narrative must therefore be used. This will always be a qualitative approach, very much like Rodriguez's (2006) life-story work.

ACTIVITY

You have designed a piece of research into the racism that is experienced by people who are of the same ethnic background, gender and class as yourself. What is the potential for bias? What impact do similarities between researcher and research participant have on the pursuit of 'truth'?

Case study: The Tuskegee Syphilis study

In the period 1932–1972, a U.S. Public Health Service carried out a study which is now famously known as the Tuskegee Syphilis study. The Tuskegee study wanted to examine the effects of untreated syphilis, a bacterial infection that is usually caught by having sexual intercourse with someone who is infected, or by an injecting drug user sharing a needle with somebody who is infected. The infection can also be passed on during pregnancy from the mother to her unborn child. In terms of moral judgements of the time, the disease was considered to be especially stigmatic and was perceived to be associated with moral decay, which had often meant it received little sympathy and understanding. The Tuskegee study focused on a sample of 600 African-American men who resided in the rural area of Macon County, Alabama. The sample were told by the clinical researchers that they were receiving free health care from the American government, which acted as a huge incentive given that health care costs in America were considered to be relatively high, and especially unaffordable given that the study began at the time of the Great Depression.[8]

Of the 600 research participants, 399 had already contracted syphilis before the study began, with the remaining 201 being free from the disease. The research, however, has been accused of being morally exploitative, as well as emotionally, psychologically and physically abusive. For instance, none of the infected men was informed that they had syphilis, and, even more problematically, neither were any of them medically treated with penicillin, which had been found to provide an effective treatment. The withholding of information and treatment was due to the study's aim of wanting to secretly experiment on infected subjects in order to examine the effects of syphilis when left untreated[9] (Marvasti, 2004, cited in Silverman, 2011: 90). The study ran for more than 40 years, and even saw some of its subjects die from the disease (Heller, 1972). Finally, in 1972 an insider leaked details of the study's failures. Ultimately, the study was halted. American laws and research regulations were introduced, including the requirement of informed consent, clear communication of medical diagnosis and the accurate reporting of all test results. Similar research regulations were developed and/or strengthened in other countries.

Research experiences like Tuskegee have had a longer negative impact on members of the black and minority ethnic community, with the result that suspicion and hostility are common responses to invitations for research participation. This is unsurprising given the exposé of exploitative projects such as Tuskegee and the extent to which some organizations and researchers will go in order to exploit subjects. This has resulted in the unwillingness of black and minority ethnic populations to participate in research studies (Corbie-Smith, Thomas, Williams and Moody-Ayers, 2001). More than this, though, it has also imprinted on the psyche of black ethnic minority populations a feeling of how little their lives are valued, and equally how there is an absence of respect for their rights. This has resulted in racial distrust and a form of heightened suspicion of the powerful, or 'paranoia',[10] among members of black and ethnic minority populations. Consider, for instance, the numerous tales of government conspiracies and racial genocide or a covert race war.

What is also interesting about the Tuskegee case is the role played by one of its field workers, Nurse Eunice Rivers, who was also black African-American. Rivers was the only member of the field study team who worked with the research subjects for the full 40 years of the study's duration. In playing a key role in the management of the sample, Rivers used her personal knowledge of the subjects and, some argue, her own black African-American background, as a direct connection to, and a source of reassurance for, the sample. It was later reported that like many of the black African-American staff on the Tuskegee study, Rivers believed that the medical experimentation was in the long-term best interests of the black African-American community in Tuskegee.

ACTIVITY

What lessons emerge from the Tuskegee study? Examine whether the study's aims and methods were necessary.

CONCLUDING THOUGHTS

This chapter has started to examine some of the key issues involved in undertaking research into race and society, especially in matters relating to race and racism. The abusive and problematic nature of previous research with/into black and minority ethnic populations has been discussed, along with the impact of this research legacy. This is, namely, the experience of abuse and further victimization by those who present themselves as authoritative and claim to be in pursuit of truth (or at least greater accuracy). Unfortunately, this has often included those working within the social sciences, such as in Criminology and Sociology. In terms of appropriate research tools for understanding race/racism and its place in society, it is argued that there are certain methods and approaches that are much better suited to expanding knowledge. This is largely because of their ability to produce qualitative data – that is, information of a more meaningful nature – and for their relatively empowering potential. A call is therefore made to invest in methodological approaches which support these desired outcomes. To illustrate some of the issues discussed in this chapter, the case of the Tuskegee Syphilis study was used. The chapter raises important questions about trust and research motives, and asks whether black and minority ethnic populations have valid reasons for still being suspicious of researchers and hostile to research participation.

MAIN POINTS

* Racialized data is used to present black and minority ethnic populations as problematic.

* Black and minority ethnic populations have a history of being over-researched, but at the same time, not having had their own voices and experiences accurately represented.

* There have recently been calls made for the use of a minority ethnic perspective for undertaking research into the subject of race and racism.

STUDY QUESTIONS

1. In matters relating to race and society, what is the value of (1) quantitative data, and (2) qualitative data?

2. Are black and minority ethnic people always disempowered when participating in research?

3. Critically assess the view that only black and minority ethnic people should do research into issues around race and racism.

FURTHER READING

Bryman, Alan (2012) *Social Research Methods*. Oxford: Oxford University Press.
Hill Collins, Patricia (2002) *Black Feminist Thought*. London: Routledge.
Robson, Colin (2011) *Real World Research*. Third Edition. Chichester: John Wiley and Sons.

REFERENCES

Afshar, Haleh, Franks, Myfanwy, Maynard, Mary Ann and Wray, Sharon (2002) 'Issues of ethnicity in researching older women', *ESRC Growing Older Programme Newsletter*, 4 (Spring), pp. 8–9.

Alexander, Claire (2005) 'Embodying violence: "Riots", dis/order and the private lives of the Asian gang', in C. Alexander and C. Knowles (eds.), *Making Race Matter: Bodies, Space and Identity*. Basingstoke: Palgrave Macmillan. pp. 199–217.

Anzaldua, Gloria (ed.) (1998) *Making Face, Making Soul*. San Francisco, CA: Aunt Lute Foundation.

Brown, Katherine E. and Saeed, Tania (2014) 'Radicalization and counter-radicalization at British universities: Muslim encounters and alternatives', *Ethnic and Racial Studies*, 38(11): 1–17.

Bryman, Alan (2012) *Social Research Methods*. Oxford: Oxford University Press.

Bulmer, Martin (2001) 'The ethics of social research', in N. Gilbert (ed.), *Researching Social Life*. Second Edition. London: Sage. pp. 46–57.

Butt, Jabeer and O'Neil, Alex (2004) *Let's Move On: Black and Minority Ethnic Older People's Views on Research Findings*. York: Joseph Rowntree Foundation.

Clark, Tom (2008) '"We're over-researched here!": Exploring accounts of research fatigue within qualitative research engagements', *Sociology*, 42(5): 953–970.

Corbie-Smith, Giselle, Thomas, Stephen B., Williams, Mark V. and Moody-Ayers, Sandra (2001) 'Attitudes and beliefs of African Americans toward participation in medical research', *Journal of General Internal Medicine*, 14(9): 537–546.

Crow, Natasha and Semmens, Iain (2008) *Researching Criminology*. Maidenhead: Open University Press/McGraw-Hill.

Crozier, Gill (2003) 'Researching black parents: Making sense of the role of the researcher', *Qualitative Research*, 3(1): 79–94.

Delgado, Richard (1989) 'Storytelling for oppositionists and others: A plea for narrative', *Michigan Law Review*, 87: 2411–2441.

Franks, Myfanwy (2000) 'Crossing the borders of whiteness? White Muslim women who wear the hijab in Britain today', *Ethnic and Racial Studies*, 23(5): 917–929.

Garland Jon and Chakraborti, Neil (2004) 'England's green and pleasant land? Examining racist prejudice in a rural context', *Patterns of Prejudice*, 38(4): 383–398.

Garland Jon, Spalek, Basia and Chakraborti, Neil (2006) 'Hearing lost voices: Issues in researching "hidden" minority ethnic communities', *British Journal of Criminology*, 46: 423–437.

Griffin, John H. (1961) *Black Like Me*. Boston, MA: Houghton Mifflin.

Hammersley, Martyn and Gomm, Roger (1997) 'Bias in social research', *Sociological Research Online*, 2(1) (www.socresonline.org.uk/2/1/2.html).

Heller, Jean (1972) 'Syphilis victims in U.S. study went untreated for 40 years: Syphilis victims got no therapy', *New York Times*, 26 July 1972. Retrieved: 15 June 2015 (http://query.nytimes.com/gst/abstract.html?res=9B0CE7D71F3EE63BBC4E51DFB1668389669EDE).

Herrnstein, Richard and Murray, Charles (1994) *The Bell Curve: Intelligence and Class Structure in American Life*. New York: The Free Press.

Home Office (1998) *Data Protection Act 1998*. London: The Stationery Office.

Home Office (2011a) *Contest: The United Kingdom's Strategy for Countering Terrorism*. London: Home Office.

Home Office (2011b) *Prevent Strategy*. London: Home Office.

hooks, bell (2003) *Rock My Soul: Black People and Self-esteem*. New York: Washington Square Press.

Jupp, Victor (2001) 'Victim surveys', in E. McLaughlin and J. Muncie (eds.), *The Sage Dictionary of Criminology*. London: Sage. pp. 312–313.

Kent, Gerry (2000) 'Informed consent', in D. Burton (ed.), *Research Training for Social Scientists*, London: Sage. pp. 61–67.

Khoury, Laura J. (2009) 'Racial profiling as dressage: A social control regime!', *African Identities*, 7(1): 55–70.

Maylor, Uvanney (2009) 'What is the meaning of black?', *Ethnic and Racial Studies*, 32(2): 369–387.

Midden, Eva and Ponzanesi, Sandra (2013) 'Digital faiths: An analysis of the online practices of Muslim women in the Netherlands', *Women's Studies International Forum*, 41: 197–203.

Moosavi, Leon (2014) 'White privilege in the lives of Muslim converts in Britain', *Ethnic and Racial Studies*, 38(11): 1–16.

NHS Choices (2015) 'Syphilis', *NHS Choices Online*, 15 June 2015 (www.nhs.uk/Conditions/Syphilis/Pages/Introduction.aspx).

Patel, Tina G. and Tyrer, David (2011) *Race, Crime and Resistance*. London: Sage.

Phillips, Coretta and Bowling, Benjamin (2003) 'Racism, ethnicity and criminology: Developing minority perspectives', *British Journal of Criminology*, 43(2): 269–290.

Rodriguez, Dalia (2006) 'Un/masking identity: Healing our wounded souls', *Qualitative Inquiry*, 12(6): 1067–1090.

Rowe, Michael (2004) *Policing Race and Racism*. Cullompton, Devon: Willan.

Russell, Kathryn (1992) 'Development of a black criminology and the role of the black criminologist', *Justice Quarterly*, 9(4): 667–683.

Said, Edward (1994) *Representations of the Intellectual*. Bath: Vintage.

Sanghera, Gurchathen S. and Thapar-Björkert, Suruchi (2008) 'Methodological dilemmas: Gatekeepers and positionality in Bradford', *Ethnic and Racial Studies*, 31(3): 543–562.

Scheurich, James Joseph and Young, Michelle D. (1997) 'Colouring epistemologies: Are our research epistemologies racially biased?', *American Educational Research Association*, 26(4): 4–16.

Scott, John and Marshall, Gordon (2005) *Oxford Dictionary of Sociology*. Third Edition. Oxford: Oxford University Press.

Scraton, Phil and Chadwick, Kathryn (2001) 'Critical research', in E. McLaughlin and J. Muncie (eds.), *The Sage Dictionary of Criminology*. London: Sage. pp. 72–74.

Silverman, David (2011) *Interpreting Qualitative Data*. Fourth Edition. London: Sage.

Silvestri, Sara (2011) 'Faith intersections and Muslim women in the European microcosm: Notes towards the study of non-organized Islam', *Ethnic and Racial Studies*, 34(7): 1230–1247.

Sirin, S. R., Bikmen, N., Mir, M., Fine, M., Zaal, M. and Katsiaficas, D. (2008) 'Exploring dual identification among Muslim-American emerging adults: A mixed methods study', *Journal of Adolescence*, 31(2): 259–279.

Skellington, Richard (1996) *'Race' in Britain Today*. Second Edition. London: Sage.

Solórzano, Daniel G. and Yosso, Tara J. (2002) 'Critical race methodology: Counter-storytelling as an analytical framework for education research', *Qualitative Inquiry*, 8(1): 23–44.

Soutar, Louise (2010) 'British female converts to Islam: Choosing Islam as a rejection of individualism', *Language and Intercultural Communication*, 10(1): 3–16.

Sukarieh, Mayssoun and Tannock, Stuart (2012) 'On the problem of over-researched communities: The case of the Shatila Palestinian refugee camp in Lebanon', *Sociology*, 47(3): 494–508.

The *Guardian* (2011) '2011 census data: Key points', The *Guardian Online*, 11 December 2011 (www.theguardian.com/uk/2012/dec/11/2011-census-data-key-points).

Vaught, Sabina E. (2008) 'Writing against racism: Telling white lies and reclaiming culture', *Qualitative Enquiry*, 14(4): 566–589.

Webster, Colin (2003) 'Race, space and fear: Imagined geographies of race, crime, violence and disorder in Northern England', *Capital and Class*, 27(2): 95–122.

Weedon, Chris (2004) *Identity and Cultures: Narratives of Difference and Belonging*. Maidenhead: Open University Press/McGraw-Hill.

Williams, Charlotte (2007) 'Revisiting the rural/race debates: A view from the Welsh countryside', *Ethnic and Racial Studies*, 30(5): 741–765.

Yates, Simeon J. (2004) *Doing Social Science Research*. London: Sage.

NOTES

1. See Yates (2004: 5–20) for further discussion of these core parts.
2. These advantages and limitations are discussed in fuller detail in any good research methods textbook, including those listed in the 'Further reading' section above.
3. As opposed to researchers' use of epistemologies.
4. By which we read, risks of radicalization and terrorist activity.
5. This includes the 'mis-examination' of race and racism, such as that undertaken by the Enlightenment approach.
6. Original use of inverted commas.
7. Although Phillips and Bowling (2003: 272) prefer using the term 'minority' instead of 'black', arguing that within the British context the first allows for consideration of wider minority experiences than those associated with race and ethnicity.
8. The Great Depression was a severe worldwide economic depression during the 1930s.
9. Today, we know that around one-third of people who are not treated for syphilis will develop tertiary syphilis. At this stage, the disease can cause serious damage to the body, including stroke, paralysis, blindness and even death (NHS Choices, 2015).
10. The term is used in inverted commas here to highlight the undetermined status of the belief itself, which means that one is not yet able to claim that that belief is fact or otherwise. Using the term in inverted commas also highlights the power of the belief and its real impact on lives, as one popular saying goes: 'Just because I'm paranoid doesn't mean they're not out to get me.'

11
CONCLUSION

INTRODUCTION

This chapter brings together the key points of the preceding chapters and summarizes the book's main arguments. In particular, there is a focus on the claim that we are living in a post-race society, and the implications of this claim for those who feel that they are subjected to discriminatory consequences of racial constructions. The case of right-wing extremism on the internet is considered as a way of examining the repackaging and commonality of racialized hate on the internet. The chapter will emphasize the need for us to rethink our approach to the study of race and society, and offer some suggestions to be factored into the analysis of newer and unresolved issues around racialized constructions and social relationships. The key question raised in this chapter is: How can we satisfy the need for a rethink of issues relating to race and society?

KEY TERMS

- Anti-racism

- Colour-blindness

- Emancipation

- Post-racial

RETHINKING RACE AND SOCIETY

The first chapter in this book opened with an introductory discussion on race and society, and argued that race in contemporary society continues to determine the experiences, opportunities and life chances of human beings. Race is very important in how identity is constructed and, from this, the access it allows to given spaces and status – namely, how race morally defines who is desirable and who undesirable, and who can access a named and/or lived title of citizen. This has been discussed in more depth in Chapter 5, which looked at how social groups continue to be formed along racial lines. In particular, it has been argued that those of black and minority ethnic background suffer disproportionately from structural inequalities. Interestingly, though, these very structures of power insist that racist practices and policies have now been removed and, as a result, we are now living in a society where equality of opportunity pervades. This claim has been further explored and challenged in each of the chapters of this book. For instance, with a focus on the representations of race, Chapter 4 considered the presentation and consumption of race in matters relating to space, locality and society, and argued that some organizations have much to gain from an intentional misrepresentation which results in panics about particular racial groups in given environments. This is not a new argument, but the chapter's discussion and illustration does demonstrate its continued presence despite claims to the contrary.

One of the arguments presented in this book is that significant events marked out by race are now presented as non-racial. In masking the salience of race, these events are embodied within a narrative that instead makes mention of 'natural' concerns in society, such as worry about security threats and pressures on services due to population increases. This permits the continued use of race and racial discrimination, with very little challenge. This has been discussed in more detail in Chapters 2 and 3, which looked at how race and citizenship are socially constructed and morally measured in society. Part of the narrative that excuses racialization and discrimination makes reference to anti-discrimination policy and race equality legislation and suggests that, as a result, racially discriminatory practice is now rare. However, this book argues that this claim is a fallacy. This has been discussed in more depth in Chapters 7 and 8, which in combination have looked at the role played by powerful social institutions and organizations in how we think about race and act on these racialized ideas, and the relative limitations of equality legislation for addressing the trend in contemporary society for palatable and acceptable racism.

It is suggested that, in Western society, the claims to being non-racial actually serve to mask the continued use of race as a marker for, on the one hand, privilege and power (largely to white subjects) and, on the other hand, the experience of discrimination, disadvantage and abuse (largely for black and minority ethnic subjects). Race therefore continues to determine social status and the nature of our everyday encounters, as well as the degree to which our basic human rights are respected and protected. In addition, though, race combines with other variables, such as gender, sexuality, age, class, geography and the urban environment, and produces a hierarchical set of experiences where one faces either more or less discrimination based on the combination of these variables and their significance in a given context. This is discussed in Chapter 6, which argues that our sociological analysis of race in contemporary society must still always take into account other social variables. In offering direction on the sociological study of race and society, Chapter 9 makes a number of suggestions on the approach best suited to studying the subject, especially in a way that accesses 'a greater version of the "truth"' and empowers research subjects, who, as the chapter discusses, have in the past experienced abuse and victimization from their participation in research.

It is useful here to remind ourselves of the key arguments that have been presented in this book.

1. The claim that an individual has one single and essential racial identity is highly problematic, given our biologically mixed nature and socially multi-racial background. Our identities are in a constant state of being negotiated and changed, and are influenced by different racial influences, in different ways, to different degrees, at different times.

2. Race is socially constructed and has an inextricable and complex relationship with society. Race continues to be influenced by power and has a meaningful and significant impact on all aspects of public and private life.

3. Society is full of social divisions and not everyone is considered worthy of membership of a given society to satisfy some of their basic rights – even when legal fulfilments for citizenship status have been met. Divisions in society may appear to be naturally occurring, but they are in reality created and maintained by those who occupy positions of power and influence.

4. Experiences of racism cannot be separated from other variables, such as gender and class, given that these variables all combine to occupy a specific position within a hierarchy of discrimination. The ways in which variables combine and their significance in any given context determine their hierarchical positioning.

ARE WE LIVING IN POST-RACE TIMES?

As noted in Chapter 1, the term **post-racial** is used to refer to a state where there are no practices of negative racial discrimination and prejudice. Sumi Cho (2009) considers post-racialism as more than a political trend, phenomenon or social fact, and argues that 'its current iteration is a twenty-first century ideology that reflects a belief that due to the significant racial progress that has been made, the state need not engage in race based decision making or adopt race based remedies, and that civil society should eschew race as a central organizing principle of social action' (Cho, 2009: 1594). In providing a relatively detailed consideration of the post-racial claim, Cho goes on to argue that post-racialists desire a 'retreat' from race, which would take at least three forms:

1. A material retreat from state-imposed remedies to racial inequality.

2. A sociocultural retreat from white liberal thinking on Black normativity and the meaning of racial equality and justice.

3. A political retreat from collective political entities organized along racial lines whose agendas focus on legitimate protest or vehicles for reform. (Cho, 2009: 1594).

ACTIVITY

Who benefits from the post-racial message?

Although the possibility of a post-racial era has been widely discussed in the academic literature for a while, the concept gained heightened attention in social and political discourse in 2009, with the election of Barack Obama as the first black President of the United States. President Obama himself famously suggested the irrelevance of race, and other divisions, in his campaign following his win of the South Carolina Democratic contest:

> The choice in this election is not between regions or religions or genders. ... It's not about rich versus poor, young versus old, and it is not about black versus white. This election is about the past versus the future. ... I did not travel around this state over the last year and see a white South Carolina or a black South Carolina. ... I saw South Carolina. (President Obama, cited in Barabak, 2007)

This and other changes, such as greater acceptability of inter-racial relationships and greater numbers of black and minority ethnic people in senior management positions within large companies and organizations, have contributed to the popular belief that we have entered a post-racial era – a key historical moment where cultural practices or political solidarities no longer predictably connect along racial lines (Mukherjee, 2011: 178).

This is an especially strong view in the USA – a nation built on cultural genocide (in its treatment of Native Americans), slavery and lynching, and racial segregation and Jim Crow. Now in the USA, iconic figures such as President Obama, Oprah Winfrey, Colin Powell and Magic Johnson are held up as evidence of a post-racial state which has supported affirmative action, and has now successfully moved to a state that treats individuals equally and rewards their efforts (Mukherjee, 2011: 179). Part of this, believe post-racialists, is also the result of policies which have adopted a colour-blind (or **colour-blindness**) approach. As an ideology that is opposite to 'affirmative action', colour-blindness disregards racial characteristics in selection processes, for instance, in the consideration of applicants for employment, meaning that (in theory) no decisions are made on the basis of race. The underlying principle behind colour-blindness is that an equal society can be achieved by treating people equally, and that this is achievable because the once racially powerful (white) group no longer has the control and influence that it did in the past. However, colour-blindness has been heavily criticized for this rather naïve claim, and has additionally been accused of actually supporting structures of racialized (white) power by permitting powerful white populations to ignore the continued disadvantaged position of black and minority ethnic people.

Support for **anti-racism**, which refers to those beliefs, actions and policies which seek to oppose racism with the goal being to end racial discrimination and achieve universal equality, has also been held up as delivering relative success and a (perceived) significant reduction in racial discrimination. Various governing bodies and allied official institutions have over the last 30 years adopted a wide range of policies which have claimed to support the anti-racist agenda. Often these approaches have been based on ideologies of motivating black and minority ethnic people and facilitating self-help for successful outcomes. As such, these approaches can be accused of being patronizing and irrelevant (Gilroy, 1990: 71), and unsurprisingly have been seen as nothing more than lip-service by disadvantaged (black and minority ethnic) populations. Similarly, anti-racism is often considered by (white) majority populations in lay society as 'politically correct nonsense', which has gone on to generate feelings of distrust and 'white victimization' among some white populations.

ACTIVITY

Does an anti-racist agenda have any place in alleviating the everyday racism that is experienced by black and minority ethnic groups?

In addition, **emancipation** from some racially discriminatory practices has been held up as evidence to support the claim of a move into a post-racial state. The term emancipation refers to a process whereby an individual or population group who have been subjected to restrictions on rights, then come to gain fulfilment of those rights. Emancipatory changes are considered to have a democratic agenda, and often run in parallel with the abolition of segregationist and discriminatory policies. Some examples of emancipation from across the globe include the abolition of apartheid in South Africa, the abolition of slavery in the USA in the nineteenth century, and the emancipation of Jews in Europe between the end of the eighteenth and the early nineteenth centuries (Valeri, 2003: 84).

However, many dispute the claim that we have reached a post-racial society, and have argued that race, or racial disadvantage, has merely been masked and reworked within the illusion of equality. For instance, in the case of President Obama and the USA, and its ever-present notion of the 'American Dream',[1] citizens are taught from a young age that each of them has an equal chance to succeed. This means that if they fail to succeed, then they alone are to blame. This is difficult for American citizens who are of black and minority ethnic background because the reality of systematic racism as a barrier to achieving success becomes an invalid excuse (Walton and Caliendo, 2011: 10). Bonilla-Silva and Ray (2009: 177) argue that research on the continued presence of laissez-faire racism, symbolic racism and colour-blind racism support their view that rather than delivering true equality, reference to a post-racial era actually means that 'whites have learned how to talk the talk, without walking the walk'. This means that we have a situation where race matters have changed in form, but not changed in substance. This explains the current contradictory situation where a 'Black' president is elected, yet forms of 'new racism' continue to pervade society, for instance, in practices of racialized anti-terror surveillance and anti-immigration/asylum hysteria (Bonilla-Silva and Ray, 2009: 177).

It appears clear that we are NOT yet living in post-race times because racial discrimination and disadvantage still exist in key areas. For instance, as has been discussed in this book, in terms of education, research shows that schools, colleges and universities continue to be more segregated. Indeed, the term 'apartheid schooling' (Kozal, 2006) has recently been used to refer to the racially divisive nature of education, which sees poor black and minority ethnic students especially suffering from inadequate facilities and poorer standards of curriculum delivery. Similarly, there continues to be significant racial difference in key areas of employment, with the evidence telling us that black and minority ethnic people continue to suffer disproportionately in terms of access to employment and with limited success in promotion to senior management positions. In encounters with the criminal justice system, too, there continue to be vast differences, with these differences, as we have seen, sometimes quite literally resulting in life and death decisions being made. These points have supported one of the key arguments presented in this book: that we do not currently have a post-racial state.

CHALLENGING THE DIVIDE, BREAKING THE RULE

Post-racialists insist that not only is race no longer significant in society, but that there should no longer be any focus on or discussion of race and racism. This is because, argue post-racialists, a condition of racial equality, and indeed racial insignificance, has been achieved. Put simply, post-racialists believe that race does not matter anymore in society (Cho, 2009, cited in Lee, 2013: 111). This book has suggested that claims to being a post-racial society in fact serve to maintain racial disadvantage. In a similar vein to Bonilla-Silva and Ray (2008), Lee (2013: 105) notes how race still matters hugely in society today, although it just matters in a different way from how it did in the past. Race matters in the lives of black and minority ethnic people who continue to experience discrimination and disadvantage based on the use of implicit racist stereotypes. This implicit racial bias influences perceptions of suspicion and threat, which go on to impact negatively on how black and minority ethnic groups are perceived and treated in society, both in lay interactions and when encountering institutions. Take, for instance, the case of Trayvon Martin,[2] an unarmed black African-American teenager who in 2012 was shot dead by George Zimmerman, a local neighbourhood watch volunteer. Lee (2013: 103) rightly notes that it would have been highly unlikely that Zimmerman would have perceived Martin to be 'a real suspicious guy' or on drugs if Martin had been white. It is argued by critics of post-racialists that implicit racial bias exaggerated Zimmerman's fear of Martin (as the black deviant subject) and motivated what seemed to him to be a reasonable decision to use deadly force (Lee, 2013: 101).

An important observation that has been discussed in this book is that sociological research has a legacy of having undertaken abusive and problematic research, in terms of access, accountability and versions of 'truth', in studies involving black and minority ethnic populations. This has also contributed to keeping black and minority ethnic populations in positions of disadvantage, by producing a body of data which has been racialized in order to present these populations as problematic, and in need of control or restriction. In addition, the black and minority ethnic research experience is one of having been over-researched and yet unheard. This book argues that there must be recognition of the sociological exploitation of black and minority ethnic populations, and an honest admission that often research has been racialized in order to satisfy agendas pertaining to the desires of wider structures of (white) normative power. This is where it would be useful to draw on the approach taken by Critical Race Theory, given that it seeks to 'honor research participants' who have suffered from the 'white lie' (Vaught, 2008: 566). This theory argues that research projects involving black and minority ethnic people should consider using narrative and life-story work (Rodriguez, 2006).

It is argued that the Eurocentric structures, especially of white, male and middle-class dominance in social scientific thinking, need to be identified, named, challenged and ultimately removed from their position of normative authority. To do this, one suggestion that has been considered in this book is the use of a minority ethnic perspective when researching race and racism. This echoes the work of Phillips and Bowling (2003) and Russell (1992). Such a perspective would move beyond single, crude and essentialized racial labels, namely 'black'. This would then limit the tendency to see a black–white dualism as a norm, and thus allow ethnic difference and cultural hybridity to be embraced (Phillips and Bowling, 2003: 271). Social scientific research must therefore ensure it challenges the (re)creation of false racialized pathologies. There are a number of ways in which this can be done, most of which involve building on and developing existing initiatives. However, any attempt to provide a truthful account of the lived black and minority ethnic experience and a full consideration of their subjection to continued practices of racism must acknowledge the repackaging of race and the impact of this on how they are viewed in society. This will involve identifying and questioning how racism has become normalized and palatable. The tendency to view and treat black and minority ethnic people in dehumanized ways, despite race equality and human rights legislation, is almost considered rational and acceptable in what, we are told, are times of increased danger, that is, insecure borders, over-burdened resources and services, and new security (terrorism) threats.

Case study: Right-wing extremism on the internet

Right-wing extremism is considered to encompass the socioeconomic and political ideology that occupies the far-right position of the political spectrum. In terms of race, ethnicity and nationality, right-wing extremism includes fascist and neo-Nazi groups, such as Germany's Autonome Nationalisten, Norway's BootsBoys, Italy's Veneto Fronte Skinheads, France's Nomad 88, and America's Aryan Nations. The ideology of right-wing extremist groups varies in its extremity, but their ideology is rooted in the view that there is a naturally superior category of people who have greater rights, including the right to dominate and rule society, and ultimately remove (often through genocide) inferior people whom they perceive to be a drain on biological progression and social (national) advance. Extreme-right politics usually involve nationalist, racist (including anti-Semitic, Islamaphobic and xenophobic), anti-integration and anti-immigration views. Traditionally, extreme right-wing groups were localized and considered relatively powerless, with some exceptions of course, for instance, the Nazi Party in Germany before and during the Second World War.

However, in more recent times the internet has provided extreme right-wing groups with a powerful tool for gathering strength and support for their ideology (Gerstenfeld, Grant and Chiang, 2003). In accompanying these groups' traditional offline activity, the internet has been used to provide instant and anonymous possibilities for propaganda. In itself, this brings the danger of inspiring and guiding criminal activity. The constant presence of these groups on the internet strengthens collective identity, by allowing virtual communities to grow and for global connectivity to be made with ease. These then lead to increased membership and financial support (Caiani and Parenti, 2009, 2013). Some groups tend to be more successful than others. For instance, Christian Identity theology is somewhat ineffective in attempts to unify via the internet, whereas Nazi sympathies are more pervasive and are able to use the internet to 'facilitate a white supremacist "cyber-community" that transcends regional and national boundaries' (Burris, Smith and Strahm, 2000: 215).

It is argued that extreme right-wing groups are able to present and gather support for their racist ideology on the internet because of the special conditions that this space brings with it. In addition, though, affiliation to these groups in a virtual community doesn't bring with it the same level of stigmatization that, say, an offline affiliation would (Koster and Houtman, 2008). However, although the internet is

(Continued)

(Continued)

fertile ground for these groups, there also needs to be a particular set of conditions in the real (offline) world that facilitates their growth. It is suggested that these offline conditions are offered by the reworked and repackaged forms of racisms that emerge within claims to living in a post-racial world. As discussed above, this allows for the common acceptability and palatability of racist views and practices to gain guilt-free momentum, as they are now presented as natural fears, for instance, about population control, an overcrowding of health and welfare support services, security threats, and so on. Indeed, those who point to the presidential election of Barack Obama as evidence that we are now living in post-race times and within an era of racial equality have their claims challenged by data which show that there was an 813% increase in American Patriot groups, including racist armed militias, following Obama's 2008 presidential election win (Southern Poverty Law Center, 2015).[3]

--- **ACTIVITY** ---

What is the power of online racist abuse and how does it differ from that experienced in face-to-face interaction?

CONCLUDING THOUGHTS

This concluding chapter has summarized the key points made in the book. It has argued that the (implicit and explicit) use of racial labels, such as 'black', continues to evoke a mental representation of a person who is of lower socio-political value, and from this ensues the very real practices of discrimination and disadvantage for black and minority ethnic people, as evidenced in education, employment and the criminal justice system, for instance. This in itself challenges the notion that we are living in a post-racial era. In addition, it highlights how we have still not truly addressed racial bias in contemporary society, yet insist on telling ourselves that a consideration of race is now unnecessary – because anti-discrimination and colour-blind measures have delivered racial equality.

MAIN POINTS

*   Claims have been made that we are currently living in post-racial times and as such reference to race and racism is no longer needed in consideration of social relationships.

*   Colour-blind approaches and anti-racist policies/practices have been held up as successful, and have contributed to the current state of post-racialism.

- Racial disadvantage continues in a post-racial state and has simply been masked and reworked.

- Sociological researchers must recognize their own abusive and problematic role in studies involving black and minority ethnic populations, and then seek to undertake research which accesses accurate and empowering data about race and society.

STUDY QUESTIONS

1. Does race (or its variants) play a role in every social interaction?

2. Can society ever escape its Eurocentric, middle-class, male structures of power?

3. Do we live in a post-race state?

4. How can sociological researchers undertake non-exploitative and empowering work?

FURTHER READING

Cho, Sumi (2009) 'Post-racialism', *Iowa Law Review*, 94: 1589–1649.
Patel, Tina G. and Tyrer, David (2011) *Race, Crime and Resistance*. London: Sage.
Song, Miri (2014) 'Challenging a culture of racial equivalence', *The British Journal of Sociology*, 65(1): 107–129.

REFERENCES

Barabak, Mark Z. (2007) 'Obama easily wins heated S.C. primary', *The Los Angeles Times*, 27 January 2007 (www.latimes.com/nation/politics/politicsnow/la-na-carolina 27jan27-story.html#page=1).

Bonilla-Silva, Eduardo and Ray, Victor (2009) 'When whites love a black leader: Race matters in *Obamerica*', *Journal of African American Studies*, 13: 176–183.

Burris, Val, Smith, Emery and Strahm, Ann (2000) 'White supremacist networks on the internet', *Sociological Focus*, 33(2): 215–235.

Caiani, Manuela and Parenti, Linda (2009) 'The dark side of the web: Italian right-wing extremist groups and the internet', *South European Society and Politics*, 14(3): 273–294.

Caiani, Manuela and Parenti, Linda (2013) *European and American Extreme Right Groups and the Internet*. Aldershot: Ashgate.

Gerstenfeld, Phyllis B., Grant, Diana R. and Chiang, Chau-Pu (2003) 'Hate online: A content analysis of extremist internet sites', *Analysis of Social Issues and Public Policy*, 3(1): 29–44.

Gilroy, Paul (1990) 'The end of anti-racism', *Journal of Ethnic and Migration Studies*, 17(1): 71–83.

Koster, Willem D. and Houtman, Dick (2008) '"Stormfront is like a second home to me": On virtual community formation by right-wing extremists', *Information, Communication, and Society*, 11(8): 1155–1176.

Kozal, Jonathan (2006) *The Shame of the Nation: The Restoration of Apartheid Schooling in America*. New York: Broadway Books.

Lee, Cynthia (2013) 'Making race salient: Trayvon Martin and implicit bias in a not yet post-racial society', *The George Washington University Law School*, 91: 101–157.

Mukherjee, Roopali (2011) 'Bling fling: Commodity consumption and the politics of the "post-racial"', in M.G. Lacy and K.A. Ono (eds.), *Critical Rhetorics of Race*. New York: New York University Press. pp. 178–196.

Phillips, Coretta and Bowling, Benjamin (2003) 'Racism, ethnicity and criminology: Developing minority perspectives', *British Journal of Criminology*, 43(2): 269–290.

Rodriguez, Dalia (2006) 'Un/masking identity: Healing our wounded souls', *Qualitative Inquiry*, 12(6): 1067–1090.

Russell, Kathryn (1992) 'Development of a black criminology and the role of the black criminologist', *Justice Quarterly*, 9(4): 667–683.

Southern Poverty Law Center (2015) *Hate and Extremism*. Southern Poverty Law Center Online (www.splcenter.org/what-we-do/hate-and-extremism).

Valeri, Mauro (2003) 'Emancipation', in G. Bolaffi, R. Bracalenti, P. Braham and S. Gindro (eds.), *Dictionary of Race, Ethnicity and Culture*. London: Sage. pp. 84–85.

Vaught, Sabina E. (2008) 'Writing against racism: Telling white lies and reclaiming culture', *Qualitative Inquiry*, 14(4): 566–589.

Walton, F. Carl and Caliendo, Stephen M. (2011) 'Origins of the concept of race', in S.M. Caliendo and C.D. McIlwain (eds.), *The Routledge Companion to Race and Ethnicity*. Abingdon: Routledge. pp. 3–11.

NOTES

1. The American Dream refers to the national ethos of the USA, which includes ideals about freedom, opportunity and success, with a particular emphasis on the pursuit of upward social mobility via self-determination and hard work.

2. After visiting a convenience store on the evening of 26 February 2012, Trayvon Martin was walking through a Stanford (Florida) neighbourhood which had previously experienced several robberies earlier that year. George Zimmerman, who was a member of the local community watch scheme, spotted Martin and called the Sanford Police to report 'a real suspicious guy' (Lee, 2013: 154). Moments later, Martin was shot in the chest by Zimmerman. Zimmerman was not charged at the time of the shooting by the Sanford Police on the basis (they argued) that there was no evidence to refute his claim of self-defence and because Florida's 'stand your ground' law provides immunity for the use of force in self-defence. However, following public protest, Zimmerman was charged and found guilty of second-degree murder and manslaughter in July 2013.

3. Although this number fell to 874 in 2014 (Southern Poverty Law Center, 2015).

INDEX